Public Relations/
Publicity

Public Relations/ Publicity

A Key Link in Communications

Lois B. Ehrenkranz
PR/Publicity Consultant
Adjunct Professor, Advertising & Communications
Fashion Institute of Technology
State University of New York

Gilbert R. Kahn
Associate Professor, Advertising & Communications
Fashion Institute of Technology
State University of New York

Fairchild Publications
New York

Copyright © 1983 by Fairchild Publications
Division of Capital Cities Media, Inc.

All rights reserved. No part of this book may be reproduced in any form without permission in writing from the publisher, except by a reviewer who wishes to quote passages in connection with a review written for inclusion in a magazine or newspaper.

Standard Book Number: 87005-449-X

Library of Congress Catalog Card Number: 83-80798

Printed in the United States of America

Contents

Preface ix

About the Authors xi

Acknowledgments xiii

1 What Is PR/Publicity? 1
   A Special Kind of News 2
   The Working Relationships 2
   PR/Publicity Is Important to Marketing 6
   PR/Publicity: Different from Advertising 8
   Kinds of PR/Publicity 8
   The World of PR/Publicity 13

2 Developing News Sense and Creative Ideas 17
   Developing News Angles 17
   Developing PR/Publicity Creativity 20
   The Importance of Research and "Listening" 25
   The ABC Company: A Case in Creative Idea Development 26

3 Knowing the Media 31
   PRINT MEDIA 32
   Newspapers 32
   Magazines 34
   Business Publications 37
   Newsletters, House Organs, and Columns 39
   Supplementary News Services 40
   BROADCAST MEDIA 41
   Television 42
   Radio 43

4 How to Write Press Releases 47
   Basic Press Release Form 47
   Publicity Writing Styles 51
   Localizing the Release 57
   Some Do's and Don'ts 62
   Some Questions to Ask Before Sending Releases 64

5 Other Written Materials 65
Fact Sheets 65
Profiles and Bios 67
Query Letters 71
Manuals, Pamphlets, Magazines, and Books 72
Letter Writing 73
Letters to the Editor and Editorial Replies 74
Guest Editorials 75

6 Working with Photos, Sketches, and Diagrams 77
Photographs Help Tell the Story 77
Outlets for PR/Publicity Photos 78
Photograph Requirements 79
Unique Standards of PR/Publicity Photography 80
Types of PR/Publicity Photos 81
Cropping and Retouching 92
Photo Releases 93
Photo Do's and Don'ts 93
Sketches, Diagrams, and Charts 94
Captions 99

7 Presentation Strategy and Placement Techniques 103
The Spoken Word 104
The Written Word—With Eye Appeal 105
The Press Kit 105
Placement Techniques 110

8 Making Contact with the Media 119
Contact Techniques 119
Establishing a Contact List 120
Media Mailing Services 125
Other Means of Reaching the Media 126
Successful Placement in Media 128
Editors Want News, Not Gifts 130

9 Events, Press Conferences, and Press Parties 133
Events 133
Press Conferences and Press Parties 144

10 Corporate PR/Publicity Functions 149
Corporate Culture, Logos, and Trademarks 150
Institutional Advertising for PR/Publicity Purposes 152
Annual Reports 152
Quarterly Reports 159
Annual Meetings 159
Speech Writing 160

11 Broadcast Techniques and Speaker Aids 163
Broadcast Techniques 163
Sponsored Films and Tapes 172
Tapes and Films for Other Uses 173
Speaker Aids 174

12 PR/Publicity Planning 177
Establishing a Plan 177
Proposals Precede Plans 186

13 Evaluating and Merchandising Results 189
Measuring PR/Publicity Programs 189
Evaluating Qualitative Programs 190
Merchandising the Results 194
Editorial Surveys 199

14 The PR/Publicity Picture Today 203
The Revolution in Communications 203
Getting a Job in PR/Publicity 205
Attitudes and Skills 207
Observations by an Assistant Account Executive 208
Another Professional View 209
Ethics and the PR/Publicity Process 210

Glossary 213

Selected Bibliography 223

Index 227

Preface

The need for publicity and public relations was never greater than it is today. Society is undergoing vast changes—family relationships, the status of women, the methods of doing business, the concepts of education, the incidence of crime—are just a few of the areas that are in great need of clarification and interpretation. A pulsating society that requires more and more interfacing with its components also calls for greater skills in the practice of public relations and publicity to clarify the changes and to interpret the news.

The setting forth of this news is primarily through the use of mass media—magazines, newspapers, television, and radio. How to deal with this media, how and what to transmit to them, is of vital concern to all who would have their products shown, their views expressed, their plans announced.

The relationship between the media and those who would use it to distribute news and information is one of mutual dependency. Media editors do not have sufficient resources to find all the news that they have time and space to publish and/or broadcast. Thus, the practice of public relations and publicity has become a key link in our communications system—with practitioners acting as silent partners of the media and both working for a common goal: the transmission of news and information.

In undertaking this book, we were well aware of the classic distinction between public relations and publicity—public relations being the "umbrella" term and publicity its subspecialty. In practice, however, we have found that the two activities employ the same techniques to generate news. Moreover, the two terms are frequently interchanged. Hence, the hybrid quality of the book's title: *Public Relations/Publicity: A Key Link in Communications.*

Primarily, this book is an introduction to the techniques used by those working in the publicity and public relations fields to disseminate news and information to the mass media. It is directed towards students taking an introductory course in publicity or public relations at the undergraduate college level. In addition, it is written in such a way as to be useful to students majoring in advertising, journalism, marketing, or communications.

The book's usefulness is not confined to the academic world, however. Those newcomers to PR/publicity, be they volunteer workers in the nonprofit sector or rising entrepreneurs seeking to promote their product, will find much solid information in these pages.

In writing this text, we have sought to eschew gobbledygook and communications theory. We have tried to make it a practical, no-nonsense handbook, heavy on a down-to-earth practical approach to PR/publicity practices. We have tried to compress the results of our experiences into simple-to-follow instructions and to give pertinent examples.

In doing the initial research, we interviewed PR/publicists and editors and solicited their opinions about the state of the field today and what skills and attitudes were needed for success. Statements from these practitioners are offered to confirm and/or modify some of the points made.

The organization of this book reflects our belief that PR/publicists must know more than how to write releases and phone editors. Success in the field reflects one's understanding of the *process* of making news through the media. Consequently, we have dedicated the opening chapters of the book to establishing a general understanding of the PR/publicity profession and the importance of creative idea development and media knowledge. Although this is a practical book, designed to introduce the communications techniques used by professionals to generate PR/publicity news and features, we firmly believe that good PR/publicists must possess more than writing and speaking skills. They must also have a thorough understanding of how they fit into the current communications scene. They must understand why the press is receptive to PR/publicity efforts.

In Chapter 1, we define and identify the PR/publicity process and discuss the PR/publicist's working relationships and areas of specialization within the industry. Chapters 2 and 3 introduce two of the most important factors in successful PR/publicity placement: a creative news sense and a knowledge of the organization and working routines of media.

Chapters 4 and 5 deal with the written materials used in PR/publicity. Detailed information is given as to the form and style requirements of press releases, fact sheets, query letters, profiles, and bios. Letters to the editor, editorial replies, guest editorials, in addition to other written means of establishing contact with both the media and specific publics, are similarly discussed.

Chapter 6 deals with photography and art used in PR/publicity with emphasis divided between style requirements and working procedures. The mechanics of writing captions are also discussed in this chapter.

Chapters 7 and 8 deal with the communications packaging and distribution of PR/publicity materials to the press. In these chapters, we offer suggestions on verbal and print presentations, discuss how to use effective graphics for press kit folders, and examine the various mail and distribution systems used in PR/publicity.

Chapters 9 through 11 deal with more involved PR/publicity activities: planning and implementing events, corporate functions (including the annual report), and broadcast and audiovisual techniques, and speaker aids. Chapter 12 discusses how an effective PR/publicity program is organized with emphasis on goal direction. Guides to plan and proposal writing are offered. In Chapter 13, we consider the documentation, evaluation, and merchandising of PR/publicity results.

In the final chapter, Chapter 14, we look to the future and consider the impact of the current revolution in communications technology on PR/publicity practices. Then, we return to the present, discussing opportunities for those seeking PR/publicity careers and offering some very practical advice.

Gilbert R. Kahn
Lois B. Ehrenkranz

About the Authors

Gilbert R. Kahn and Lois B. Ehrenkranz have a combined total of almost forty years in the communications field. Dr. Kahn has been a trade editor, a newspaper correspondent, a sales promotion specialist, a Madison Avenue agency executive, and a television production company principal. Lois B. Ehrenkranz has been the publicity director of a national corporation, has operated her own public relations and publicity organization, and has had extensive experience in handling national and regional accounts as well as a number of nonprofit organizations.

Dr. Kahn is on the faculty of the Fashion Institute of Technology, State University of New York. He has a BSS from the College of the City of New York, an MS from the School of Journalism, Columbia University, and a Doctorate in Education from Temple University. He is currently active as a consultant in marketing communications.

Lois B. Ehrenkranz is a specialist in consumer motivation, working in product development, public relations, and publicity. She is on the faculty of the Fashion Institute of Technology and has a BA in Psychology from Barnard College.

Acknowledgments

As no man is an island, so is no book of this nature the product of the thoughts and experiences of one or two people. The authors wish to acknowledge indebtedness to their colleagues in the Advertising and Communications Department of the Fashion Institute of Technology, and to those individuals in the public relations and publicity field who have given of their time and effort to make this book a reality: Richard Magat, currently senior consultant to the Council on Foundations; Hal Davis, formerly president of Grey & Davis; Jack Hyde, formerly with *Men's Wear* magazine, now a member of the FIT faculty; Chester Burger, Chester Burger & Co.; Edward Starr, Hill & Knowlton, Inc.; and Annette Green, Annette Green Associates.

Also: Elias Buchwald, Burson-Marsteller; Victoria Lucas, Victoria Lucas Associates; Will Barbeau, Barbeau Associates; Robert Cherneff, formerly with Hill & Knowlton; J. Wilfrid Gagen, J. Wilfrid Gagen Associates; Susan Ehrlich, formerly with The Rowland Company; Susan Kornfeld, The Rowland Company; Marion Benedek, graphic designer; Sol Kunis, S.R. Kunis & Co.; Phyllis Levine, the International Center of Photography; Quentin McDonald, the Bobby-Mac Company; Sue Hartman, Jackson-Hartman Associates; Diana Goldin, Margaret Moore, and Felicia Narvaez, New York Hospital—Cornell Medical Center; Ed Meyers, Edward M. Meyers Associates, Inc.; Kathy Hyett, Public Relations Society of America; and Carol Sirinek, Collins & Aikman Corporation.

The authors also want to express their gratitude to their students, particularly Betsy Haak, Susan Maxson, and Eva Pfaff, for their ideas and suggestions and for providing a pretesting ground for much of the material contained in this book.

The authors also wish to acknowledge the talents and efforts of those connected with the publication of this book: Angelo J. Virgona, editor; Walter Lindell, production manager; Janet Solgaard, book designer; and Karen Wiedman, illustrator.

Finally, the authors owe a debt of gratitude to their respective spouses, Lucille E. Kahn and Sanford B. Ehrenkranz, for their encouragement, help and, above all, forbearance.

1
What Is PR/Publicity?

The terms *public relations* and *publicity* are often confused. Part of the difficulty is that, in operation, they both employ the same basic techniques to create news and reach a desired group of people. Also both processes form a key link in the chain of communication that joins carriers of news (media outlets) with receivers of news (viewers, readers, listeners).

The vital difference, at least theoretically, is that public relations (abbreviated *PR*) refers to the *total* image projected by an organization or individual. Advertising, packaging, customer relations, and all corporate policies are part of public relations. PR practitioners concern themselves with broad programs to establish, maintain, and improve the image of the company or individual. In comparison, publicity may be defined as an organized effort to make *known* some person, product, place, or idea, either by word of mouth or by being featured as news in media: newspapers, magazines, television, and/or radio.

In practice, these processes overlap to the extent that publicity is often considered to be a tool of public relations. Moreover, the terms, public relations and publicity, are commonly used interchangeably to identify the techniques and procedures used to make news in media. They are also used as the designation for the whole group of career professionals who work at the business of creating links in the chain of communications, and as the labels for news that features a product, service, or idea in media.

Because the emphasis here is on the basic techniques used by practitioners in both fields to generate news, these skills will be referred to as *PR/publicity* techniques.

A Special Kind of News

News is information that people see, hear, or read about. It is a report of changes in events or situations and the significance of these changes. News is information that interests people; what they want to think about, talk about.

The news that PR/publicity techniques produces is a special kind of news—news that involves a company, individual, or idea and makes them better or more favorably known to an interested public (a group of people having something in common).

PR/publicists use both written and verbal techniques to generate news for the organizations and clients for whom they work. Written techniques include press releases (the basic written tool used to present a concept to media editors), fact sheets, query letters, profiles, biographies, captions for photographs and illustrations, and scripts for interviews. Verbal techniques include person-to-person and person-to-group presentations, announcements at press conferences, product presentations, and phone solicitations. These written and verbal techniques will be discussed in subsequent chapters of this book.

Whatever techniques are used, the best results come from matching the organization's or individual's news to those media outlets whose readers, viewers, or listeners are interested in that type of information.

The Working Relationships

PR/publicists can work *in-house* as full-time employees for organizations (companies, individuals, or institutions) seeking to make news. They can also work as *account executives* at PR/publicity agencies and advertising agencies, or independently as *free-lance consultants.* In the case of account executives and free-lance consultants, the company, individual, or institution seeking to make news is referred to as the *client.*

In-House. PR/publicity managers or directors work on the executive level helping to set company policy and directing a PR/publicity staff on a day-to-day basis. Their responsibilities include conceiving campaign strategy and formulating corporate positions on commercial as well as public issues. They maintain contact with editors and producers of media and help develop all writing, photography, and art work for distribution. In addition, they supervise the production of annual and periodic financial reports. They are also responsible for newsletters and promotional booklets and pamphlets used to generate PR/publicity news.

At a PR/Publicity Agency. Account executives at PR/publicity agencies have a function that is similar to their namesakes at advertising agencies. They usually handle the PR/publicity program for two or three clients simultaneously. In

PR / PUBLICITY AGENCY ORGANIZATIONAL CHART

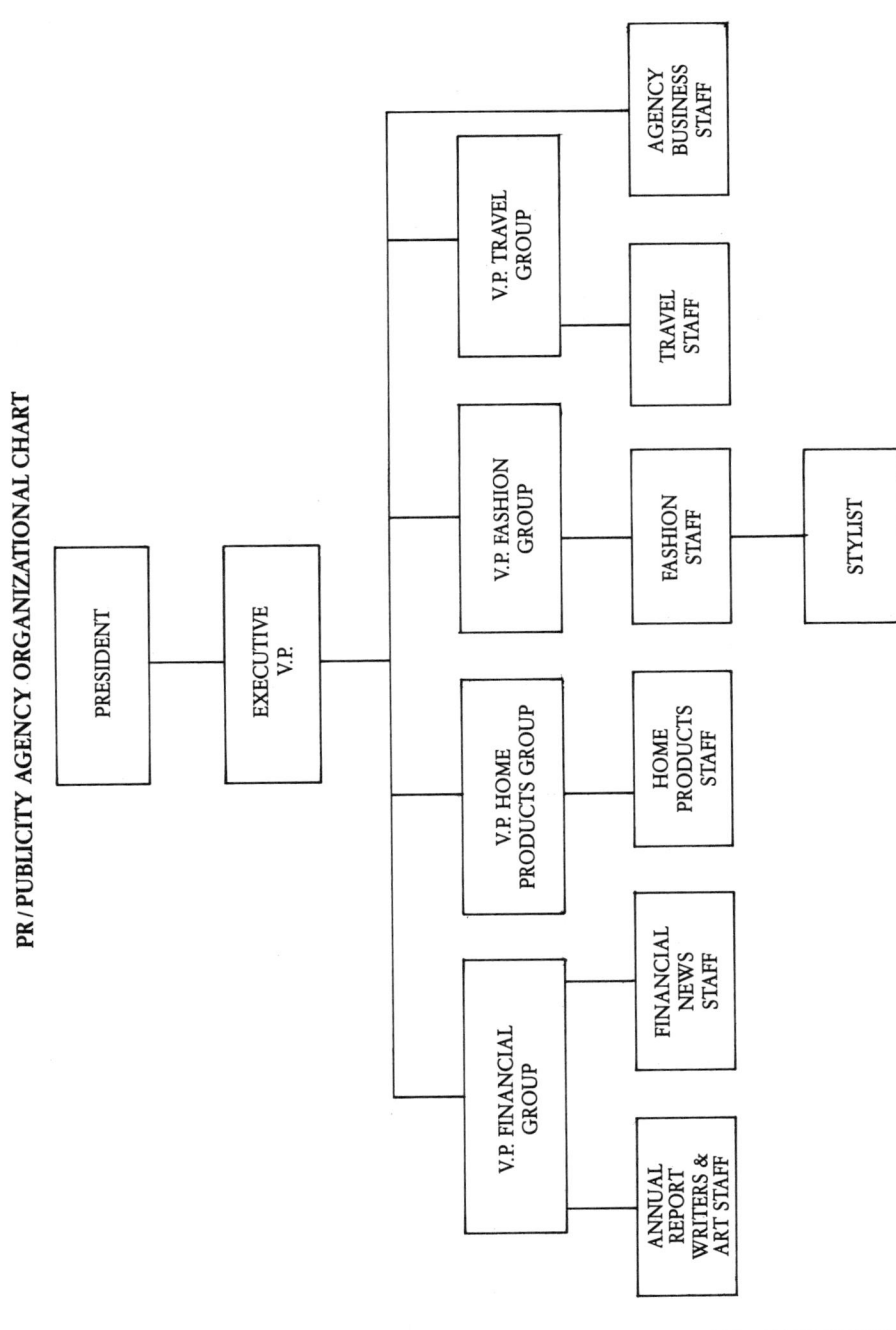

1-1. *This chart represents the typical organization of a PR/publicity agency specializing in financial, home products, fashion, and travel industry news.*

some cases, however, PR/publicity account executives will work on only one account which has a great volume of activity and pays the agency a fee large enough to justify individual attention.

Agency PR/publicists have day-to-day responsibility for the accounts they are assigned and spend a considerable amount of time planning strategy. They usually have assistants who follow-up on the details.

Similar to the structure of an advertising agency, PR/publicity agencies are organized by groups with senior management supervisors directing the activities of account executives. Often, these groups handle clients in the same industry or merchandise category with the supervisor being a specialist in that area. PR/publicity agencies are paid by retainer based on work volume and time expended. They are also reimbursed for out-of-pocket expenses for entertaining, printing, and so on.

At an Advertising Agency. Some advertising agencies have PR/publicity departments that plan and execute campaigns for agency clients and other organizations or individuals. Such departments usually evolve from the agency's belief that PR/publicity coordinated with advertising can maximize a client's image. PR/publicists working in such departments usually work for a salary. The agency bills a time-based fee to clients. The organization and working routines of such departments are similar to those of the PR/publicity agency.

Consultants and Free-lancers. These PR/publicists work independently and bill on the basis of time expended; they are reimbursed for out-of-pocket expenses, etc. Consultants and free-lancers can work for a client directly or for other PR/publicists to help structure their programs. They can assume full responsibility for a PR/publicity campaign or be hired to run a special event. Such individuals can also be hired just to write PR/publicity material.

Consultants and free-lancers work from home or their own offices. Occasionally, they are given office space at the client's headquarters while on assignment. They usually have considerable experience, having worked either for a PR/publicity agency or in-house. They are often hired as specialists on the basis of experience in industry or a nonprofit area—fashion, financial, home furnishings, educational institutions, community health campaigns, political issues, and so on.

WHO EMPLOYS PR/PUBLICISTS?

PR/publicity is an important function in the modern company or organization. Fiber producers, apparel manufacturers, retailers, cosmetic companies, political parties, governments, and hospitals are just a few examples of the organizations that employ the services of PR/publicity professionals to generate news. It is estimated that these professionals supply the media with well over 50 percent of the information printed and broadcast each year.

Professionals work in industries and fields as varied as consumer products, government programs, and entertainment. In some cases, these practitioners are called "publicists," in others they are "media and consumer relations experts"; in still others, they are referred to as "public affairs representatives" or "press agents." The variety of job titles used by professionals in this field reflects the growing importance of the field. Today, a majority of companies in the profit and nonprofit sector employ people to perform PR/publicity duties.

PR/PUBLICISTS HAVE TWO BOSSES

PR/publicists have two bosses: the company or individual seeking exposure and the press working for the media outlet that is the object of their newsmaking efforts. PR/publicists must carefully and diplomatically cater to these two bosses. They must generate stories that accomplish the company's or individual's goals while appealing to the media as well.

While PR/publicists labor under circumstances that produce a dual alliance and responsibility, in a real sense, they can be considered silent partners of the press. They supply journalists with new story ideas, completed articles, photographs, tapes, and films. They do research, leg work, and much of the writing; yet, their by-lines or credits are not the ones the public sees.

The relationship between the PR/publicist and the press is one of mutual dependency. Media editors use PR/publicity stories and pictures because they do not have sufficient resources to find all the news they have time and space to publish and/or broadcast. On the other hand, PR/publicists depend on the press to furnish an outlet for the stories they wish to place. This partnership is an integral part of our communications system.

Discussions with professionals in the PR/publicity field have confirmed the view that the relationship between public relations and publicity is close and often confused; that the PR/publicists must work for two bosses to make news—the client or organization who employs them and the media editor through whom they must work.

Below are statements from professionals which are directed to these points:

> *Public relations is really the totality of a whole company... what a company is, what the products are, what its employees are, what its policies are, its history, how it behaves toward unions, how it behaves toward consumers, what kind of service it gives its products.... If you say public relations, and you are a public relations counselor, that means you have a voice in the management in terms of policy. Now, nine times out of ten that is not true; most public relations people are publicity practitioners. They use publicity to execute and carry out policies that have been set down by the company, and once you get that in your mind, you realize that most public relations people are really publicity people, and there's nothing wrong with that.*
>
> Hal Davis, former President
> Grey and Davis, PR/publicity arm of
> Grey Advertising

6 PUBLIC RELATIONS/PUBLICITY

In all my years in the field, I have been called a "publicity gal" and a "PR lady," interchangeably. I and other professionals know the textbook distinction between the two terms, but in the real working world even those who should know better, constantly confuse the terms. Whatever I and my counterparts are called, we are all in the same business—that of generating favorable news for our clients and presenting any unfavorable news as diplomatically as possible. This is true whether you call yourself a fashion publicist, a financial public relations counsel, or a press agent.

> Lois Beekman
> Lois Beekman Associates
> Publicity Services Co.

In publicity you have two bosses which you have to satisfy, at least. One is the client who is paying you directly or indirectly for writing about his company or his product. You have to say nice things about him; you have to present part of what he considers, not *what you consider, in the best possible light. By the same token, your story has to be acceptable to the editor, and the editor's interests are not always the same as the client's interest. So you have to, in some cases, draw a pretty narrow line between making the story an obvious "puff," which might please some clients, and at the same time you have to consider the editor.*

> Sol Kunis, President
> S.R. Kunis & Co.,
> publicity-public relations agency

If you ask the top executives of almost any company what publicity is, nine out of ten will tell you it's free advertising. Well, publicity isn't free. And it isn't advertising. When you buy a page of advertising you own that page and you control its contents. Publicity appears on editorial pages which are owned by the publication.

> Carol Sirinek
> Director, Sales Promotion & Publicity
> Collins & Aikman Corporation

PR/Publicity Is Important to Marketing

Marketing means the movement of goods and services from producer to seller to consumer. It encompasses research, planning, distribution, and all promotional activities, including PR/publicity.

PR/publicity is an important part of a good marketing program because it provides visibility and credibility for the product, service, or idea being marketed. In addition, it is a flexible tool that can accomplish different objectives. For example, it can be used to build an image, attract attention, establish authority, increase public awareness, forestall negative customer reaction, and create the opportunity for product promotion.

The message that the customer receives from PR/publicity is potentially more believable than anything marketers can say in advertising or a salesperson can say to his or her customer. This is because customers are selective and consciously differentiate between news in an article and appeals in an advertisement or sales "pitch." When customers read, view, or listen to the news produced by PR/publicity, they are aware of the implied third party endorsement by the medium in which it is printed or broadcast. That implied endorsement generally makes the message more believable.

The news resulting from PR/publicity efforts for an industry, client, or organization can help a marketer attract new customers and reinforce on-going business relationships. To the producer of raw materials seeking to influence a manufacturer to buy his or her goods, a single, positive story in a trade journal has the potential of generating thousands of dollars worth of business. To the retailer looking to attract attention to a storewide promotion, pre-opening news in a local newspaper or on a television show can bring the customers out in droves. To the manufacturer of a nationally branded product, network television coverage of a sports event that bears the corporate name can project the company image nationwide and help support sales for their products and their stock issues. PR/publicity is a highly effective, cost-efficient tool that marketers can depend on to help generate sales to consumer and trade alike.

For example, a broadcast interview with the author of a new book will usually produce more book sales than a full-page newspaper ad or a radio spot for the book. In addition, if one were to calculate the value of unpaid PR/publicity space to a marketing plan, the figures would be astonishing. A three-page fashion story about a designer in a major women's interest magazine is equivalent to many thousands of dollars worth of advertising space and has the additional credibility provided by the implied endorsement of the magazine's editors. A ninety-second TV news story about an event such as a marathon would be equivalent to many thousands of dollars worth of air time that the company sponsoring the event could possibly never afford to include in their advertising budget.

In addition, PR/publicity provides marketers with exposure in media that do not accept advertising, such as industry letters. Print clippings and broadcast mentions of a product that are generated by PR/publicity can be used to inspire a sales force or impress potential customers. The number of stories generated and the potential reach, i.e., the number of people exposed to the news, can be reported with pride. Reprints of PR/publicity results can also be distributed to employees either directly or through a company newsletter and can serve to enhance motivation, productivity, and company spirit.

Similarly, nonprofit institutions and political figures depend on the strength of their image for success. PR/publicity is essential to the marketing of that image to the public. To the nonprofit organization seeking to help the general public better understand the need for continued financial support, a series of articles in general news magazines or local newspapers can make the difference between a successful fund-raising drive and a failure. To the politician seeking to pave the way for future candidacy, a series of radio and TV interviews can build recognition of his or her name and policies.

PR/Publicity: Different from Advertising

With advertising, a company pays to secure commercial space or time in media. Because the insertion is guaranteed by a signed contract, advertisements and commercials run exactly the way they have been created. In PR/publicity, companies do not buy space or time, but offer stories to the media as news. PR/publicity stories will appear *only* if editors feel that the information will be of interest to their respective readers or audiences. Moreover, these stories can be changed by the editor to suit the medium's requirements.

Do advertisers get automatic PR/publicity exposure in commercial media? In most cases, they do not. The majority of publications and broadcast media strive for a sharp division between editorial and advertising departments. This is because media keep their readers' interest by featuring what is new, *not* what is being advertised. Their influence and financial success depends on circulation, and they need a fair and news-oriented reputation to keep their readers. In some cases, an editor will seek to feature a major advertiser, if possible, but rarely if the news or product must be directly related to the media audience. Of course, there are always a small number of exceptions, but the percentage is low, and rarely will a major medium risk its reputation by compromising news standards.

Kinds of PR/Publicity

In PR/publicity, as in other large and multifaceted vocations, there are areas of specialization. Because there are so many PR/publicity professionals working in infinitely varied industries, the variety of subspecialties is considerable. Most often the classification of a special kind of PR/publicity reflects the types of clients or organizations represented. PR/publicists develop areas of specialization as a result of experience working in one or more industries. The following are some of the areas of specialization or kinds of PR/publicity:

Product. Product PR/publicity generates news about new products and changes in old products directed to the trade as well as the ultimate consumer. Product PR/publicity techniques can be used in virtually any industry from sporting equipment to machinery parts.

With Which We Serve

Silver-plated flatware by Ricci comes with a 50-year warranty. A thick layer of silver is bonded to its alloy base metal to keep the silver from wearing off. The manufacturer encourages buyers to clean this flatware in the dishwasher. $149 for a five-piece place setting. At Bergdorf Goodman

DANSK DESIGN...18/8 STAINLESS AT 40% OFF 5 PC. PLACESETTINGS.

Odin: Sugg. Retail $55.00 **Carl's $32.95**
Elsinore, Classique, Variation V: Sugg. Retail $32.50
Carl's $19.50
Thistle: Sugg. Retail $37.50 **Carl's $22.50**
86 West Palisade Avenue   New Location: **The Galleria**
Englewood, N.J. 07631   Main Street, White Plains, N.Y. 10601
(201) 568-5990   (914) 428-7878
N.J. M-Sat 9:30-5:45 N.Y. M-Sat 10 a.m.-9:30 p.m., Sun 12-5 p.m.
Add $3.50 for Shpg. plus appropriate Sales Tax.

Carl's HOUSE OF SILVER

82   Home Entertaining

1-2. *In the advertisement for Carl's House of Silver, above, the store paid for the part of the magazine page on which its ad was run. The ad was planned, photographed, and written under the supervision of the store and its advertising agency. The decision as to which issue the ad would appear in was also made by the store and its ad agency. Note that the store's name is in prominent type, quickly identifying it as the advertiser. In fact, the store name is as clearly visible as the headline.*

In the PR/publicity for Bergdorf Goodman, on the left, the store did not *pay for the part of the magazine page on which their flatware is pictured and they are mentioned. The piece was planned, photographed, and written under the supervision of the magazine's editorial staff, and they decided in which issue it would appear. Note that the mention of the store appears in small print at the end of the description of the flatware and is clearly not as important as the headline.*

Fashion. Fashion PR/publicity produces a special kind of product news. It is used by companies in industries such as apparel, cosmetics, and home furnishings, where style trends change many times a year. One of the most important ways people learn about these new styles, and are motivated to buy them, is through stories generated in the media.

Financial. In financial PR/publicity, news is developed for companies that issue stock or wish to "go public." The technique is used to generate stories about such companies in business publications, business sections of newspapers, and occasionally on talk shows. The resulting news includes announcements of profit and loss, new manufacturing techniques, and management changes. Financial PR/publicity also encompasses the preparation of annual and other periodic reports, plus appropriate brochures and broadsides.

Personality. Personality PR/publicity is used mainly in the entertainment, publishing, and political fields, and sometimes to build a designer's name or an executive's image. Arranging interviews in print or on television and/or radio is the technique most frequently employed.

Nonprofit. Nonprofit PR/publicity techniques generate news about the worthiness of organizations such as charities, hospitals, and schools. Issuing reports, running conferences, and raising funds are among the special methods employed in this field.

Image/Issue. Image/issue PR/publicity efforts attempt to change the way people think about a high-profile commercial organization or a concept or idea of social or moral significance. Professionals working in this specialized area must be well-informed about the issues involved as well as public sentiment, keeping up with current trends through careful research.

THE "PUBLICS"

PR/publicity may also be categorized in terms of "publics," or specific audiences to whom the message may be directed. These publics can either be broadly based or very narrow. There are some practitioners, who by virtue of their experience with these publics, can be considered specialists in one or more areas. These publics include those defined by sex, age, e.g., youth, middle age, senior citizens; those defined by profession, e.g., doctors, lawyers, teachers; those defined by ethnic background and race, e.g., black, Hispanic, Oriental; those defined by their interest or hobbies, e.g., stamp collecting, gardening, and so on.

In addition, some PR/publicists specialize in dealing with internal, or in-company, employee publics as compared to external, or out-of-the-company, publics. This area of specialization is closely related to personnel responsibilities. Practitioners in this field can be called upon to communicate the company message and policies to the employees in a variety of ways: through in-house newsletters, seasonal and special parties or events, award programs for achievement and length of company service, an incentive program for new ideas, etc. When a company must relocate offices or manufacturing facilities must be closed down, internal PR/publicity specialists may be engaged to relate the company reasons to the employees in the most favorable terms and to offer aid in relocation or assistance in job changes.

Companies that employ vast numbers of people, in numerous locations, usually have a person responsible for internal relations. In a large company, employee relations are important, and the attitudes of the employee public are of considerable value in enhancing goodwill and employee team spirit and productivity. PR/publicists who direct their attention to internal publics write and distribute employee newsletters, maintain suggestion boxes and award programs, run events from holiday parties to retirement dinners, etc.

PR/Publicity and Advertising Compared

PR/Publicity	Advertising
Editors as objective source write or talk about organization or client.	Organization or client talks about itself and its products.
Organization or client does not buy the space or time in which it is mentioned.	Organization or client pays for advertising space or commercial time in which to run its message.
Editors have control over the story and can make changes affecting the news angle, etc.	The organization or client who places the ad controls its messages.
Editors can use as much or as little of the story as they want in accordance with what they feel would be of most interest to their readers and viewers.	The organization or client who places the ad controls length of its message.
Organization or client has no control over date the story runs.	Date ad runs is guaranteed by signed contract.
Editors are interested in story's news angle. Unless a new one can be developed, a story is usually used only once.	Theme in ad can be repeated many times.
Editors rarely show stories to PR/publicists before they are run.	Proof of ad can be seen and corrections made.
Developed by editor from concepts submitted by PR/publicist or from spontaneous news.	Prepared by advertising agency or advertiser.

1-3. KINDS OF PR/PUBLICITY

Product PR/publicity for RST tennis racquet in the weekly sports section of a newspaper.

Fashion PR/publicity for handbag in a trade newspaper.

Fashion PR/publicity for necklace in a national magazine.

Financial PR/publicity in a national business newspaper.

Image/issue PR/publicity on radio.

Personality PR/publicity in national news magazine.

Personality PR/publicity on television for author and product publicity for book.

Nonprofit PR/publicity of special event on the society page of a newspaper.

Nonprofit PR/publicity for a medical center in their own newsletter.

The World of PR/Publicity

The job of the PR/publicist is multifaceted, calling for a variety of skills and a flexibility of attitude perhaps unequaled in any other vocation. Yet PR/publicity's purposes and functions are, for the most part, only dimly perceived by the ordinary citizen who, if he or she thinks about it at all, categorizes the field as having something to do with parties, the press, and the pursuit of name mention in mass media.

One of the problems leading to this misunderstanding is that the PR/publicity function takes many forms in different organizations. In addition, the function goes under many names, including public information, corporate communications, marketing or product publicity, customer relations, press relations, and so on. The list goes on and on.

Practitioners, themselves, have difficulty in defining the scope of their activities—there are so many. An idea of the vocation's complexities can be determined by considering the following characteristics of the field:

The PR/Publicity Office: A Busy Place. The volume of work that goes on in most PR/publicity offices is very heavy, with schedules constantly interrupted by phone calls, meetings called and cancelled, and creative sessions with photographers, artists, and printers.

More often than not, PR/publicity programs operate against deadlines with the result that office hours, normally 9AM to 5PM, frequently go far, far into the night. Often the office is only a stopping-off place between a round of business lunches with editors, meetings with clients, company functions, community affairs, travel assignments, fund-raising speeches, television interviews, and the myriad activities that could ultimately result in client-mentioning space or time.

PR/Publicity: Little Personal Credit. While PR/publicists work closely with media, they rarely get credit or recognition for news stories, features, and promotional concepts that might have appeared in print and/or broadcast. While not completely altruistic—most practitioners are fairly well compensated—the sense of reward for many PR/publicists comes in the number of times and places their releases are picked up as well as the satisfaction of having followed a program to the successful achievement of goals and objectives.

A PR/Publicist Is Not a Social Butterfly. There are misconceptions that in order to be successful in PR/publicity, the practitioner must like people. While it is helpful for the practitioner to have the ability to like people and in return to have them like him or her, these qualities are not the most crucial. What is important is for the PR/publicity practitioner to be sensitive to the moods of people and to be able to understand their reactions to any set of circumstances.

Similar misconceptions abound as to the necessity of extensive party-going and socializing with the client. While social contact is not necessarily a bad thing, and many practitioners have achieved the status of "friend" with a client of long-standing, such a relationship, again, is not of paramount importance. As a matter of fact, most successful practitioners draw a very firm line between a business relationship and a personal relationship with a client. More important is the ability of the practitioner to accomplish for the client the objectives laid out in his or her basic PR/publicity program.

The Menial Job Leads to Better Things. The order of activity in most PR/publicity offices calls for a myriad of menial tasks. The individual starting off in the field should have no preconceived ideas as to what, within reason, he or she should or should not be asked to do. These could range from answering the phone, to delivering intra-office mail, acting as a secretary, pasting up scrapbooks, opening letters. In PR/publicity, as in other fields, aspirants must "pay their dues."

The Beginning Salary Is Not the End. While the salaries paid to entry-level job holders in PR/publicity are competitive with those found in other branches of the communications industry, some entering the field are disappointed with their wages.

Salaries paid to beginners depend on such factors as the individual's qualifications, the size and strength of the organization, and the state of the economy. Location, too, is an important factor, with personnel in such metropolitan centers as Los Angeles, Chicago, and New York usually getting higher salaries. Salaries paid in nonprofit PR/publicity are usually less than those in business and/or industry.

The PR/Publicist Must Be a Diplomat. Because the PR/publicity practitioner has to cater to two bosses (the client who is paying for the service and the editor of the medium into which he or she is trying to get a story), and because their interests do not always coincide (the client wants his or her company mentioned in the best possible light; the editor is looking for news of greatest value to the readers or viewers), the practitioner is often confronted with problems in strategy. In those cases, the PR/publicist has to draw quite a fine line between making the story a puff and providing the basic material for which the editor is looking. In short, the PR/publicist has to be a skillful diplomat.

Attention to Detail and Follow Through Needed. While many PR/publicity plans are filled with ingenious ways of promoting a product or organization, it is not necessarily the extent of their creativity that makes them successful. More important is the degree to which the details of that plan have been carried out. Most practitioners agree that it is better to have a fair idea that is carefully followed than to have a highly imaginative, creative one that is simply "floated" without any detailed planning or follow through.

Good News Is Not Always "Good." Most often the job of the PR/publicist is to find ways of emphasizing the most favorable aspect of the client's program or product. However, there are instances where less than pleasant information, i.e., a fire at the factory, an accident, etc., has to be given to the press. Under those circumstances, it is better to state the facts openly along with a credible explanation of what occurred. This will result in much less harm than to have an unfriendly source spring the bad news at a later date.

Despite the factors given above, the field of PR/publicity is flourishing. The U.S. Department of Labor estimates that there are 125,000 people employed in the field at this time. Indications are that with the continued growth of large organizations and the increasing complexity coinciding with their expansion, the field will continue to grow.

Things a PR/Publicist Might Be Called on to Do

- Do research
- Write news and feature releases
- Hold press parties
- Write/make speeches
- Write TV/radio scripts
- Direct photography sessions
- Arrange media market tours for clients
- Arrange personality TV tours
- Create special events
- Arrange newspaper, magazine interviews
- Edit house organs
- Handle scholarship and award programs
- Hold press conferences
- Write and edit pamphlets, newsletters, employee publications
- Write annual reports
- Prepare institutional advertising
- Arrange special convocations and seminars
- Organize visitor and tour bureaus
- Administer corporate donations
- Give advice on company and organization activities that affect corporate image.

2
Developing News Sense and Creative Ideas

News angles help determine success in PR/publicity efforts. The news angle around which a particular story is developed is the key factor in attracting the interest of media editors who judge and select which PR/publicity stories will be printed or broadcast as news.

To make news, a PR/publicist must develop a story from an angle that is relevant and exciting to a selected medium. A well-written story can be and often is rejected because it is not developed around an interesting news angle or "peg." Consequently, a first step in any PR/publicity effort is to find one or more news angles that are appropriate for the client and of potential interest to the media. To do this successfully, a PR/publicist must also possess a special sense or instinct for what will make news. PR/publicists can stimulate this awareness by being conversant with trends in the areas in which they are working and by studying relevant media.

Developing News Angles

All PR/publicists start developing news angles by asking some basic questions:
1. *Is it new and different?* Something that has not been done or happened before.
2. *Is it timely?* Something that is happening now or tomorrow.

3. *Are prominent people involved?* Names make news.
4. *Is there local significance?* Something that affects a defined local area.
5. *Is there human interest?* Something that evokes emotions—joy, humor, fear, sorrow, pride, love, lust.
6. *Is there political significance?* Something that affects the state of government or public affairs.
7. *Is there social significance?* Something that has a potential impact on how people relate to each other and society.
8. *Is there conflict?* The clash of people or ideas and the threat of violence.
9. *Are there scientific, medical, or ecological implications?* New life forms, disease cures, space exploration, and erupting volcanoes make news.

CREATING THE NEWS ANGLE

It has been estimated that between 1.3 and 1.4 million press releases are received by the news media in the United States every week from people anxious to get their stories into mass distribution. Of this number, a pitiful few achieve their goals. The press releases that are used are the ones that contain news angled to the particular media to which they were sent; where the editor felt that the information contained in them would be of interest to his or her readers.

Figuring out an angle is not as difficult as it may sometimes appear. The thing to remember is that the release must have news value—either the inclusion of recognized names, an event with significance for a specified community, a sense of immediacy or urgency or human interest—to mention just a few of the attributes that an editor would look for in a press release.

For example, if a release was written saying that the XYZ Manufacturing Company has been in business for seventy-five years, busily making rustproof storm windows, and that its employees are happy because they live in an area good for recreational sports, and the release was sent off to the local press, chances are that it would not be used. But, if the story contained the information that the XYZ Manufacturing Company was just named a subcontractor supplying parts for a new space vehicle and that they were planning to double their work force, chances are the release would be used by the press. The news angles here would be: local significance because of increased job opportunities; scientific and social significance because of the relationship to the national space program. In addition, it is new and different because XYZ has never expanded in this direction before. Of course, one cannot create information of this type if it did not actually happen. But the range of activities that one could capitalize on is circumscribed only by one's imagination and creativity. Stories based on colorful personalities doing the unexpected, awards for service beyond the norm, employees who are active in the community, employees who have unusual hobbies—all are grist for the PR/publicist's mill.

2-1. TYPES OF NEWS ANGLES

New and different

Timely

Prominent people

Local

Human interest

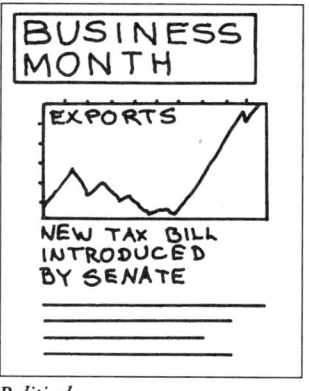
Political

Conflict

Social significance

Medical significance

EVALUATING THE NEWS ANGLE

Successful PR/publicists approach each project with the objective of finding or creating as many relevant news angles as possible. In this way, they maximize the pick-up potential of their stories. The idea is to go beyond the obvious and find unique aspects of the story in order to have the broadest possible appeal to the media editors and their publics.

For each of the five examples given below, select the news angle ("a" or "b") that is more important. Compare your answers with those at the end of the exercise. Consider how the importance of a news angle can affect media coverage and public interest.

1. (a) The Jones Store closes down for two weeks for major alterations. All employees get two weeks with pay.
   (b) The Jones Store closes down and goes out of business.
2. (a) The Northside Bank offers a $1,000 scholarship for the best essay on "Keeping the City Clean."
   (b) The Northside Bank organizes and finances a campaign to set up local "block teams" to clean up empty lots, making them fit for growing flowers and vegetables.
3. (a) Local college basketball team wins state title after leading the league all season.
   (b) Local college football team wins surprise bid to Orange Bowl.
4. (a) $10,000 worth of merchandise stolen from menswear factory.
   (b) $10,000 worth of clothing stolen from patrons of Turkish bath.
5. (a) Mayor's wife sues him for divorce on grounds of adultery.
   (b) Local merchant granted divorce from second wife.

Answers: 1. (b) 2. (b) 3. (b) 4. (b) 5. (a)

Developing PR/Publicity Creativity

There is a special kind of creativity needed for PR/publicity. People who are successful in this field seem to possess a unique ability for developing new ideas and finding news angles.

Creativity has been defined as seeing something that everyone has seen, but thinking something that no one else has thought. It involves the ability to recognize the relationships and to make connections between seemingly unrelated concepts. It results in original thought.

What kind of creative processes do PR/publicists go through in order to develop ideas that can fulfill the client's or organization's desire to make news and stimulate the press to print a story as well? Where do the newsmaking ideas come

> **Some Things that Make News**
>
> - Known people appear in the news much more often than people who are "unknown." Studies done over the past decade show that more than 70 percent of the people in the news are known personalities. (Herbert Gans, *Deciding What's News,* Vintage Books, 1980).
> - Political or entertainment celebrities make easy news. The public never seems to tire of knowing what the President ate for dinner and with whom. The same with movie stars. The popularity of restaurants and resorts are often the result of the PR/publicity they receive from having famous people visit them.
> - The fashion world makes news, too. Women like to know about changing apparel styles—the new skirt length, the popular colors. Men like to know about style changes as well, but perhaps not so obviously.
> - Events in the fashion world attract interest as well. Fashion shows, design awards, store apparel promotions—they all make news regularly.
> - People like to read about profit and loss. They want to know who is making big money and who is losing it. Not only the industry executive or the stock market analyst, but the man-in-the-street is interested in the intrigue of high finance.
> - New technology and new products make news. The public is fascinated by what applied science can produce in computers and new machines to perform business and domestic tasks—from assembly line robots to ordering groceries using a television set.
> - Scientific and medical breakthroughs make news. The cure for cancer, the fight against the aging process, childbirth by artificial means—all find an eager audience.
> - New art forms make news. Modern paintings, experimental music, unique multimedia presentations, and computer graphics are grist for the public's never-ending urge to be "in the know."

from? How does one summon them up? How do PR/publicists learn to think creatively?

One way to answer this question is to consider the three levels of communication that affect the development of ideas: *interpersonal, intrapersonal,* and *mass communication.* Interpersonal refers to our communications with others on a one-to-one basis or in a small group. It involves an exchange of ideas through the use of a common language. Intrapersonal refers to our communications within ourselves; to those ideas we develop in our own minds; to times when we "kick the idea around" on our own and almost seem to talk to ourselves internally without spoken language. Mass communication refers to the messages we receive as a group through the media. Although our perception and understanding of mass media messages is colored by individual experience, this level of communication is not as consciously active as the other two.

PUBLIC RELATIONS/PUBLICITY

BRAINSTORMING: A TECHNIQUE FOR CREATIVITY

Brainstorming is a conference technique (interpersonal communication) in which one of the members of the group presents the other participants with a problem which is then explored through unrestrained discussion. The goal is for one member to inspire another so that ideas "hitchhike" on each other. Professionals in the PR/publicity field use this technique frequently.

The rules for brainstorming include the following:

1. The problem is stated.
2. All ideas are acceptable no matter how "far out."
3. Ideas are not characterized as good or bad.
4. Effort is made to combine ideas of a similar nature and to spark additional ideas.
5. Ideas that have evolved are evaluated in terms of the original problem.

Below are five news angles for a company manufacturing disposable shirts and tops for men and women. The garments are made from a newly developed, reinforced, tissue-like, woodpulp product and are sold in small, medium, and large sizes. The items are packed in 4-inch by 5-inch plastic pouches. They cost $2.65 per set and are available at drug stores and supermarkets.

Figure 2–2 illustrates what took place in a brainstorming session to determine a series of news angles for the company described above. Each extension represents an idea that "hitchhiked" on a basic suggestion presented by a member of the group.

As you can see, the result is five different approaches that could produce news for the product. It is doubtful that any one person working alone could have come up with all these ideas.

2-2. FIVE APPROACHES TO DEVELOPING NEWS ANGLES FOR DISPOSABLE CLOTHING PRODUCT

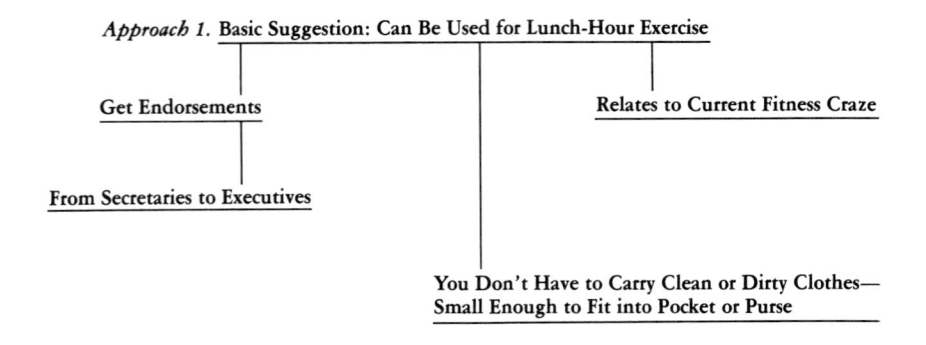

Approach 1. Basic Suggestion: Can Be Used for Lunch-Hour Exercise

Get Endorsements

From Secretaries to Executives

Relates to Current Fitness Craze

You Don't Have to Carry Clean or Dirty Clothes—Small Enough to Fit into Pocket or Purse

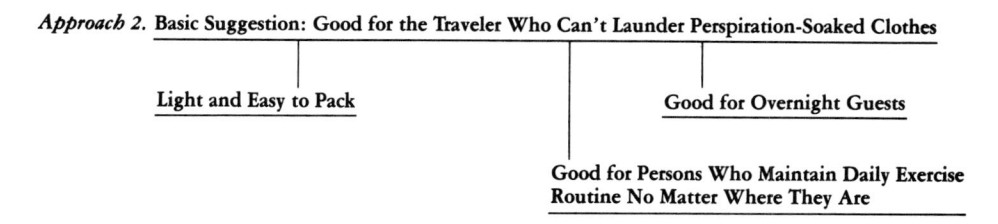

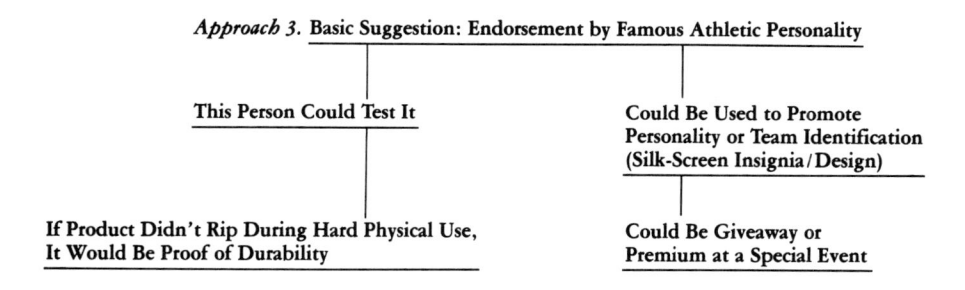

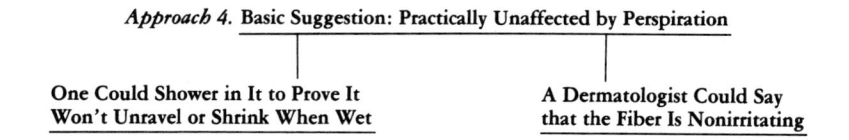

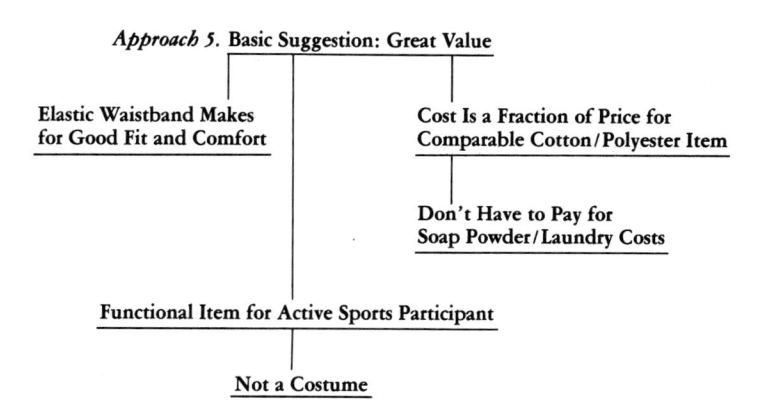

DEVELOPING NEWS SENSE AND CREATIVE IDEAS

Approach 2. Basic Suggestion: Good for the Traveler Who Can't Launder Perspiration-Soaked Clothes

- Light and Easy to Pack
- Good for Overnight Guests
- Good for Persons Who Maintain Daily Exercise Routine No Matter Where They Are

Approach 3. Basic Suggestion: Endorsement by Famous Athletic Personality

- This Person Could Test It
- Could Be Used to Promote Personality or Team Identification (Silk-Screen Insignia/Design)
- If Product Didn't Rip During Hard Physical Use, It Would Be Proof of Durability
- Could Be Giveaway or Premium at a Special Event

Approach 4. Basic Suggestion: Practically Unaffected by Perspiration

- One Could Shower in It to Prove It Won't Unravel or Shrink When Wet
- A Dermatologist Could Say that the Fiber Is Nonirritating

Approach 5. Basic Suggestion: Great Value

- Elastic Waistband Makes for Good Fit and Comfort
- Cost Is a Fraction of Price for Comparable Cotton/Polyester Item
- Don't Have to Pay for Soap Powder/Laundry Costs
- Functional Item for Active Sports Participant
- Not a Costume

TECHNIQUES FOR DEVELOPING PERSONAL CREATIVITY

Brainstorming is a good way to encourage one's creativity in a group or with another individual. There are times, however, when PR/publicists must find news angles and creative ideas for a project on their own. At such times, it is difficult to control or predict the mind's ability to produce a good idea. Surely, one can run the project through a checklist of questions used to develop news angles such as the one on pages 17–18, but what else can be done? The terrific catchy idea, the ones that make for distinctive and successful PR/publicity campaigns do not necessarily come to mind on demand.

Just as brainstorming with others can encourage the flow of ideas and usually lead to new insights, so free association (unrestrained thoughts) and word analogies (list of words bearing a relationship to the main thought) can help to stimulate the individual mind (intrapersonal communication). Sometimes, it seems as if our minds work like organized computers, lining up the facts in a logical sequence and then determining the facts and the solution to a given problem. But other times, the facts do not seem to fit any sequence, and the ability to find a solution seems hopeless. We feel we are at a dead end. Then suddenly, while playing a sport or relaxing with a book, the answer we have been seeking just seems to "come to us." It often feels complete and correct even though we have not yet put it into words. How do we explain this? How can we improve our ability to find these insightful and complete solutions more regularly?

There is no specific answer. Most creative thinkers cannot fully explain how "the great idea" comes to them. Most say fill your mind with as much information on your subject as possible. Then forget about it. Relax. Let your subconscious go to work. From time to time, make a conscious effort to rethink and reexamine the problem. But do not strain. Gradually, the idea will come to you.

If this approach does not work, do not give up. Try others. Many of the following techniques can stimulate the brain and encourage creativity:

1. Consider the basic facts in new and varied combinations.
2. List random words, phrases, rhymes, jingles, etc., that relate to the idea.
3. Think about how people with varying interests and lifestyles relate to the idea.
4. Test the product—use it yourself, ask family and friends to use it. Think about its performance.
5. Find analogies. Consider what properties the product or idea would have if it were an animal, a car, a machine, a food, a type of music.
6. Develop your ideas by asking: *Who?, What?, When?, Where?, Why?,* and *How?*
7. Feel free to use intuition and hunches to find links and connect ideas.

The Importance of Research and "Listening"

The more PR/publicists expose themselves to information relating to a project, the better chance they have of coming up with an interesting and useful story idea or news angle. It is helpful to do research—not just to plunge in and try to be creative, but rather to take the time to read and listen to others in order to gather all the information available from mass communication sources that is relevant to a given project.

Most successful PR/publicists are skilled researchers who make placements in a variety of publications regularly and are used to adapting an idea from one field to influence a project in another.

In addition, good PR/publicists are usually excellent listeners who know how to get the most from spoken information. This is because they must know how to "read" intent as well as word content in order to get the most direction from their clients or management and the most feedback from press contacts. To accomplish this, they employ one or more of the following techniques of "active listening":

1. Think ahead of the speaker and try to anticipate what he or she is going to say.
2. Weigh evidence used to support points made and consider its validity.
3. Mentally review and summarize each point.
4. Watch for nonverbal behavior. Facial expressions, gestures, etc., can be clues to meaning.
5. Keep an open mind. Try to avoid evaluating until you have heard all the points the speaker has to make.

It is not always possible to accomplish totally "active" listening, but studies have shown that we think at a faster rate than we talk. Therefore, there is usually time to use the aforementioned techniques when we play the role of listeners.

Professionals in the PR/publicity business know that to be successful they have to be creative and able to develop ideas that can be placed in print media and broadcast. Following are some thoughts from PR/publicity pros on what it takes to make it in the field. Note how much these practitioners stress idea development skills and creative approaches to problem-solving.

> *I would say generally that people who are successful in the agency I am with are rather extroverted, involved kind of people. They are curious; they are very involved. I think current events is an important part of public relations, being able to capitalize on something that's in the news, so as trends develop you can tie them in with your client's product.... If you are not up to date with what's happening in the world you can't tie it in with something that's going to be interesting to editors who are barometers of public tastes. In*

other words, presumably what you read in magazines or newspapers is what the editors of those publications think the public wants to read about.

Susan Ehrlich
Executive Vice President
The Rowland Co., Inc.

You have to be able to see a mundane product, you have to be able to see the potential for something other than just a release; you have to see something that can create excitement, consumer interest as well as trade interest. A textile company like ours is mainly interested in publicity for our customers—we are not selling directly to the consumer. If we do consumer publicity, it's as a service to our customers.

Carol Sirinek
Director, Sales Promotion & Publicity
Collins & Aikman Corporation

Discovery, someone said, consists of seeing what everybody else has seen and thinking what nobody else has thought. That, it strikes me, is an excellent description of the process of creativity in PR as in many other fields. Creativity, I think, is not a mystical, murky process arising from some innate ability. Rather, I think it is working with raw materials that everyone else has seen, but making somewhat unconventional connections. It isn't mystical—it's hard work. It also entails knowledge of the materials you're working with, and knowledge of where you want to go. It's "figuring angles," to use jargon. There is an element of daring in it, enthusiasm that leads to the question: "Why not?"

Dick Magat
Director of the Office of Reports
The Ford Foundation

The ABC Company:
A Case in Creative Idea Development

The ABC Company, a large manufacturer of bed and table linens, was the first company to commission a fashion designer to do a collection of sheet and towel designs. They successfully promoted the collection with a combination of techniques: in-store appearances by the designer, advertising, and PR/publicity. The results that the PR/publicity effort produced were exceptionally good. This was because a fashion designer collection of sheets and towels was unique: it had not been done before; the products were new; they had a new design concept; and the designers were already well-known personalities whom the public found interesting. In short, the company had lots of news angles to use.

ABC ran these fashion designer promotions over a period of three years. The public they reached with the news of these promotions and the public who, in turn, bought the designer linens was an affluent, urban, and relatively sophisticated one. This public represented a new, younger, and more avant-garde customer for ABC products than the company had attracted previously.

Soon after ABC ran the first designer collection promotion, other companies in the industry, impressed by ABC's success in generating news and sales, began to do the same type of promotions. At the end of three years, virtually every competitive company in the industry had designer promotions of one sort or another. These were all fairly successful, but such promotions were no longer new or unique and, consequently, the news angles, which had made them so interesting to the press and, in turn, produced such stunning PR/publicity results, were no longer as effective.

At this point, ABC management realized that their marketing strategy for going into the designer promotions had been realized—they had drawn attention to their brand through PR/publicity techniques and they had attracted a new, younger, urban, more sophisticated customer. They also realized that their business success had been built by catering to an older, more conservative customer whom they could not afford to lose. They concluded that they should attempt to create a PR/publicity concept that would reach these older customers and make them feel secure in their allegiance to the ABC brand. This realization was the result of market research and analysis directed by the vice president of marketing for ABC.

A series of brainstorming sessions were called to discuss the results of the designer promotions and to develop ideas for the future. At the first meeting were the company vice president, marketing; the vice president, communications; the PR/publicity director, and the advertising director. The advertising agency was represented by the account executive for ABC, members of the agency marketing staff, and a secretary to take notes. Through a give-and-take of ideas in the brainstorming session, the following points were initially established:

1. ABC was the leader in the industry and it was important that they maintain that aggressive position in terms of their trade and consumer publics.
2. They were the first company to do designer collection promotions, and they should try to be the first to do another type of promotion.
3. They had successfully captured a new, younger, sophisticated, urban customer through their fashion designer promotions. They should maintain product lines and PR/publicity and promotion to keep that customer interested.
4. They must turn their PR/publicity strategy to their major consumer public—the more conservative, older, suburban customers, and create a

concept designed to reach them and encourage their continued brand loyalty.
5. Whatever promotion they embarked upon should be done quickly—within one year to eighteen months, if possible.

In addition, they analyzed the elements that had made their designer promotions successful:

1. Known designer personalities in whom the press and the public had significant interest.
2. Unique and different designs of their standard quality products.
3. The status of a "designer" item.

The brainstorming session that produced these conclusions was the result of the participants using each others' ideas to inspire new ones. Its progression was more involved, but similar to the disposable clothing session discussed previously on page 22. After the meeting, the conclusions were organized by ABC's marketing vice president and distributed to each of the participants for review and study. The notes, which were distributed within one day of the meeting to ensure recall and clarity, were accompanied by a directive that the participants should consider as many ideas as possible for a new promotion directed at the conservative, suburban customer.

The next meeting was scheduled for one week later. During the week, the participants used both interpersonal and intrapersonal communications techniques to develop their ideas. In addition, one researched the mass media to better understand the market involved. Some had lunch together to "kick around some idea" (interpersonal communications). Still others went over the elements that made for the success of the designer promotions in their own mind (intrapersonal communications). One focused on the type of celebrity who might appeal to the customer they were interested in reaching by skimming through the magazines (mass communications research) directed to the conservative housewife and reading market research profiles on her.

At the next meeting, all had run the problem over in their minds many times and were sufficiently immersed in it to understand what they were looking for in a PR/publicity idea. It was the PR/publicity director who had the idea that the company eventually used. She said it "came to her" in the shower the morning of the meeting, and knew it would probably work even before she had thought it out completely. At the meeting she presented her concept as follows:

> *We should engage a celebrity because known people have proven that they can make news for us. We need someone who can really appear to be involved in the product because, if not, the press will think of the promotion as just another label and not be very interested in writing about it. We need another person that the customer we want to reach can relate to and identify with. It probably should be a woman since so many of the fashion designers we've promoted have been men.*

DEVELOPING NEWS SENSE AND CREATIVE IDEAS

The brainstorming session continued with the participants running through various personalities until they arrived at one who fulfilled all the criteria. She was a very famous, retired movie star who had a conservative style. She happened to be a needlepoint expert and had many designs which would be suitable for adaptation to linens. She was acknowledged as a gracious hostess who had a lovely and comfortable home and a style to which the desired public could relate. She had appeared in many world-famous films, and themes for these could be used to influence design motifs. The story of what she had been doing in the ten years since her retirement from films would be of significant interest to the press, making it probable that the opportunities for PR/publicity would be great. As an experienced performer, she had the presence and stamina to do a national promotional tour which would multiply the PR/publicity opportunities. She was available and interested when contacted.

What developed was a PR/publicity campaign that worked and produced thousands of dollars worth of valuable news and exposure for the ABC Company. Months were spent by the PR/publicity staff researching all the details and creating stories and ideas that could be used to create news about the promotion. Once the actual campaign was launched, the results were excellent. There were feature length television and radio interviews, parties in selected cities across the country, and many newspaper and magazine articles.

In conclusion, it is important to note that creative insight, that ability to put the facts together in a new and exciting way, is an important part of the PR/publicist's profession. The techniques introduced in this chapter were intended to illustrate the special kind of creativity needed for success in PR/publicity and to encourage readers to develop their own.

3
Knowing the Media

A knowledge of media is of vital importance to PR/publicists. Without a clear understanding of the characteristics of the individual medium, including a blueprint of the various job functions involved, working routines, and deadlines, PR/publicists cannot work with media editors efficiently.

Effective PR/publicists regularly study the print or broadcast media with which they are working, noting style, content, and length of news items, stories, and features. In addition, they learn the hierarchy at each of the mass media outlets, and how to establish contact.

Basically, media can be divided into two areas: *mass media* and *specialized media*. Mass media, in its academic sense, can be subdivided into newspapers, magazines, television, radio, books, motion pictures, and advertising aimed at a broad spectrum of consumer publics. Of these, the most widely used by PR/publicists are newspapers and magazines in the print category; television and radio in the broadcast category. Specialized media, for the most part, deal and cater to those publics with a very special interest usually associated with a business, profession, trade, or occupation.

Another way of looking at media is to consider it as either *external media* or *internal media*. The former are those forms of communication that circulate outside of their originating source; e.g., a newspaper leaves its plant and is circulated throughout the entire city. Internal media are those forms of communication whose circulation is restricted to their originating source; e.g., a house organ, a college newspaper circulated on campus, and so on. But media, no matter how classified, are the lifeblood of PR/publicity. Therefore, a close study of various types of media outlets is in order. (Refer to Chapter 8 on how to select appropriate media sources and the techniques for contacting and working with them.)

PRINT MEDIA

Print media offer great opportunities for PR/publicity campaigns. The variety of print media and the scope of the publics they reach give the PR/publicist innumerable opportunities for placement. Whether defined by locale, industry, or special interest, whether issued daily, weekly, or monthly, print media offer the PR/publicist a constant outlet for news stories and features.

Newspapers

Newspapers are an important outlet for PR/publicists because of their wide readership—80 percent of all people eighteen years of age and older read a newspaper—and newspapers can expand or contract in relation to the amount of news they carry. Regardless of where the newspaper is distributed, there is a constant need for "new" news.

Newspapers can be broken down into a group of categories. Knowing how newspapers are classified is of help to the practitioners who want to work with them. They can be divided according to the interest to which they cater. There are newspapers of general consumer interest (*The New York Times*), special consumer interest (*AFL-CIO News*), business interest (*The Wall Street Journal*), and trade interest (*Women's Wear Daily*).

Newspapers can also be classified as to day of issuance (daily, Sunday, semi-weekly, weekly, monthly) and time of issuance (morning or afternoon). There are approximately 1,800 daily newspapers and about 7,500 weekly and semi-weekly newspapers.

Newspapers generally have geographic areas of influence. Most consumer papers are local in appeal and their content is geared to the community in which they are published. A few, such as *The New York Times* or *The Los Angeles Times*, which are large metropolitan dailies, place heavy emphasis on the national and international scene as well as reporting local news.

While daily newspapers usually get a good deal of attention from practitioners, the weekly and semi-weekly newspapers are often forgotten, despite the fact that they represent a highly effective means of reaching people who live in suburban and rural areas. Many authorities feel that because of the interest with which they are read, these papers exert a far greater impact on their readers' opinions in relation to their circulation than do the average daily newspapers.

The daily newspaper, for the most part, is produced under great pressure, sometimes leading to unintentional distortion of fact—a situation that the PR/publicist must recognize and live with. Newspaper deadlines are important. The wise PR/publicist keeps a deadline chart (which might also contain a list of preferred news angles) to which he or she can easily refer. Although individual schedules differ, the first edition of an afternoon paper usually closes in the late morning, and the first edition of a morning newspaper in the early evening of the day before.

NEWSPAPER ORGANIZATION

The organization of a newspaper is rather complicated. It is usually divided into three areas: editorial, business (which includes running the internal operation at a profit as well as soliciting advertising revenue), and mechanical. The ordinary daily newspaper has the difficult marketing assignment of coming up with a "new product" 365 days a year.

The most important executive jobs on the editorial side include editor, managing editor, city editor, and such "specialty editors" as editorial, sports, financial, features, drama or entertainment, Sunday, women's page, and society. In many instances, the job titles overlap, and the alert PR/publicity practitioner keeps a record of who is responsible for what or, at least, keeps aware of any shifts in responsibilities.

In terms of job activity, every newspaper has a publisher, who might be likened to the president of a corporation. The publisher's job is to keep the paper going; for the most part, he or she is concerned with the business side of the operation. Sometimes, the publisher wears two hats, and is the editor-in-chief as well.

The editor-in-chief is in charge of the editorial staff and the editorial tone of the newspaper. Under normal circumstances, the PR/publicist will have little to do with the editor or with the managing editor, whose function varies but whose usual responsibility is coordinating the various editorial departments so that the paper comes out on time. On many papers, the managing editor also performs the job of news editor.

The flow of news is directed by the city editor, who works with reporters handling local news, and state editors and wire editors who screen state and national news. The PR/publicist will have some contact with the city editor if the story involves "hard news," but he or she will most likely have more contact with the specialty editors, such as the women's page editor or the financial editor.

Photographers are usually assigned to the city editor, although, on a number of newspapers, there are special photographers assigned to the sports staff. Photographers are not assigned to all stories; to do so would be too expensive. Therefore, it is a good idea for the PR/publicist to take pictures and have them ready for publicity purposes whenever possible.

Sunday editions of newspapers, because of the leisurely manner in which they are usually read, will accept stories, particularly features, that will not be included in the daily edition. The Sunday editor, then, if there is one, is a good person to know.

While the traditional typewriter and hot-lead Linotype machine are still in evidence in many newsrooms throughout the country, the advent of the video display terminal (looks like a typewriter upon which has been mounted a television screen), computerized typesetting, and photo composition have forever changed the newspaper printing process. One of the major benefits of this transition has been an increase in production speed, allowing reporters and editors to work more closely to their deadlines. This, in turn, has given publicists more time to get material to the press.

Magazines

There are approximately 9,000 weekly, monthly, and quarterly magazines published each year. These can be divided into consumer and business classifications. Of this number, only approximately 1,000 are targeted toward general consumer interests; the rest are targeted toward more specific business areas.

Although consumer magazines are the most visible and many have enormous circulations, business magazines offer the PR/publicist a highly efficient way to reach specific publics with stories directed to the commercial or professional interests of the publications. In addition, such magazines are generally receptive to materials from PR/publicists because many have small staffs and tight budgets which may limit their ability to cover all the areas of interest to their readers.

Of all media, with the possible exception of radio, magazines are the most specialized. Within the consumer field, for example, magazines may be classified as fashion (*Vogue, Harper's Bazaar*); home service (*McCall's, Redbook, Good Housekeeping*); news (*Time, Newsweek*); shelter (*House and Garden, Better Homes and Gardens*); general interest (*Reader's Digest*), and so on. In the publishing industry, magazines are often referred to as "books."

Magazine circulations vary from those in the thousands to such giants as *Reader's Digest* and *TV Guide* with circulations in the millions. In addition, magazines increase their sphere of influence by virtue of their "pass-on" quality, i.e., several people, besides the initial receiver, usually read a magazine.

Magazines are sold in two ways: at the newsstand and by subscription. Sustained and increasing newsstand sales indicate considerable pulling power and specific reader interest in individual issues. An impressive subscription renewal rate is a sign of continued faith in the publication and a loyal and consistent reader audience. Both of these points are often advanced in magazine promotion.

The magazine reader is different from the newspaper reader. The magazine reader absorbs at a much slower pace, and while magazines are constantly being started (and ended), magazine readers, for the most part, are loyal and long term, and the magazines they read reflect their approach to life. Consequently, they react more noticeably than newspaper readers to product information and news found in magazines. For example, *New York Magazine* attracts readers who are interested in issues relevant to life in and around the metropolis; *McCall's* provides answers to what many suburban women believe are their problems; *Seventeen* reflects the teenage girl's lifestyle.

Magazines, because they are read at a more leisurely pace than newspapers and usually offer a more luxurious environment (quality paper, good color reproduction), can provide an indexing of information (i.e., cutting and filing that particular article) which is more effective and inclined to be more long-lasting than that provided by newspapers.

Preparing stories for magazines requires careful planning. With the possible exception of the news weeklies that have a shortened lead time, most magazines plan their editorial lineups months in advance. PR/publicists should not only have their written ideas ready to conform to such a schedule, but they should also have product samples for photography ready at that time.

A magazine keeps its readers interested by providing a distinct "slant" or "angle" to its editorial material. Consequently, it is important that the PR/publicist know who the reader of the magazine is (age, income, sex, lifestyle, etc.) and what slant the magazine takes in presenting information to the reader. The PR/publicist can get this information by reading the magazine carefully and regularly and from the statistics about readership issued by the magazine itself.

Basically, every magazine is edited according to a "formula," a basic concept that distinguishes it from its competition. Most magazines are devoted to a special interest, such as current news, photography, apartment living, or the general interests of a well-defined audience, such as teenage girls, brides-to-be, executives. Magazines tend to appeal to higher economic groups and, consequently, they are a powerful and influential force in reaching those people.

Magazines constantly research their readers and offer editorial articles and features that meet their readers' current interests. Because of the greater length of time between issues, magazines, unlike newspapers, can present more in-depth features and aim for "better writing." To be successful, magazines must have either a large national circulation or an intense local circulation.

MAGAZINE ORGANIZATION

The central figure in the magazine organization is the editor-in-chief who has the final word in what goes into the publication, even though other editors are often given a good deal of freedom in accepting material. Most magazines have a managing editor who oversees the day-to-day operation. Other staff functions include a copy editor, art director, and a group of editors charged with specific responsibilities.

Some magazines are organized with department editors, such as articles, beauty, home fashions, etc., with the specific editor charged with the responsibil-

GOOD HOUSEKEEPING

959 EIGHTH AVENUE, NEW YORK, NEW YORK 10019

JOHN MACK CARTER
Editor in Chief

MARY FIORE
Managing Editor

MINA W. MULVEY
Executive Editor

HERBERT BLEIWEISS
Art Director

A. ELIZABETH SLOAN, PH.D.
Director, The Institute

MEMBERS OF THE EDITORIAL STAFF

VICE-PRESIDENT AND TECHNICAL DIRECTOR: GEORGE S. WHAM, Ph.D. ASSISTANT MANAGING EDITOR: MARGARET R. DE MEO FICTION: NAOME LEWIS, *editor*; LEONHARD DOWTY, *senior associate*; ARLEEN L. QUARFOOT, *associate editor*; SARA CHRISTIANSEN, *editorial assistant* BOOKS: LEONHARD DOWTY, *editor*; ALIX HARPER, *editorial assistant* ARTICLES: JOAN THURSH, *editor*; DIANE BROWN, *senior associate*; PATRICIA GADSBY, TONI GERBER HOPE, *associate editors*; ROSEMARY LEONARD, MARY ANN LITTELL, CAMILLE MANDLER, *editorial assistants* THE BETTER WAY: ERIKA REIDER MARK, *editor*; MARY H. J. FARRELL, *senior editor*; MIDGE LASKY SCHILDKRAUT, *associate editor*; JEFFREY W. MILLER, *writer*; CLAUDIA RIEMER, *editorial assistant* HOME BUILDING & DECORATING: GENEVIEVE FERNANDEZ, *director*; BOB COLLINS, JUTA RISTSOO, *associates* FASHIONS: ANN ELKINS, *director*; RUTHANN COGGINS, *associate director*; BRIDGET DEMSKI, *assistant* COPY: RUTH ARNSTEIN, *editor*; PHYLLIS SCHILLER, *senior associate*; HELEN CEGLIA, *associate* EDITORIAL PRODUCTION: JAMES M. LOPEZ, *director*; JUANITA G. CHAUDHRY, MARY MALGIERI, *associates*; SUZANNE LA ROSA, *editorial assistant* ART: BRUCE DANBROT, *design director*; ELLEN SCHWARTZ, *associate*; PAT McBRIDE, *cartoon editor and art coordinator* ART PRODUCTION: ANN PEARSE, *director*; JOANNE WINEMAN, *assistant* REGIONAL EDITIONS: SHIRLEY HOWARD, *editor, associate travel editor*; CANDACE BUSHNELL, *assistant editor* TRAVEL EDITOR: STEPHEN BIRNBAUM BULLETIN SERVICE: BERTRAND J. GILMAN, *director*; MARGARET ALFARO, *manager* CONTRIBUTING EDITORS: JEAN LIBMAN BLOCK, DR. JOYCE BROTHERS, JANE KEELY, CHARLOTTE MONTGOMERY, ALAN E. NOURSE, M.D., ELIZABETH POST SPECIAL PUBLICATIONS: ROSEANN HIRSCH, *director*

NATIONAL AFFAIRS: MARGARET ADAMS, *senior editor*; BARBARA KOLK, *assistant*

THE GOOD HOUSEKEEPING INSTITUTE

A. ELIZABETH SLOAN, Ph.D., *director*
GEORGE S. WHAM, Ph.D., *technical director*
MARY E. POWERS, *associate director*
APPLIANCES & HOME CARE: JOAN MEES, *director*; RUTH LAUMAN, *associate director*; SARAH E. REPKE, *associate*; SALLYANN TYSK COSGROVE, *assistant* BEAUTY CENTER: NANCY ABRAMS, *editor*; LAURIE M. CYBUL, *associate editor, director, Beauty Laboratory*; LEE LOBEL, *associate*; ELIANA LIMARDO GARCIA, MATILDA M. McLAUGHLIN, *beauty stylists* THE BUREAU: KRISTEN W. McNUTT, Ph.D., *director*; AMY BARR, M.S., R.D., *nutritionist*; CAROL WAPNER, *home economist*; ELAINE GARSKE, *nutrition fellow*. *Nutrition and Diet Center*, CHRISTIAN C. HANSEN, *special-projects officer*; YVETTE GH BANKS, *supervisor, Bureau Laboratory*; MARJORIE C. HORTON, MARY KLIAUGA, ROBERT KORMENDI, *chemists* CONSUMER RESEARCH LABORATORY: MARY E. POWERS, *director*; PATRICIA QUIGLEY, *associate director*; M. KELLY RUANE, *associate* ENGINEERING: ROGER G. COOK, *director*; DAVID QUENTZEL, *associate director*; KENNETH MILLER, CHARLES W. MONTPLAISIR, JR., *engineers* FOOD: MILDRED YING, *director*; SUSAN DEBORAH GOLDSMITH, *associate director*; ELLEN H. CONNELLY, JOYCE A. KENNEALLY, *associates*; DIANE SIMONE DIXON, NORMAJEAN SARLE, VICTORIA SCOCOZZA, *assistants* NEEDLEWORK & SEWING CENTER: CECELIA K. TOTH, *director*; MARY CAROLYN WALDREP, *associate*; VALENTINA ANASTASIA SNELL, JANET HUFFMAN AKHTARSHENAS, *assistants* TEXTILES: JEANNETTE VAN LEEUWEN, *director*; CAROL BETH LIPMAN, *associate director*; CAROLYN E. HUGHES, *assistants*; LUCY TERENZIO

Published by The Hearst Corporation,
Frank A. Bennack, Jr., President
Randolph A. Hearst, Chairman
Gilbert C. Maurer, President, Magazines Division
Raymond J. Petersen, Publishing Director, *Good Housekeeping*
GORDON J. SEMERAD, Advertising Director
WILLIE MAE ROGERS, Special Adviser to the Publisher
RICHARD E. DEEMS, Publishing Consultant

NEW YORK

Editor
Edward Kosner

Managing Editor
Laurie Jones

Design Director
Robert Best

Executive Editors
Richard Babcock, Deborah Harkins

Senior Editors
Frederick Allen, Peter Devine (Copy)
Peter Herbst, Rhoda Koenig, Molly McKaughan
Nancy McKeon, Anna Wintour, Carter Wiseman
Photography Editors
Karen Mullarkey, Jordan Schaps
Contributing Editors
Jennifer Allen, Julie Baumgold, Alexis Bespaloff
Marie Brenner, Seymour Britchky, Sharon Churcher
Orde Coombs, Barbara Costikyan, Michael Daly
Peter G. Davis, David Denby, Jack Egan
Linda Bird Francke, Gael Greene
Anthony Haden-Guest, Pete Hamill
Bernice Kanner, Jesse Kornbluth, Michael Kramer
Kay Larson, Mary Ann Madden, Nicholas Pileggi
Henry Post, Alan Rich, Tony Schwartz, John Simon
Tohi Tobias, Craig Unger, Lally Weymouth
James \ olcott, William Wolf, Linda Wolfe, Vic Ziegel
Around Town Editor: Ruth Gilbert
Sales & Bargains Editor: Leonore Fleischer
Associate Editors: Florence Fletcher, Ouita McMath
Assistant Editors: Georgia Gunn, Richard Mineards
Corky Pollan, Mayer Vishner
Editorial Assistants
Ellen Hopkins, Fran Kessler, Caroline Law
Tanya Lenkow, Sarah Lewis, Deborah Mitchell
Evelyn Norman, Eric Pooley, Laurie Schechter
Jennifer Seabury, Jeannette Walls
Cue Listings: Gillian Duffy, Madeline Johnson
Howard Karren
Editorial Publicity: Suzanne Eagle

Art Director
Patricia Bradbury
Art Production Manager: David White
Assistant Art Director: Don Morris
Assistant Photo Editor: Susan Vermazen
Assistant Art Production Manager: Shelley Lefkowitch
Art Staff: Christine Lang (Art Assistant)
Deane Folsom, April Garston
Jeff Pappalardo, Vivette Porges, Joan Ranieri

Publisher
Cathleen Black

Circulation Director
Vince Dema
Circulation Business Manager: Harold Shain
Staff: Linda Cortese, William Donaldson
Nora George, Ellen Goldwasser, Bella Hopkinson
Amy Kirson, Ann Llewellyn
Production Director
Frank Sullivan
Production Manager: Richard Muehleman
Staff: Dolores Liberto, Kathy Tomlin
Controller
Sidney Ferenc
Credit Manager: Molly Strauss
Staff Accountants: Ruth Chamberlain, Carmine Tiero
Staff: Lisa Anselmo, Teresa Ferri
Jeffrey Nozile, Mark Sabb
Advertising Sales Director
David O'Brasky
Advertising Manager: Marvin Krauss
Promotion Director
Elaine Shindler
Promotion Manager: Anthony Irving
Research Manager: Ken Meitener
Staff: Anne Lewis, Jilann Picariello
Jane Podhoretz, Chris Shea
Sales Representatives
Alan Berman, Larry Burstein, Elinore Carmody
Mary Joe Cassidy, Carol Crellin, Betsy Cronen
Patricia Drazan, Nan Elmore, Thomas Florio
Jack Kaduson, Alan Tigner, Lori Zelikow
Advertising Coordinator: Nancy Pollock
Computer Operations: J. McGehee
Staff: Theresa Bresnihan, Helen Fajerman
Patricia Herberich, Kathy Kontiles
Mimi Moskowitz, Marilyn Taerstein
Chicago: Heidi Grumley, Manager
Classified Advertising Manager: Mel Worby
Staff: Michael Rousseau
Information Services Manager: Valerie Taylor
Personnel Manager: Mary O'Connor
Office Services Manager: Mary Ann McCarthy
Staff: Paul Abrams, Andrew Cruz, Jacqueline Dees
Stan Katta, Rodney Madden, Joseph Markfelder
George Pogue, Anna Preato
Special Consultant: Mort Glankoff

News Group Magazines
President: Marty Singerman
Director of Finance: Alan Greene
Coordinator: Lucille Piccoli

3-1. *A comparison of the mastheads from* Good Housekeeping *and* New York *reveals the difference in the way personnel and departments at the two publications are organized. At* Good Housekeeping, *responsibilities are defined by topic covered in the magazine, such as fashion, fiction, decorating, etc. At* New York, *editors and writers are listed by level of responsibility with no topic breakdown.*

ity for producing a specific part of the issue. Some magazines have regional editors whose responsibilities involve a wide spectrum of subjects in the region they cover. Others have a combination of regional and department editors.

Much of the writing and research connected with magazine publication is done by free-lancers. Magazines would find it too expensive to employ, on a regular basis, the many writers needed to fill their columns. Despite their unofficial status, free-lancers are recognized as important members of a magazine's staff, and the varied expertise and writing styles they provide bring vitality to a magazine's editorial content.

Business Publications

Practically every profession, business group, industry, or vocational area in the country is serviced by a business paper or magazine. In terms of aggregate numbers, business publications greatly outnumber consumer magazines. As such, they represent great opportunities for the PR/publicist.

Like consumer publications, business periodicals can be broken down into a number of subgroups:

1. Trade publications concerned with marketing and merchandising functions. Examples: *Men's Wear, Advertising Age.*
2. Professional publications oriented toward people in recognized professions, such as law, medicine, dentistry. Examples: *Journal of the American Medical Association, Journal of the American Dental Association.*
3. Institutional publications aimed at institutions, such as hospitals, and other service organizations, such as hotels and nursing homes. Examples: *Modern Health Care, Hotel & Travel Index.*
4. Industrial publications aimed at those individuals and institutions engaged in some form of manufacturing or production. Examples: *Mechanical Engineering, Appliance Manufacturing.*

Stories prepared for specific editors of business publications require a detailed knowledge of that area by the writer. However, trade editors are usually very cooperative and have been known to be willing to spend time with PR/publicists setting forth the requirements for acceptable material.

In addition to spot news and stories of a broad, general nature pertaining to developments in the specific field, business publications give much space to the introduction of new products and services, personnel changes, transfers, and promotions. Additionally, it is frequently possible to interest an editor in an article (under a company by-line) on the development of some phase of the industry as exemplified by the specific company's progress.

For MEMBERS ONLY

A newsletter for American Express Cardmembers

Now Travel Accident Insurance increases to $100,000 (page 2)

Feb. 1983

Viewpoint: William F. Buckley, Jr.

The rewards of adventure travel

There is a growing appetite among many Americans for active vacations that teach them a new outdoor skill or provide a close encounter with nature. The corporate world is also becoming cognizant of this trend and is experimenting with adventure vacations for executives, to help them work together more effectively. The *For Members Only* newsletter gained some additional insights on adventure travel from an unexpected source, William F. Buckley. As an author, editor and host of TV's *Firing Line*, he is well-known as an explorer of ideas. But he has also become an explorer of physical realms on his vacations. He has twice crossed the Atlantic in a small boat, most recently with six companions (the subject of his new book — *Atlantic High*). Here are some of his adventurous thoughts.

Why do some people like adventure vacations?

"Life and work must have a certain keenness, or they become banal.

"Winston Churchill defined a vacation as a time for 'doing something different.' There may be a great deal of physical effort involved in an adventure trip, but the physical effort is transcended in the memory by the totally new environment and respect gained for the physical world.

"An adventure trip gives you the feeling *you* are in charge of your life and not simply a pawn of nature."

Are there skills or attitudes learned on adventure trips that are applicable to the workplace?

"Any shared adventure trip can create a bond between people. It can accelerate the development of relationships.

"You also quickly learn that cooperation with other people is absolutely essential. If you are on a mountainside holding the rope for someone, you're very aware that he will be holding the rope for you in the next minute.

"When adventure travel is used by companies as a form of corporate lubrication of working relationships, such experiments tend to prove themselves out empirically. The companies can quickly see whether or not executives are working together more smoothly after such a trip."

Are there any lasting effects on business people who choose adventure vacations?

"There is a resonant impact of any adventure trip. Sometimes you are not always sure of what it is until you've run the trip through your metabolism several times after you've returned home. After my voyage

continued on page 4

3-2. *PR/publicity in a newsletter. An article in the "For Members Only" newsletter, distributed to American Express cardmembers, provides PR/publicity for William F. Buckley's new book. It was a good choice because the book deals with adventure vacations and, therefore, could inspire readers to think about traveling and using American Express services.*

By and large, business publications are interested in covering as many relevant stories as possible because they have a real stake in promoting the health and expansion of the area they serve. And readers are looking to these publications for news and information that will help them in their profession or vocation.

Newsletters, House Organs, and Columns

Newsletters. One of the most popular and efficient means of dealing with a specific public is the newsletter, a written report that usually provides forecasts or analyses of information to a special audience. Used by governmental agencies, schools, banks, and other organizations of all kinds, the newsletter can fit almost every situation.

Newsletters are relatively easy to reproduce. The reproduction method depends on the extent of their circulation. For a small distribution, they can be mimeographed; for a larger circulation, dittoed or photo offset. Artwork is not essential, but the judicious use of illustrations will make a newsletter more attractive.

Newsletter items should be short and written in an informal manner. Although newsletters have time flexibility, they are most effective if they are produced on a regularly scheduled basis, i.e., weekly, monthly, semi-monthly.

House Organs. According to personnel surveys, the thing that employees complain about the most is a lack of communication within their company. "No one tells me anything" is a popular refrain. An opportunity for alleviating this situation is the house organ or company magazine which many times becomes the job of the company PR/publicist.

In its beginnings, a medium for chit-chat and gossip, the house organ has become more sophisticated, more concerned with presenting general information about the company and the views of the employee, in addition to management's policy and philosophy.

House organs are usually produced in magazine format or, in some instances, newspaper style. The writing is informal. The publications are usually sent to the home.

House organs can be divided into several categories: (1) the strictly internal publication which is distributed within the company; (2) the publication sent to employees, but also to people not on the payroll whom management feels it worthwhile to cultivate—current and prospective customers, government officials, stockholders, and so on; (3) the strictly external publication targeted at business people outside the company.

Columns. In dealing with columns, the PR/publicist has two ways to go. One, particularly if he or she represents a nonprofit organization, is to write a column on a regular basis. The other is to provide information to an already established columnist. Both approaches can present opportunities for the placement of news and information of value to the client.

Columns written by PR/publicists, under a by-line, have their best chance of being used in newspapers catering to smaller markets or rural areas. While there are many different types of columns, those best suited for PR/publicity purposes are educational and informational in nature. This type of column can be used to publicize events, to promote continuing programs, and to provide up-to-the-minute information.

Already established columns most likely to be receptive to the PR/publicist are largely in the entertainment/show business area. Here, it often becomes a "you scratch my back and I'll scratch yours" situation. The columnist, in payment for a number of items submitted by the PR/publicist, will generally insert a favorable "plug." The items submitted must be completely accurate and exclusive.

Supplementary News Services

These are services that provide news and features to other media. Several have large national and international reporting staffs which enable them to deliver fast and in-depth stories on events no matter where they occur. Others provide feature materials and photos.

Wire Services. Known as *wire services* because their stories were originally circulated via telegraph wires for rapid delivery, today these organizations use coaxial cable (telephone lines) leading from central offices to teletype outlets of subscribing media. News from such services is received in long sheets known as *wire copy*. Future plans for transmitting such information include direct broadcast satellite service and the use of video discs. Of the group, the best known are UPI (United Press International) and AP (Associated Press), each of which services several thousand other media as subscribers—newspapers, television stations, and radio stations. Most major newspapers and broadcast stations make some use of these services to supplement their coverage, while smaller papers and stations really depend on them for out-of-town, foreign, and special interest news.

The wire services have bureaus situated in most of the important cities in the United States as well as throughout the world. Each service has reporters who gather news which is edited at local bureaus and put on leased wires to go out on local, state, or regional networks. While teletype machines are still in use, much of the material is composed on video display terminals and later, after being electronically edited, sent out to various subscribers on their circuits.

Deadlines for getting PR/publicity material to wire services vary greatly, but generally the local bureaus accept material on a continuous basis. Material so accepted may be distributed locally, regionally, or nationally, depending on its news value. For the PR/publicist, the best approach to the wire services is through the local bureau.

Of great importance to the practitioner are the *day books,* or listings of newsworthy events which are compiled by the wire services and transmitted by teletype to newspapers, broadcast networks, and individual television and radio station newsrooms. These provide the various media editors with a blueprint for upcoming story assignments. The PR/publicist who is successful in getting an event noted in the day book has increased the chances of its placement.

The wire services also provide radio stations with news and feature material in audio form. These *cuts* are often inserted in local newscasts to add realism to the newscasts.

Publicity Wire Services. In large cities, many publicists use commercially operated publicity wires to send releases to city newsrooms. Practitioners pay so much a word for their use. An advantage of this type of service is that releases are provided to the news media simultaneously, eliminating charges of favoritism. A leading company of this type, the PR Newswire, services more than 250 news media in more than 50 cities of the United States.

Feature and Specialized News Syndicates. Newspapers and, to some extent, broadcast media obtain additional material from the several hundred syndicates of various sizes that specialize in the distribution of features and specific kinds of news coverage. In their distribution, these associations will include appropriate publicity material.

Among the material provided are news features, sports features, editorials, columns, women's page features, comics, cartoons, and other services. Leading organizations include: Newspaper Enterprise Association, AP Newsfeatures, King Features Syndicate, United Features Syndicate.

Photo Syndicates. Publicity photographs that are accepted by national photograph syndicates usually have a good record of placement in the media. Because pictures are considered a permanent and very memorable record, photo syndicates are very careful in what they accept to distribute to their clients. Accepted pictures must be able to stand alone, to tell a story with no accompanying words other than an appropriate caption. Additionally, pictures should show imagination, have universal interest, be well composed and technically correct—sharp with good contrast. Unlike individual newspapers, photo syndicates require that the PR/publicist submit negatives as well as prints. Leading national photo syndicates include: Wide World Photos, Black Star, Globe Photos, Associated Press News Photos, UPI Newspictures.

BROADCAST MEDIA

Millions of people watch television and listen to radio. The images seen and the messages heard exert great and immediate influence. Broadcast PR/publicity takes the form of news coverage of a story or an event, personal appearances, airing of tapes, movies, slides, and the use of demonstration material by an announcer.

The opportunities for PR/publicity placement in broadcast, however, are more limited than in print. Most of the editorial matter in a newspaper is of an informational nature, and as such, it represents an opportunity for news and information supplied by PR/publicists. Not so in broadcast; the average television or radio station can use such material only in brief newscasts, various interviews, and some in-depth treatments. There are some exceptions to this—those television stations called *independents,* which are situated in smaller markets and not affiliated with a network, and those radio stations where news makes up most or all of their programming. But because of the inherent qualities of both television and radio and their sense of immediacy, involvement, and impact, any effort to gain broadcast placement is well worthwhile.

Television

There are approximately 1,000 television stations at the present time with about 70 percent of them commercial—that is, they accept paid advertising. The remaining 30 percent are noncommercial, made up of public television stations or those operated by school systems, universities, or other not-for-profit organizations.

Most of the commercial stations belong to one of the three major networks—American Broadcasting Company (ABC), Columbia Broadcasting System (CBS), and National Broadcasting Company (NBC)—as *affiliates* which get a large part of their programming through their network connection. The remaining commercial stations, the independents, create their own programming or sometimes carry programs from one of the networks. Often these nonaffiliated stations will buy shows from syndicators. Most syndicated programs are in the entertainment field, but some are interviews, game shows, and documentaries. As such, they present opportunities for story placements.

Almost all of the commercial stations have news departments that originate local programs, but the average station gets its state, national, and international news from the Associated Press, United Press International, or the news outlets of the network with which it is affiliated.

Commercial television reaches approximately 90 million homes, or about 98 percent of the nation's total. Approximately 75 percent of the viewing audience are adults.

TELEVISION STATION ORGANIZATION

In terms of contact, the PR/publicist has a choice, depending on the organization of the individual station. Most stations have a news director and a program director, both of whom usually report to the station's general manager.

While situations may vary, the news director is usually concerned with all locally produced newscasts and the coverage of events. Working under the news director is the assignment editor, who, many practitioners believe, is the key to coverage because he or she sets up the camera crews and assigns reporters for work in the field. Programs other than news are usually the responsibility of the program director. These programs include interview and variety shows and coverage of events not always related to news, i.e., contests, competitions, and so on. Where a program has been purchased from a package producer (an "outside" individual who puts together a TV program—usually on a speculative basis), it is usually the producer of that program who has the authority to accept ideas and guests, which might be suggested by the PR/publicist.

Contacts at television stations can be obtained by checking *T.V. Publicity Outlets* or any one of the other services that provide names. As with newspapers or magazines, it is best to phone and make sure before sending off material.

It is important to keep in mind that there is a difference between local and national network newscasts. Networks have separate news departments and news personnel. In addition, each important news program or documentary series has its own producer. The networks operate regional news staffs in key cities all over the world. These staffs are independent of those news staffs connected with the network's affiliate in the same city. Consequently, any material sent to a network regional office should also be sent to the affiliate's newsroom in the same city.

CABLE TV

Originally, simply a method for carrying the television signal to homes that were unable to receive one (because of some obstruction, e.g., a mountain), cable TV has developed muscle of its own. These systems distribute programs from local television stations as well as television programs from nearby cities and various syndicators. Some cable systems, originating in a specific city, originate programs and these can offer placement possibilities to the PR/publicist, particularly as cable television grows in popularity. Examples of syndicators who specifically service cable systems nationally include cable news networks, health news networks, movie networks, and sports networks. These cable syndicators are springing up rapidly and offer excellent PR/publicity opportunities to the practitioner. Currently, there are more than forty different networks available to operators of cable systems.

Radio

Radio is the country's number one user medium with more than 450 million sets in use. These were in 99 percent of the nation's homes, in most of its automobiles, and many of its public gathering places—bars, stores, and so on.

> **Working with Media Successfully**
>
> - If you are in the same local area as the media you wish to reach, mail in simple items, but call in a more involved story. This will give you the opportunity to "sell" an idea on the phone and get direction from the editor before writing.
> - Know deadlines. Keep a record of the most important ones you will have to meet.
> - Do not, as a rule, badger a newspaper editor to see if the material will be used. With broadcasters, because of the constantly shifting scheduling, it is a good idea to keep checking.
> - When calling newspaper editors, do your own dialing. Most do not have secretaries, and answer their own phones. Broadcasting has a greater bureaucracy, but do your own dialing anyway.
> - Use "exclusives" sparingly.
> - Check and recheck your written materials for typos, spelling errors, and correct figures. Editors depend on your materials being 100 percent accurate.

There are more than 8,000 radio stations in the United States—both AM and FM. Of this number, approximately 90 percent are commercial stations, the remainder being noncommercial. Unlike television, most of the commercial stations are unaffiliated with networks.

In the network category, there are four important organizations. Of these, three of them—National Broadcasting Company, Columbia Broadcasting System, and the American Broadcasting Company—have the same structure as their television counterparts. The fourth major network, the Mutual Broadcasting System, is the largest with more than 700 affiliates. Many regional networks also operate.

Like magazines, but unlike television and newspapers, radio is an extremely selective medium appealing to specific groups of people by virtue of its programming. Radio stations can be classified as talk, news, ethnic, rock and roll, semi-classical, classical—to mention just a few of the categories. This specialization requires the practitioner to study the outlet carefully before attempting to provide it with appropriate information.

RADIO STATION ORGANIZATION

Radio stations are organized similarly to television stations with station managers, news editors, assignment editors, and program producers, although they may not be known by such titles. Some stations have both AM and FM facilities. In those instances, the same staff usually services both.

As with television, the NBC, CBS, and ABC networks provide their affiliated stations with programming. Nonaffiliated stations produce their own programming, use the facilities of syndicators, or utilize the services of such groups as National Public Radio, RKO Radio Network, or the Black Radio Network.

Radio programming falls roughly into two categories: information and entertainment. Information programming usually includes news, special events, and public service information shows. Entertainment programming covers interviews, panel shows, audience participation programs, reviews, and dramatic presentations. These divisions are not mutually exclusive, i.e., sometimes an interview can be considered information programming. While both of these categories present the PR/publicist with opportunities, practitioners are of the opinion that information and public service programs offer the greatest possibilities for placement.

4
How to Write Press Releases

PR/publicity writing is intended to interest an editor in a story and to stimulate that editor to pass the story on to readers, viewers, or listeners in the form of news. The passed-on news may appear just as the PR/publicist wrote it, or it may be revised or rewritten by the media. The style and form used in press release writing evolved from practices used in journalism which reflect the reporter's need to get a story across quickly, clearly, and objectively.

Because PR/publicity writing had such a specific function, it has special form and style requirements. All stories written by PR/publicists are called *press releases,* or *publicity releases.* There are three types of releases: (1) the news release; (2) the feature release; and (3) the news-feature release. These types of releases are discussed and illustrated starting on page 53. The form requirements for all three are the same; however, the writing styles vary.

Effective PR/publicity writing takes skill and patience to develop. The words must work together to interest media editors in using the story, and to "sell" the client's product or idea to the ultimate reader as well.

Basic Press Release Form

A press release is written in a standard way to aid an editor to use the material for publication or broadcast. The basic release form shown in Figure 4–1 is number-keyed so that the function of each of the elements can be readily understood. All copy is typewritten on 8½ x 11-inch, white bond paper, on one side of the page only.

The following elements are included in every basic press release form:

1. The *name and address of the company* releasing the news appears in the upper left-hand corner, permitting the editor to know instantly what organization sent the release.
2. The *name and phone number of the contact person* appears below the company name so the editor knows whom to call for further information or clarification of a point. The contact person is usually the publicist responsible for writing the release.
3. A *specific date of release* or the words *"For Immediate Release"* appear in the upper right-hand corner so that the editor knows when the information in the release can be printed.
4. *"Special To:"* means it has been written especially for the medium. *"Exclusive To:"* means that no other outlet in the circulation area has the same story. Either one of these phrases appears below the release date. If they are absent, the editor knows the material has probably been sent to many publications.
5. The *headline in capital letters* is underlined and centered approximately one-third down the page. The headline summarizes the release. The space around it gives the editor room to make headline changes and/or general notes on how the story is to be used.
6. The *actual copy of the release* starts approximately one-half down the page. It is double-spaced so that it is easy to correct and revise.
7. Indent five spaces to start a *paragraph*. Add an extra single space to the double space between each new paragraph—three spaces in all. Paragraphs should be kept short with no breaks at the end of a page, i.e., the paragraph should not be split between one page and the next.
8. *Subheadings* are indicated to the left, above the paragraph they introduce. They are in upper and lower case letters, underlined.
9. *Margins* are generally one inch on the sides and two inches top and bottom. This varies depending on how much goes on the page. The PR/publicist usually wants the release to look as succinct and concise as possible and will try to keep it down to one page. Some practitioners have two different typewriters with different typefaces and will use one (pica) or the other (elite) depending on the circumstances.
10. *"More"* goes at the end of each page when the release continues onto the next page.
11. The *page number and name of the company* are, after the first page, typed at the top of each continuing page for easy identification in case the pages become separated.
12. The *end of the release* is indicated by the marks *###* or *30*. This is particularly helpful if the release ends at the bottom of the page.
13. Some PR/publicists will put a date on the bottom lower left-hand corner of the release which is the date it has been distributed.

① Company name or agency
Street address
City and State
(Phone if different from contact no.)

② Contact: Name
Phone No.

③ For Immediate Release
or
For Release: Date

④ Special To:
or
Exclusive To:

⑤ HEADLINE IN CAPS, CENTERED
AND UNDERLINED, ONE-THIRD DOWN PAGE

⑨ 2 in.

⑨ 1 in.   ⑨ 1 in.

⑥ Lead paragraph starts about halfway down the page, indented five spaces. Double space between typed lines.

⑦ Paragraphing is standard with an extra single space added to the double space between each new paragraph--three spaces in all.

⑧ Subheads Are Indicated to the Left

Xxxxxx xxxxxxxxxxxxx xxxxx xxxxxxxx xxxx xx xxxxxxxxxxxx xxx xxxxxxxxx xxxx xxxxxxxxxxxxxx. Xxxxxxx xxxxxxxxx xxxxxxxxxxxxx xx xxx xxxxxx xxxxxx xx xxxxxxx xxxxxxxxxxxxx xxxx xx xxxxxxxx xxx xxxxxxxx xxxxxxx. Xxxxxxxxxxx xxxx xxx xxxxxx xxxxxxxxx xxxxx xxxxxxxxxxxxxx.

⑬ Code no. of date mailed

⑩ More   (If release is continued)

⑫ # # #   (If release ends on this page)

⑪ Company   -2-

(second page)

⑨ 2 in.

4-1. *Basic press release form. This form is number coordinated to the listing in the text and to the release example in Figure 4-2. Note the placement of every element of the press release.*

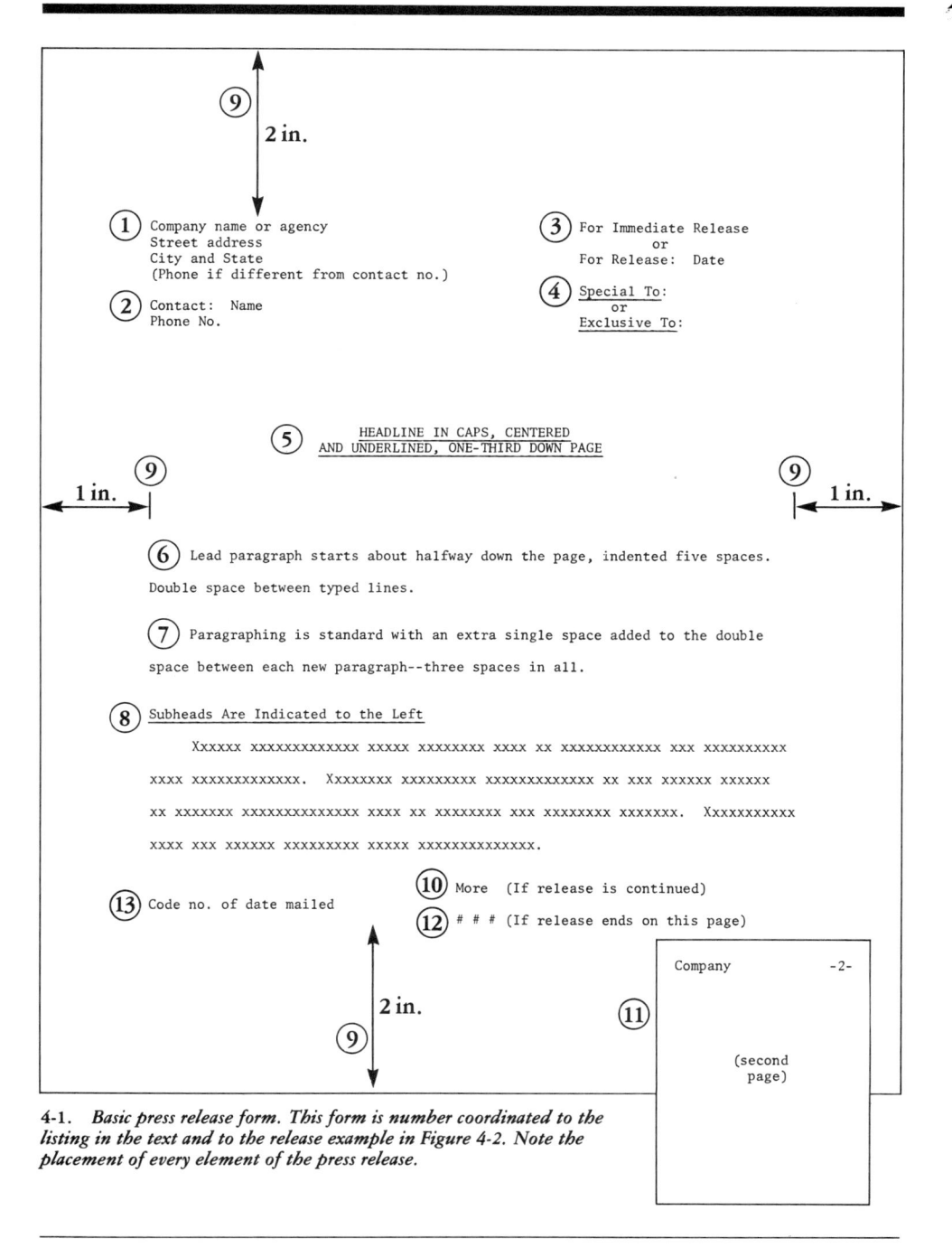

50

(9) ↕ 2 in.

(1) Amulets and Talismans
33 Christopher Street
New York, N.Y. 10003

(3) For Immediate Release

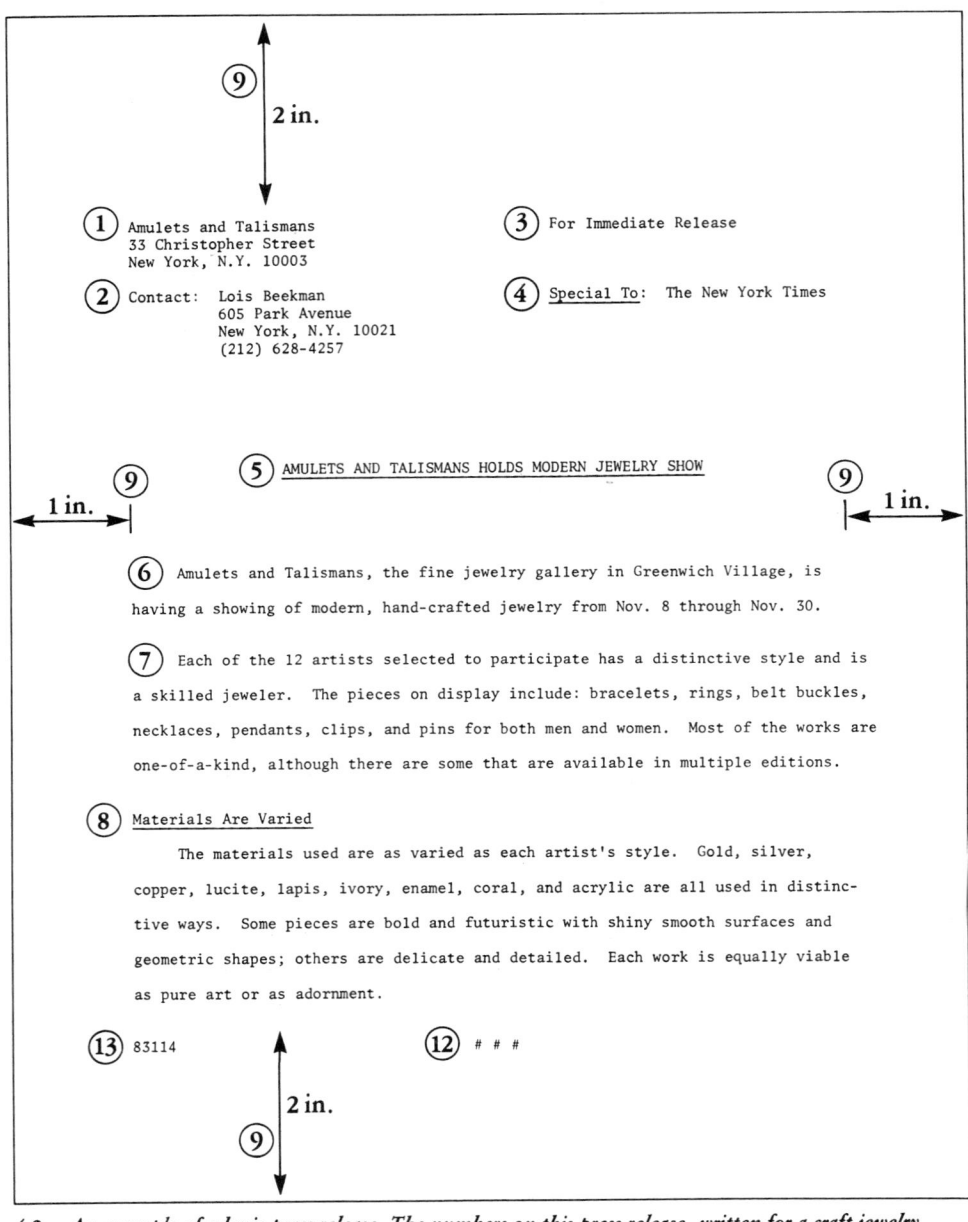

(2) Contact: Lois Beekman
605 Park Avenue
New York, N.Y. 10021
(212) 628-4257

(4) <u>Special To</u>:   The New York Times

(5) <u>AMULETS AND TALISMANS HOLDS MODERN JEWELRY SHOW</u>

(9) ←— 1 in. —→   (9) ←— 1 in. —→

(6) Amulets and Talismans, the fine jewelry gallery in Greenwich Village, is having a showing of modern, hand-crafted jewelry from Nov. 8 through Nov. 30.

(7) Each of the 12 artists selected to participate has a distinctive style and is a skilled jeweler. The pieces on display include: bracelets, rings, belt buckles, necklaces, pendants, clips, and pins for both men and women. Most of the works are one-of-a-kind, although there are some that are available in multiple editions.

(8) <u>Materials Are Varied</u>

The materials used are as varied as each artist's style. Gold, silver, copper, lucite, lapis, ivory, enamel, coral, and acrylic are all used in distinctive ways. Some pieces are bold and futuristic with shiny smooth surfaces and geometric shapes; others are delicate and detailed. Each work is equally viable as pure art or as adornment.

(13) 83114   (12) # # #

(9) ↕ 2 in.

4-2. An example of a basic press release. The numbers on this press release, written for a craft jewelry boutique, are coordinated to those that appear in the text discussion of the elements of a press release on page 48 and the basic form shown in Figure 4-1. Note that items 10 and 11 are omitted because the release is only one page long.

VARIATIONS IN FORM

Sometimes, the rules of form are "bent" for practical reasons. For example, a publicity release may be typed and reproduced on preprinted stationery which has the company name, logo, and address on it. In that case, that information is not repeated in the heading. Another example would be when margins and spacing are altered in order to get a long release to fit on one page or to make a short one appear to fill out a page. Still another would be the use of colored paper.

In general, however, one should stay as close to the standard form as possible. When it makes sense to bend the rules, care should be taken that the form of the release still functions in terms of usefulness to the editor.

DATES ON RELEASES

Dates can appear on a release in three different places.

A date or the phrase "For Immediate Release" in the *upper right-hand corner* of the heading of the release is used to indicate the period after which the information in the release applies. This is important because PR/publicists send releases out in advance of the effective date in order to accommodate the advance planning of editors.

For example, if the weekly business review of a newspaper is planned on the Monday, six days before the Sunday the section is ordinarily published, and a significant management change is about to take place at a major corporation, the PR/publicist will mail out the release with news of the change well in advance of the actual publishing date. He or she trusts the editor not to release the story prior to the designated date the change is to become public knowledge.

A date is sometimes used at the *beginning of the first sentence* of the release's lead. This is called the *dateline* and is used to indicate when the story was written. It is most useful when handling releases of a current, but ongoing event.

Finally, a date recorded in number form (e.g., 12/1/84) or code form, and usually placed at the *bottom left* of the release, indicates the day that the release was mailed and is useful for filing and record-keeping purposes.

Publicity Writing Styles

Each of the three types of press releases—the news release, the feature release, and the news-feature release—has its own unique style. These styles are developed in anticipation of the eventual use of the materials by a particular type of medium. Descriptions of the writing styles for the three types follow. Each

4-3. VARIATIONS ON THE FORM OF A RELEASE

Company name and address appear on stationery—they are not typed in.

Release starts high on the page and margins are narrowed so that the entire release fits on one page.

PR/publicity firm used its own paper for the release. The company about which the release is written is typed in on the bottom.

COVER   **BACK**

Long release is made into a folder with art work on the cover and a store list on the back.

description is accompanied by an example based on a publicity campaign for the Bobby-Mac 3-in-1 Baby Chair pictured on page 54.

THE NEWS RELEASE

The function of a news release is to highlight some item of current or future interest about a person, place, product, etc. This type of release is news and has a limited time of relevance. It is meant to be "released," i.e., printed as news either immediately upon its receipt by the publication or at a specified date not too far in the future.

The style and requirements of a news release include the following:

- A summary headline, usually on one line, giving the essence of the story.
- A lead paragraph which summarizes the story completely and answers the "five W's": *who, what, why, when,* and *where;* and sometimes a sixth point, *how.*
- Release is written in order of diminishing importance; the most important facts are stated first and the less important ones last, so that the story can be cut easily from the bottom.
- Simple and direct writing style.
- An easily identifiable, relevant news angle.

A well-written news release depends on *organization,* a *relevant news angle,* and *careful vocabulary selection.* It is often a tedious job of putting ideas together, over and over again, until the final release says exactly what it should. Even for the most experienced publicity writer, some stories are hard to organize and take hours of rewriting to get right. The following "formula" can be used to organize facts in such a way as to make it easier to develop a news release:

1. Write down all pertinent information in brief phrases or sentences. The information can be from a fact sheet, notes, or an interview.
2. Identify the news angle around which the release is going to be developed.
3. Rank these phrases or sentences according to their diminishing importance as related to the news angles you have selected. The statement that contains the most important information is first, the one that contains the least important information is last.
4. In keeping with the ranking from most important to least important, develop a lead paragraph that covers the five W's and reflects the news angle.
5. Following the lead, develop subsequent paragraphs according to the ranking of the individual sentences.
6. Now write a headline that summarizes the story and indicates its news relevance.

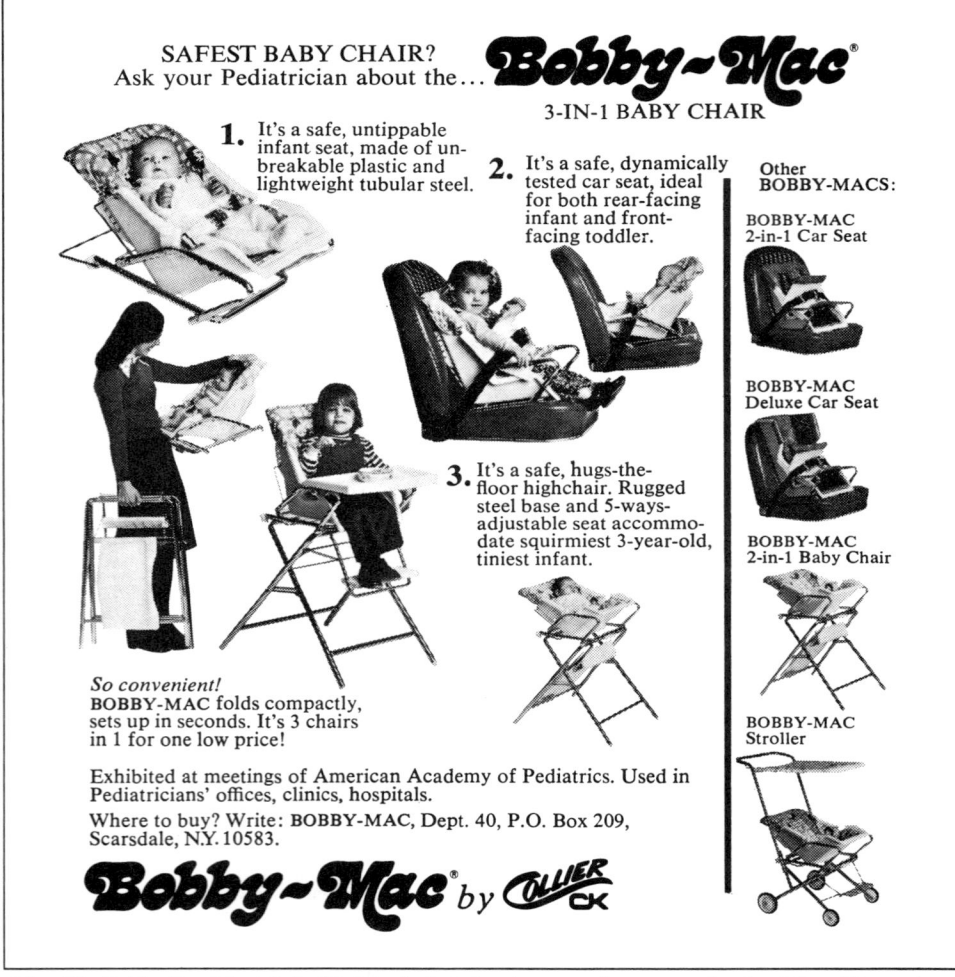

4-4. The Bobby-Mac 3-in-1 Baby Chair is the basis for the press release examples that follow (Figures 4-5, 4-6, and 4-7). Note the product features and highlights that are mentioned in the advertisement pictured above.

Lois Beekman Associates
767 Fifth Avenue
New York, N.Y. 10022

For Immediate Release

Contact: Maryanne Moore
(212) 249-7841

For Bobby-Mac Company

BOBBY-MAC COMPANY ANNOUNCES SUCCESSFUL RESULTS
OF CRASH TESTING OF CHILDREN'S CAR SEAT

Quentin McDonald, president and designer of Bobby-Mac juvenile furniture and safety products, has announced impressive results from crash tests given to ascertain the safety of the company's car seat for children. These tests were conducted at the Highway Safety Research Institute of the University of Michigan, Ann Arbor.

A set of 12 simulated crashes called "dynamic impact sled tests," which demonstrate the results of collisions from various angles when cars are moving at different speeds, was conducted under the supervision of the Technical Advisory Service. The tests were conducted as a performance check of the present Bobby-Mac seat, checks of lap belt and shoulder harness anchoring, and as research for possible product modifications.

Mr. McDonald conceived the idea of the car seat in 1955 as a safety device for his own son. Today's Bobby-Mac is made of strong, padded plastic and tubular steel. It is sold throughout the United States.

# # #

4-5. *The Bobby-Mac news release. This release about the Bobby-Mac Company announces a timely event with immediate news significance. Consequently, it is prepared in the news release form with a summary headline and lead, written in order of diminishing importance. Possible accompanying materials for this release would include: a picture of the Bobby-Mac chair, a photograph of the actual test situation, a copy of the official test results, and promotional materials about the company and its product.*

THE FEATURE RELEASE

The function of a feature release is to highlight a person, place, or thing in a manner that emphasizes human interest more than a straight news release. This "interest" can take many forms: a personal profile, corporate background information, an interview, and so on.

While the feature release may be written within a specific time frame, it usually lacks the sense of urgency and immediacy associated with a news release. It may be longer than a news release because it provides a broader treatment of its subject. Often a feature release will stimulate an editor to ask for more information or even to assign a staff writer to explore the topic further.

A feature release article does not have to be based on current news, but the more removed it is from the current news scene, the more it needs to have some significant point of interest and relevance to an outlet and its public.

The practitioner can write a feature release in any commonly accepted style. It is not necessary to write so that the paragraphs fall into an order of diminishing importance. What is important is human interest. It dominates the theme of a good feature story. The feature editor will allow a livelier, more flavorful style than the news editor, but will not accept subjective "sales pitch" writing. For example, in a feature you could write:

> *Have you ever wished you could have a food processor that would cook as it purees and chops? Imagine the one-step convenience of making soup or vegetable puree this way. The XYZ Company has just come out with a processor with a heat and beat feature....*

However, if you were to write:

> *The XYZ heat and beat food processor that cooks as it purees and blends is a must for every kitchen in the USA. You can't cook well without it. Go out and buy one at your local hardware or department store today....*

you would be going too far, and the article would probably be rejected because it appeared to read like an advertisement.

A potentially successful feature release depends on an *interesting lead* with which the reader can identify, a *timely theme,* and *good writing.*

There is no simple rule to developing a good feature. However, it is a good idea to plan a feature with a particular medium or media in mind and to use a theme that is similar to other feature themes that have been used in that type of medium. Examples of feature ideas include: profiles of personalities behind a company, history of an industry, the opinions of a company executive on a matter of importance in the industry, and so on.

Editors usually demand exclusivity on feature articles. In the case of newspapers, they will allow the article to be sent to other editors in other cities in which their paper is not distributed. In the case of magazines and trade publications that are distributed nationally, the article must be written especially for the publication in order to be used.

The style and requirements of feature releases include the following:

- An intriguing headline.
- Lead paragraph should be provocative. Does not have to summarize the story.
- Writing can build to a climax. Information does not have to be in order of diminishing importance.
- Writing style is more "creative," but still objective and direct.
- One or more news angles can be identified.

THE NEWS-FEATURE RELEASE

The function of a news-feature release is to provide additional or background information about a current situation or happening. Such a release often appears shortly after the news event has occurred. The basis of a news feature is usually an item of current news, but the treatment of that news item is more detailed and elaborate than in the ordinary news release.

In writing a news feature, the PR practitioner attempts to develop *human interest angles* about the company or people involved in a current news story. If the feature is developed around a created news event, there is time to develop it carefully in advance. It is also possible to develop news features around a spontaneous event.

The style and requirements for news-feature releases include the following:

- A headline that relates to the current news.
- A provocative lead that relates to the current news.
- Writing is objective, can be in order of diminishing importance or not.
- A relevant news-related angle should be developed and highlighted.

Localizing the Release

Localizing a release means writing a story with emphasis on the news that is relevant to the public in a specific local area. The same story can be localized in a variety of ways by organizing the facts around different news angles. The angles and facts that can make news in one city often are not those that will make news in another.

For example, consider the situation of a PR/publicist trying to get the maximum news exposure for the New York City Mayor-for-a-Day College Competition. Suppose that the student winning the essay competition is a political science

Lois Beekman Associates
767 Fifth Avenue
New York, N.Y. 10022

For Immediate Release

Contact: Maryanne Moore
(212) 429-4178

For Bobby-Mac Company

<u>THE STORY BEHIND BOBBY-MAC</u>

 Behind the success of the Bobby-Mac Company, a leading producer of children's safety products and furniture, lies more than 25 years of planning and preparation by one man. The man is Quentin McDonald of Scarsdale, New York, and his story is both a business saga and a crusade for infant safety.

 The Bobby-Mac is an ingenious piece of juvenile furniture that functions as a high chair, an infant carrier, and a car seat. Designed with a child's safety in mind, it is made of strong, padded plastic and tubular steel.

 McDonald conceived the idea of the Bobby-Mac when his son, Bobby, was born in 1955. Shocked by the inadequate and unsafe juvenile furniture products on the market, he designed and built the Bobby-Mac for the protection and comfort of his son--it was simple, practical, and durable. Above all, it was absolutely safe.

 Bobby McDonald used the first chair until he was four years old. By then, it had named itself Bobby-Mac, and the idea of mass production was growing in his father's mind.

More

4-6. The Bobby-Mac feature release. This release about the Bobby-Mac company provides background information and a brief history of product development. Consequently, it is prepared as a feature release with an intriguing headline and a provocative lead, in chronological order. Possible accompanying materials for this release would include: a photograph of the wooden prototype Bobby-Mac safety chair, a photograph of the contemporary steel and plastic version, a photograph of Quentin McDonald, a copy of the sled testing results, and promotional materials about the company and its product.

Bobby-Mac Company -2-

It remained only an idea until 1966, when Quentin McDonald left his job as Vice President, Management Supervisor of the Post Cereals account at the Benton & Bowles Advertising Agency. He had decided to put all his time and effort into producing, marketing, and promoting the Bobby-Mac.

The Bobby-Mac is now produced by a leading juvenile furniture manufacturer, within the terms of an unusual contract-licensing agreement. Under this agreement, McDonald owns all the tools, dies, and molds necessary to produce all Bobby-Mac products. No changes in the Bobby-Macs can be made without his approval. This allows him to maintain the product's quality and safety standards.

In 1971, he initiated a rigorous system of dynamic car seat testing as part of the Bobby-Mac Research and Development program. The tests used by the Bobby-Mac Company are conducted at one of the nation's leading testing centers and are similar to those used by automobile manufacturers. Called "sled testing," they demonstrate the result of collision from various angles when cars are moving at different speeds. Apart from the auto companies themselves, the Bobby-Mac Company is probably the heaviest user of such testing of all car seat manufacturers.

The Bobby-Mac story is far from over. With numerous foreign patents granted or pending, McDonald's crusade promises to become worldwide. The Bobby-Mac was recently approved by Germany's Volkswagen for sale in Volkswagen dealerships.

From Bobby-Mac come other stories that have equally happy endings--stories from parents whose children survived accidents because of the Bobby-Mac. They provide a continuous source of gratification to the inventor.

# # #

Lois Beekman Associates　　　　　　　　For Immediate Release
767 Fifth Avenue
New York, N.Y. 10022

Contact: Maryanne Moore
(212) 342-7685

For Bobby-Mac Company

BOBBY-MAC SEAT HAS PROVEN SAFETY RECORD

The Bobby-Mac Company's announcement of impressive results from recent crash testing for their juvenile car seat adds to their reputation for high product standards and quality control. The Bobby-Mac is the first juvenile combination safety seat to have earned the approval of the Committee on Accident Prevention of the American Academy of Pediatrics for exhibiting at Academy meetings. In addition, the company has received many grateful letters from parents who have found that the seat protected their children from injury and possible death in auto accidents. Pediatricians have also written letters lauding the product.

The following statement made by Diane Atkinson of Santee, California, is representative of the type of letters Bobby-Mac received from parents:

". . . when Jennifer was three years old, she and I were involved in a head-on collision with another car which had crossed the center lane. Although I was wearing a seat belt, I still suffered cuts, bruises, and broken bones from hitting the steering wheel. Jennifer was riding on the front seat in her Bobby-Mac car seat facing the rear, and other than being upset at being so rudely awakened, she suffered no injuries whatsoever."

More

4-7. *The Bobby-Mac news-feature release. This release provides information about the Bobby-Mac Company that is related to the results of the crash tests reported in the news release. Consequently, it relates to the current news, but then goes into other aspects of the company, its products, and history. Possible accompanying materials for this release would include: a picture of the safety chair, a picture of the chair in use, and copies of promotional materials about the company and its product.*

Bobby-Mac Company   -2-

Although physicians ordinarily shy away from recommending any product, a large number of pediatricians are familiar with the Bobby-Mac and as a result are recommending it to the parents of their young patients because of its many features.

The Bobby-Mac is also used in doctors' offices, hospitals, and clinics. One such case is the Pediatric G.I. Unit, University of Rochester, New York, whose former head, Dr. Clinton B. Lillibridge, says:

> "In our Pediatric G.I. Unit, we used the Bobby-Mac exclusively. When emergencies arose requiring that a nurse discontinue feeding a child abruptly, she could leave the child unattended with complete confidence. The built-in safety of the Bobby-Mac and its ease of use have now been borne out through three years of very hard use."

The Bobby-Mac was invented by Quentin McDonald in 1955 because he couldn't find a safe car seat for his own infant son. Today, the strong, padded plastic and tubular chrome seat has passed series after series of dynamic impact (crash) tests and static load (weight and strength) tests. McDonald, who has been awarded both United States and foreign patents for the seat, continues work to improve the product and runs more of these tests than any other company except the car manufacturers.

# # #

> **Release Writing and Preparation—Tips from Pros**
>
> - Never send carbon copies; "clean" photocopies are fine.
> - Try to include a release date.
> - Check the "time peg" relative to releases. Tie in with holidays, commemorative days, etc. Use the almanac for ideas.
> - Use a thesaurus to help you select effective words.
> - Additional pages of a release can have "Add One" on the second page, "Add Two" on the third page, etc., together with a *slug line* with the key word of the story or company name.
> - If you discover an error after the release is mailed out, call in the correction and then follow up with a corrected version.
> - Avoid releases that run over two pages whenever possible.

major and a junior at Columbia University whose family comes from Portland, Oregon, but was raised in Washington, D.C., because his father was a Democratic Congressman.

In order to have the best chance of making news in New York, Portland and Washington, it would be necessary to localize the facts and news angles in three different releases.

A release sent to the New York City news media would have to emphasize the facts that interest the city public: what it is like to be mayor for a day, the history and purpose of the Mayor-for-a-Day College Competition, the student's background. A story sent to the Portland media would need to emphasize the student's Portland background and Oregon family origins and connections. A release sent to the Washington media would need to focus on the student's relationship to the political world in Washington, his father's influence, and any part-time or summer jobs involving politics.

In addition, in order to pursue every news-making opportunity, the story would have to be reworked to accommodate the readership of publications as diverse as the Columbia University undergraduate newspaper, *The Spectator,* and the newsletter of the Democratic National Party.

Some Do's and Don'ts

The Third Person. *Do* write in the third person, i.e., from the point of view of an objective reporter describing an event or situation. *Don't* use "I," "we," or "you." Always refer to the company or people mentioned by name or pronoun. ("I" or "we" or "you" may be used in quoted material.) For example:

Do write: William Jones, president of Regal Industries, will be honored as the textile industry's "Man of the Year" at the Waldorf-Astoria Hotel in New York City on Thursday evening, May 1, according to an announcement by the company.

Don't use: We, at Regal Industries, are very proud to announce that our wonderful president, William Jones, will be honored as "Man of the Year in the Textile Industry." You really must attend the dinner where he will be given the honor this Thursday. We expect all of Regal Industries' clients and friends to celebrate with us.

Use of Quotes. *Do* use quotes to show company personality or accomplishment. It is the one way you can speak subjectively of an individual or organization in a release. *Don't* overload a release with irrelevant and confusing quotes. If the person you feel should be quoted does not come up with a remark that you believe is suitable for your release, create an appropriate quote and then check back with that person. For example:

Do write: William Jones, president and founder of Regal Industries, said of his company's 50 percent increase in profits this year, "We took a tremendous financial and technical gamble when we converted to computer knitting, but, by George, it paid off. I'm so proud of the Regal technical team."

Don't use: "I said to Jake one day back a few years, 'You know Jake, Phil told me that he read an article in the Journal that computers were the wave of the future in our business.' Well, being a bit of a gambling man, I tossed a coin: Heads, I would switch. Tails, I would not. The coin came up heads. So then, I called six different computer companies and had each do a report on...."

Make It Simple, But Interesting. *Do* write simply and informatively, making the description of complicated matters as easy to understand as possible. *Don't* forget to use a few descriptive adjectives and phrases to make the story interesting. While they should be held to a minimum, it is these well-chosen modifiers that will develop the interest of the editor and the ultimate reader, listener, or viewer. For example:

Do write: At Regal Industries, its 110-member development group works on the basis of indirect proof to determine whether something is practical or not for the company's nationwide chain of quality distributors.

Don't use: At Regal Industries, the R & D Department works on the premise of the null hypothesis which specifies hypothesized values for one or more of the population parameters.

Attribution. *Do* be objective and reporter-like when reporting facts or accomplishments. If you report accomplishments, "attribute" the knowledge of those accomplishments to some source. *Don't* brag about accomplishments, but refer to them in a dignified and flattering way. They will seem more believable. For example:

Do write: Regal Industries, New York-based manufacturer of double knit polyester apparel fabrics, has announced a 50 percent increase in profits over the past year. This remarkable growth has been attributed to the company's conversion to computer-operated knitting machines.

Don't use: The fantastic Regal Industries of New York, the world's leader in the manufacture of double knit polyester apparel fabrics, has announced an unprecedented, colossal 50 percent increase in profits in the past year. This incredible growth has been attributed to the company's trend-setting conversion to computer-operated knitting machines.

Some Questions to Ask Before Sending Releases

The following are questions that a PR/publicist should ask before mailing out press releases. These questions can serve as a checklist to help develop releases that have the best possible chance of being used:

1. Is the individual or organization featured in a way which is consistent with its image?
2. Is the story consistent with the long-term PR/publicity goals set for the client?
3. Are all names spelled properly?
4. Are all numbers and statistics correct?
5. Can you identify one or more exciting news angles that will motivate an editor to run a story based on the materials?
6. Is the headline provocative and sufficiently reflective of the story that follows?
7. Is the release date realistic?
8. Is the language as simple and clear as possible?
9. Can you and the client be proud of the typing and the grammar used in the release?

5
Other Written Materials

A PR/publicist must know how to develop other written materials in addition to press releases. Fact sheets, profiles, biographies (often called "bio's"), query letters, scripts—each of these is an important tool of the PR/publicist. Each has a definite function, style, and form. The nature of the PR/publicity project and its goals determine whether one or more of these materials is required.

For example, bio's are required only when soliciting an interview or feature about a person. Query letters are used to stimulate interest in a proposed magazine piece or appearance on a TV talk show. Fact sheets are used so that the interested editor has the freedom to develop a story in the style that best suits him or her.

As in release writing, these materials must be developed with the media outlet and its specific requirements in mind. They must be objective, report-like, as well as flattering to the news-seeking organization or client. They must be in a form that is easily adaptable to the media involved. In addition, it is important to note that when writing specifically for broadcast placement, suggested scripts and special adaptation of the basic release forms are a necessity.

Fact Sheets

Fact sheets summarize information in an easy-to-understand way. They are most often used to explain details of a special event, press conference, or a new product or development. They are usually written in a terse, almost list-like style covering the five W's. Fact sheets are typed on one side of the paper, usually single-spaced, with margins large enough for necessary notes.

Contact: Mark Gianni   For Immediate Release
           Publicity Associates
           33 S. Michigan Ave.
           Chicago, IL 60603
           (312) 557-3000

Fact Sheet: CARIBBEAN FLOWERS COLOGNE

Products: A trio of delicate floral fragrances imported
                 from the islands of the Caribbean.

                 * Orchid Spray, a delicate, lingering scent

                 * Bay Blossom, an up-beat, spicy scent

                 * Palm Bud, a refreshing, invigorating scent

Description: Each fragrance was inspired by a native, Caribbean
                 island flower. All three are made from pure in-
                 gredients and natural extracts that enrich the skin
                 as they add scent.

                 Each scent is available in an all-purpose lotion,
                 a skin care creme, and a liquid soap.

Packaging: Each lotion is packed in its own distinctive crystal
                 flask with a crystal stopper. The cremes are in
                 elegant crystal containers with screw-on tops to ensure
                 their freshness between each use. The liquid soap is
                 packaged in a self-dispensing crystal flask. All
                 packages are wrapped in Caribbean floral motif tissue,
                 tied with golden cord and placed in a clear plastic
                 cylinder with distinctive silver lettering.

Prices: All-purpose lotion, one size only, 4 oz. $20.00
                 Creme, one size only, 2.5 oz. $15.00
                 Soap, large size, 4 oz. $12.00
                      small size, 2 oz. $ 6.50

5-1. *This fact sheet summarizes all the information about the colognes made by a cosmetics company. Note the simple outline style, which makes it fast and easy to grasp all the facts listed. Also note that the contact information is on the fact sheet so that points can be clarified and additional information requested.*

It is helpful to have one or more persons who know nothing about the subject read the fact sheet to see if it can readily be understood. Characteristics of fact sheets used for various situations are as follows:

For Special Events. Fact sheets for events tell location, time, and purpose of the "happening." They are useful to the media as a reminder of the event's time frame and to provide the press with an outline of the vital statistics. Fact sheets are often sent ahead with the invitation to attend the event, and are particularly useful when the activities occur over a period of time, such as the week-long opening of a new shopping mall with several "happenings" occurring each day. As such, they help the press to organize its coverage.

For New Product Development. Fact sheets for new products summarize the product's features and history of development. Usually featured is such information as: product name, function, contents, patent and corporate information, and distribution rights, both foreign and domestic.

For New Services. Fact sheets detailing the inception of new services, such as new routes for an airline, bus, or train, would highlight such facts as the name of the new service, date of its commencement, point of departure, intermediate stops, number of people expected to be accommodated, and the company reasons for the service's institution.

Profiles and Bios

Profiles and bios (biographies) are used primarily to give background information—profiles on companies, bios on individuals. For the most part, they are an introduction of the company or individual to the press. They should be brief, easy to read, well organized, and in an objective way, project the facts about the company or individual seeking to make news. Bios, as well as profiles, may take the form of a news-feature release, but a one-page rundown, simply stated, is usually more desirable.

Bios, for the most part, indicate an individual's current position in a company, a brief tracing of his or her industry career, some mention of activities at clubs or charities, and some personal information concerning age, marital status, children, and, sometimes, hobbies. Photos (head shots) of the individual are often included.

Profiles usually are brief background pieces in the business history of a client or organization. Factual and concise, they are more or less case histories and contain information on the organization's management and its methods of marketing, production, and distribution. Profiles are a source of detailed information for the press as well as governmental agencies and security analysts. They should be updated frequently. Sometimes, they include the company logo or trademark.

BILL FLINK ASSOCIATES, INC.
LEE WRIGHT DESIGNS

128 CENTRAL PARK SOUTH, NEW YORK CITY 10019 (212) 265-0222

LEE WRIGHT

Lee Wright, winner of the Coty American Fashion Critics "Winnie," and twice nominated for the Cutty Sark Men's Fashion award as "outstanding U.S. designer," is a native of New York City. He attended Pace College in Westchester County, New York, and finished his education at the University of Miami. He is 32 years old, and now resides in Manhattan.

Lee has been designing menswear since 1973 when he left a career in show business to join Bill Flink in a company which distributes menswear throughout the United States. He appeared frequently on the Broadway stage and in road companies around the country before settling on menswear design as his chosen profession.

In his design career, Lee has travelled and worked extensively in Europe, particularly in Italy, and has been influenced a great deal by the flexible and experimental approach to fashion which is common there. In addition, he has had the opportunity of using extravagant fabrics from the world's greatest mills--most of which are still in Europe. As a result, his designs are characterized by a combination of truly original uses of fabric, color, and texture with modern and flattering silhouettes. Lee is now widely recognized for this truly unique signature. And, he designs specifically for the American man. . . the new, progressive, establishment American man who resists stereotypes and fads, but who wants clothes that are distinctive, young, comfortable, and sexy.

5-2. *This biography of men's fashion designer Lee Wright highlights his professional accomplishments and the other parts of his life that have affected his career. A biography of the same person for different purposes—his election to the board of a charitable institution, for example—would highlight different aspects of his life. No contact has been typed in because this information is included in the letterhead.*

Growth, Challenge Characterize Eastern Airlines' First 50 Years

It took all of its first 25 years for Eastern Airlines to chalk up its first 25 million passengers, but today the Miami-based airline carries more than that in just one year — over 30 million in 1977 alone.

This rapid growth has lifted the 50-year-old airline to the rank of the Free World's second-largest carrier of scheduled air passengers.

Eastern, which started on May 1, 1928 as a tiny mail carrier, today operates a fleet of 250 jetliners over a 35,000-mile route system. Last year, it carried 31.3 million travelers a distance of more than 20 billion revenue passenger miles.

When it started flying, Eastern was called Pitcairn Aviation, Inc. and its route system stretched just 792 miles from New Brunswick, N.J. to Atlanta.

Pitcairn Aviation, started and owned by aircraft manufacturer Harold F. Pitcairn, consisted of eight single-engine, open-cockpit biplanes when it began hauling mail for Uncle Sam under a $3-a-pound contract.

To fly his fleet of PA-5 Pitcairn Mailwings, the aircraft manufacturer enlisted a handful of pilots, World War I veterans and barnstormers among them. Even before operations began on the original run, Pitcairn received a second mail contract, covering the 641-mile Atlanta-Miami route, thus creating a 1,411-mile "eastern airline."

Encouraging Start

When May 1 arrived, the airline found so much mail on hand it had to operate double schedules, both northbound and southbound. Two planes took off from Atlanta that day, heading north, while another pair left Hadley Field in New Brunswick, N.J., the northern terminus, for the southbound flight.

Crowds numbering in the hundreds turned out at the

Curtiss Jenny

Pitcairn Mailwing

scheduled stops along the way — Washington, Richmond, Greensboro and Spartanburg. Pitcairn, who left nothing to chance, also had prepared emergency fields every dozen miles or so along the route.

On Dec. 1, 1928 Pitcairn extended its mail route from Atlanta to Miami, via Jacksonville.

During 1929, the airline added stops in Daytona Beach, Orlando and Tampa/St. Petersburg, Fla., and Macon, Ga.

In July 1929, Pitcairn decided to concentrate on his plane manufacturing business. He sold the airline to North American Aviation, Inc. In January, 1930, the airline's name was changed to Eastern Air Transport, Inc.

Eastern began passenger service Aug. 18, 1930, between what is now LaGuardia Airport at North Beach, Long Island, and Richmond, Va. The first route included stops at Camden (serving Philadelphia), Baltimore and Washington, D.C.

The flights operated daily except Sundays over the 310-mile route, using 10-passenger Ford Trimotor aircraft. The new mode of transportation grew so rapidly that Eastern added six 18-passenger Curtiss Condors to the fleet and extended service to Atlanta on Dec. 10.

Passenger service reached Florida on Jan. 1, 1931, when Eastern's 120-mile-per-hour Condors began flying to Miami and St. Petersburg.

By 1932, it had become possible to fly from New York to Miami in one day. An Eastern plane left New York at 8 a.m. and arrived in Miami at 9:50 p.m. The airline promoted the feat with a radio jingle, "From Frost to Flowers in 14 Hours."

Long Trip

By today's standards, the trip was a grueling one. The plane stopped at Philadelphia, Baltimore, Washington and Richmond, where lunch was served. Then passengers went back aboard for stops at Raleigh, N.C.; Florence and Charleston, S.C.; Savannah,

5-3. *In this first page of a profile of Eastern Airlines, written at the time of its fiftieth anniversary, details of the airline's history are presented in a printed pamphlet illustrated with various photographs of airplanes and graphic symbols used over the years. If this detailed profile had been typewritten in the standard format, it would have been many pages longer and the visuals could not have been included. In pamphlet form, this profile is attractive and concise.*

DANISH NATIONAL TOURIST OFFICE • 75 ROCKEFELLER PLAZA, NEW YORK, N.Y. 10019 • TEL: (212) 582-2802

Denmark
Famous For Food, Fun & Fairytales

Dear Travel Writer:

Your Denmark photo file may need a face lifting. Here are some new photos that may interest you just before what looks like a record year for American visitors to Denmark!

Please fill out the enclosed order card and we shall be happy to send you the requested glossy prints immediately.

Thank you and best regards from us all at the

        DANISH NATIONAL TOURIST OFFICE

5-4. This query letter "sells" the PR/publicist's materials by identifying what is available and by giving a reason that they might be of interest to an editor—in this case, new photographs of tourist attractions in Denmark for travel editors. Note how the whimsical and eye-catching drawings on the stationery add to the impact of this letter. Such drawings are appropriate for the fun-loving image that the country of Denmark wants to project. Most query letters, however, ordinarily appear on a more traditional letterhead.

Query Letters

Query letters are used to introduce a potential story idea to an outlet editor in order to determine whether the idea stirs interest. If so, the editor responds and the PR/publicist then knows that it is worthwhile to spend the time researching and writing the story and preparing accompanying material.

Query letters can save time and "sell" the story. They are used with magazines, sometimes with newspapers, often with television and radio stations.

Queries are most useful in selling an article or a broadcast interview concept. Both of these situations require a lot of preparation time on the part of the PR/publicist, and a query response gives some indication of the degree of the outlet's interest. Also, a positive response to a query usually gives the PR/publicist some direction and indication of the editor's interest in the slant, or angle, for the proposed story.

The response that a query gets depends on the strength of the query itself. The query has to "sell" the story concept. In order to do so, it must be well written and establish why the client's story should be of interest to the outlet. In addition, it should suggest several different news angles around which the idea could be developed. The tone must be professional and undemanding. Ideally, queries are not longer than a single page. They are neatly typed, singled spaced, and set up like a standard business letter.

A poorly written query is a straight road to refusal. When writing a query, one follows the same basic rules that would be used in writing any important business letter. Sentences should be short, clear, and to the point. Clichéd phrases, such as "This is to inform you," "Enclosed please find," or "I remain," should be avoided. English should be perfect, without spelling or grammar mistakes.

In addition, it is best to be cautious in the use of slang or colloquialisms. Remember that contemporary jargon can become quickly outdated. Editors relate better to a straight-forward, professional business style. If it is appropriate, use humor, but do so carefully.

Query letters are meant to inform and sell. Unless you know the editor very well, do not attempt to be too familiar. Your query is a business letter, and your writing should reflect that. It is best to put yourself in the place of the recipient; write a letter that would truly impress *you*. Above all, be accurate and be careful what you say. Your success depends on it.

When you write a query letter, remember the following points:
1. *Get to the point quickly.* Summarize the idea in one paragraph before going into details. If you can do it in one sentence, so much the better.
2. *Give alternate angles.* If possible, indicate different approaches to your main story idea. This may prevent an immediate negative response.
3. *Explain the story's importance.* Tell the editor why readers/viewers should be interested in the story.

4. *Be specific and persuasive.* More than summarizing the subject, the query should indicate the approach and main points. If the subject is controversial, it is important to get a point of view established.
5. *Give source(s) of material.* State if the concepts presented are based on statistics, interviews with authorities, man-in-the-street observations, etc.
6. *Tell how the piece will be written.* First person? Scholarly? Chatty style?
7. *Keep it short.* The shorter and more concise the query, the easier it will be for the editor to evaluate. A long, drawn-out query will seem complicated and may discourage interest.
8. *Tell when the story you are trying to place will be ready.*
9. *Indicate if there will be illustrative materials.* Will the story be accompanied by photos, charts, graphs, sketches?
10. *To speed up the reply,* include a stamped, self-addressed, return envelope to make a quick reply easy for the editor.
11. *Explain your credentials.* If the editor has not had any contact with you before, state your responsibility and the relevant aspects of your background.

Manuals, Pamphlets, Magazines, and Books

PR/publicists are regularly called upon to write and produce all kinds of written material for business organizations. These take many different forms, and some require months of research and additional writing and art talent to execute. In general, organizations require their literature to project both their business style and a favorable image.

Examples of such materials are books, reference guides, indoctrination booklets, employee benefit handbooks, consumer information pamphlets, and the like. The books produced are usually company histories or opinion and position statements of executives who are acknowledged leaders in their fields. The kinds of business organizations that produce books are usually established enough in the public eye for people to be interested in reading the story of their development and the opinions of their management.

Since all of these projects are supplementary to the everyday routine of a PR/publicist, they are considered as special projects for which there is usually a separate budget and plan. However, because they are costly to produce, the PR/publicist should consider the following points before undertaking production:

1. Does the proposed literature fit the company's needs?
2. If it is a book, is it to be sold or given away?
3. Should it be a hardcover or paperback?
4. What are the possible tie-in promotional opportunities?

5. Does the project further the major PR/publicity goals of the company?
6. Is the anticipated expense equivalent to the value of the results the project is expected to produce?

Pamphlets and booklets are relatively hard to write. They look easy, but to be effective they must offer a substantial amount of information in a brief and easy-to-read format.

Pamphlet and booklet writing is like writing a short story. You must begin with a provocative lead to entice the reader; use of an attractive type layout and cover illustrations can set the stage for this. Next, when you have the reader's interest, you unfold the story in logical, concise sections, often broken up by subheadings. You must be exact in this kind of writing. Every word has to count.

Either a summary or "call-to-action" should be used as a conclusion. A summary is best, for example, if the pamphlet has explained a complicated process like filling out insurance forms or putting together an intricate wall system. A call-to-action, in a series of steps, is best, for example, if the subject is about the danger signs of a disease or a community program that needs citizen support. The call will give simple steps for the reader to take to avoid the disease or catching it in the early stages. In the case of the community program, the call-to-action will give facts on how readers can express their sentiments on the community issue, whom to write, address, etc.

The graphic design and layout of these materials are vitally important. The PR/publicist must be able to interpret the information and the company's style in the layout as well as in the words. Professionals should be used to assist in the selection of typeface and colors for maximum impact. The layout must combine the color, graphic motifs, and typeface with illustrations or photography to support the copy.

It takes part instinct and part experience to produce an effective booklet. Important considerations in the graphic design include the choice of one or more colors to be used; paper stock that is appropriate and within budget requirements; available photographs and illustrations; suitable typeface(s); necessity of including trademarks, logos, pictures of company buildings, key management, and so on. Above all, all pages should work together; there should be a natural flow from page to page and a consistent style throughout.

Letter Writing

The ability to write a letter is often taken for granted. In the hands of some writers, it can become an art. Exceptional letters have produced exceptional results—raised money, changed lives, obtained jobs, reversed opinions, gotten orders, turned negatives into positives. Being able to write a good letter is important to the practitioner in all phases of PR/publicity activity.

A letter ordinarily has three major divisions: *salutation, body,* and *closing.* Unless the person to whom the letter is addressed is known to you and can be addressed by name, the salutation can become a problem. Do you say "To Whom It May Concern" or "Dear Friend"? Many professional letter writers have discarded the concept of a salutation and begin with either a provocative lead sentence or a headline. The body of the letter is where you put the essence of what you want to say—simply, honestly, naturally. The close of the letter is simplicity itself. The familiar "Sincerely yours" or words to that effect still work.

Good letters take time to write. There is the story about the well-known author who started a letter to his friend in this way: "Please pardon this long letter; I did not have the time to write a short one."

Here are some points to follow when writing letters:

1. Be natural, but not too familiar, unless you know very well the person to whom you are writing.
2. Be careful of slang and humor.
3. Be careful about what you say. It may haunt you later on.
4. Avoid any inaccuracy.
5. Write short, clear sentences.
6. Avoid awkward phrases.
7. Follow standard business form.
8. Make your letter writing style consistent for a long-term impression.
9. Make letters impressively neat. Messy typing is unprofessional.

Letters to the Editor and Editorial Replies

Letters to the editor in print and editorial replies via broadcast are usually stimulated by an article or commentary in the specific media. Many are written spontaneously to express the opinions of concerned individuals. Some are developed as part of an organized PR/publicity effort.

In either case, such pieces should be concise and relate specifically to the article or program that inspired them. Brevity cannot be stressed enough. Space and times for these are limited. The writer has a greater chance of making the point by keeping the piece short than by submitting one that is too long, running the risk of having sections edited or deleted by the media. Obviously, fast action is required so that the letter or editorial reply can be submitted while the issue of interest is still timely.

Also, the writer must have an important point to make. Media will not accept pieces that use a current issue as a self-serving vehicle.

Guest Editorials

Many media outlets run guest editorials on topical issues. In publications, these usually appear near the editorial page or section. Broadcast media air guest editorials as well. These editorials, both print and broadcast, are usually written by an individual considered to be an authority in the field. In some cases, the editorial staff of the medium will seek an individual to write such pieces. Very often, PR/publicists will identify an issue on which they feel a company or individual they represent is qualified to comment, and after getting approval from their client, will make contact to try to "sell" the guest editorial to the appropriate medium. In addition, sometimes, extracts from books or speeches written by the guest editor are used for this purpose.

Guest editorials offer both visibility and prestige to a client or organization as well as an opportunity to expand on a point of view. Issues that are complicated, controversial and, above all, timely are most appropriate.

The development and placing of guest editorials is a sophisticated area of PR/publicity. Successful placement demands creativity, in-depth knowledge of the issues and appropriate media, and swift follow-through. The PR/publicist's responsibility for a particular placement may vary from just placement and advice to full responsibility for idea development, contact, and ghostwriting.

Guest editorials are almost always "specials," appearing only in the selected medium.

6
Working with Photos, Sketches, and Diagrams

We live in a visually oriented society. Newspaper and magazine editors, as well as TV producers, have found that visual materials create interest and help get important messages across to readers and viewers.

As a result, editors of all media are open to the use of photographs, sketches, and diagrams that have news value. To truly take advantage of these opportunities, PR/publicists must have, in addition to a good nose for news, a good visual sense—a knowledge of basic aesthetics which permits them to judge the quality of a visual and its appropriateness to a medium.

Some people are born with a good visual sense; others must acquire it. A PR/publicist who feels deficient in this area can remedy the situation by entering into a routine which includes attendance at art shows, reading books on graphic design, visiting museums, reading magazines that feature graphic design developments, and/or taking a course in photography or design.

Photographs Help Tell the Story

Photographs are an invaluable means of communicating a message and producing PR/publicity. The message is delivered instantly. Often, the communication seems more believable than a written statement of the same situation. In addition, the impression created by the photograph is usually remembered for a longer time.

The press regularly uses PR/publicity photographs. Because good pictures attract attention, create interest, and help tell a story that words, by themselves, cannot, there are many outlets for PR/publicity photos. Consequently, editors' desks are regularly flooded with PR/publicity photos, and the competition for placement is keen. The shots chosen are those that reflect the finest technical quality and have the most news value.

No matter what the story, photographs can add zest to its telling. Consider the following examples:

- *Personnel changes:* election of officers, photos of newly appointed sales personnel.
- *Introduction of new machinery:* photos comparing the new and the old; the installation of machinery (e.g., crane lifting machinery shot from above showing a watching crowd in the street).
- *New store announcement:* photo of the site in juxtaposition to an artist's rendition of the structure or photo of a scale model.
- *Development of a new fiber:* photo of the chemist who worked on the new fiber, photos and sketches showing the various stages of its development, and so on.

Outlets for PR/Publicity Photos

Newspapers regularly use pictures on style pages, business pages, and entertainment pages, in addition to photos that supplement stories in the general news section.

In some cases, editors run photo feature sections on a regular basis, using many photos for such features. These are often related to news concerning fashion or home furnishings. Occasionally, they will be based on a unique event, such as the Winter Olympics, or one of local significance, such as a new convention center and surrounding area facilities.

Wire services and syndicates, besides being sources for written material, also distribute photographs to subscribing papers. In most instances, these syndicates require exclusive photos taken just for them. Here the competition is extremely stiff, but one selected photo has the potential of appearing in hundreds of newspapers simultaneously. Therefore, the extra expense and effort of taking exclusive photos for syndicates and wire services can really pay off for the PR/publicist and the client. The PR/publicist usually establishes phone contact in advance with editors for these photos; they are rarely sent without some expression of interest by the editor.

Magazines are also a good outlet for PR/publicity pictures. Many magazines have a distinct photo style and will require the PR/publicist to simulate it before accepting a photograph for publication.

In almost all cases, a magazine will require exclusivity so that it will appear that the photos were taken by the magazine itself. This agreement not to offer the same pictures to any other publication might run up the cost for the practitioner.

However, such an expense is often worthwhile; a photo in a magazine reaches thousands and, in many cases, millions of people.

Television programs will use PR/publicity photos, especially those showing a new product, a current style, or a unique human interest item. Often, these are used to accompany a personality to be interviewed or are offered to the show's producers with an accompanying script.

Local TV talk and news feature shows are the productions most interested in such materials, particularly if the product shown is available in an area store or if the event described has local significance (e.g., a movie filmed in the area). In such cases, the materials will have an excellent chance of being accepted and used. Again, the competition for such exposure is stiff, and some prior query as to potential interest on the part of the show is necessary.

Photographs can also be used in annual reports, brochures, newsletters, and bulletins. Photos that have a natural look and some human interest will enhance the story being told and capture the flavor of the company, person, or concept being described.

For example, a brochure describing a new knitting technique for an apparel manufacturer will be much more interesting if there are photos of the machine that produces the new technique, of the product produced, and the people involved with it; e.g., a company executive admiring the finished product and perhaps a model wearing the item.

Similarly, an annual report of a company in the accounting business can be made much more exciting by photos of people at work, volumes of processed cases stacked up, clients being interviewed, and so on.

Photograph Requirements

PR/publicity photographs are usually 8 inches x 10 inches, black and white, with a glossy finish. This is the standard size used for most newspaper and magazine placement although 5 inches x 7 inches or even 4 inches x 5 inches is sometimes used.

A size of 8 inches x 10 inches scales easily into the columns of most newspapers and is also proportioned properly for magazine use. *Glossy* prints are best for reproduction although some magazines prefer a *matte* (dull surface) finish. Borders around the print are often used by editors to indicate where the picture should be cropped. Borders also protect the picture to some extent.

Color reproduction is very expensive and few publications are able to use color PR/publicity photos regularly. Before any action is taken, a query letter explaining the color shot should be sent to the editor to see if there is some interest in using it. The letter is most often accompanied by a relatively inexpensive black-and-white print of the shot. If the editor is interested, he or she can request a

35mm. transparency or a 4-inch x 5-inch or 8-inch x 10-inch color print. Transparencies are most often requested.

Unique Standards of PR/Publicity Photography

Rarely, if ever, can a photograph taken for an ad be used for PR/publicity. The emphasis is quite different. PR/publicity photos must seem natural, believable, editorial—almost as if they were taken on the spot by a roving reporter with a camera. They should never look "perfect" or posed, and the best photos usually have some human interest and reflect one or more of the news angles discussed in Chapter 2.

Producing photographs that have these qualities and that also tell the desired PR/publicity story is hard. It usually requires the services of a highly skilled professional photographer working together with a PR/publicist who has a good sense of visual taste.

The PR/publicist has to be able to judge both the technical and aesthetic quality of the photograph as well as its appropriateness. While this is a skill that grows with experience, one can develop this ability by studying the media with an eye to understanding the kinds of photos that are used and what they have in common in terms of style and technical quality.

One can also learn from contact with professional photographers, observing their techniques and approaches so as to arrive at a "feel" for the kind of photos that editors will use.

WHAT THE PRESS EXPECTS FROM PR/PUBLICITY PHOTOS

Editors look for pictures that tell a story. If possible, most of the message should be discernible from the photograph itself. The caption accompanying the photograph should only add more meaning.

There should be logic and plausibility in a PR/publicity photograph. If people are included, they should be placed in "normal" situations, ones in which the reader would expect to find them. For example, a woman in an evening dress in front of a theater or at a formal dance is fine, but a woman in an evening dress posed in daylight at a football stadium is not appropriate.

While the idea behind the photograph is important, equally important is the technical quality. PR/publicity photos should have good detail in the shadow as well as the highlight areas, with a range of sharp contrast tones from jet black to clear white. Because of the differences in reproduction techniques, photographs sent to newspapers need more contrast than those submitted to magazines. This has to do with the size of the engraving screen used and the fact that ink spreads more on newsprint than on magazine paper stock.

Good photos are essential to any PR/publicity effort at media placement. But "good" means more than simply technically good. For the PR/publicist, it can involve the essentials of the client relationship and the on-going association with specific media. Here are some questions the PR/publicist should ask before distributing a photograph:

1. Does the photo project the desired image?
2. Is the photograph aesthetically pleasing?
3. Is it appropriate for the photo style of the media to which it will be sent?

WORKING WITH A PROFESSIONAL PHOTOGRAPHER

Because the PR/publicist must meet a high quality standard, professional photographers are usually used. Even the best pro and the PR/publicist working together may require as many as twenty-five "takes" to get one good shot. These takes reflect changes in lighting, camera angles, a model's expression, and so on.

After a photo session, the photographer marks the takes that he or she likes on the *contact sheets* (unretouched prints which are the same size as the developed film—usually 35mm. or 2¼-inches square) and sends them to the PR/publicist who makes the final selection. These contacts are then enlarged, usually to 8 inches x 10 inches, spotted (to eliminate white hairlines created by dust on the negative) or retouched (to soften lines or get rid of unsightly areas) if necessary. Sometimes, if there are several possibilities, the PR/publicist will request two or three unfinished blowups and then make the final choice.

The fees charged by photographers doing PR/publicity work vary greatly. Most get paid per take in a session. In general, the more experienced photographer will get paid more than the novice. Other factors that affect the price are whether the session is in a studio or on location, whether a stylist is required, and whether any special processing techniques are necessary.

Types of PR/Publicity Photos

It is possible to classify PR/publicity photographs into various categories and, in general terms, discuss those qualities that would make them more acceptable to editors. Photos can be broken down as follows:

- Executive and personality
- Product
- Fashion and beauty
- Special news events
- Offices, factories, and stores
- Transportation
- Locale and scenic.

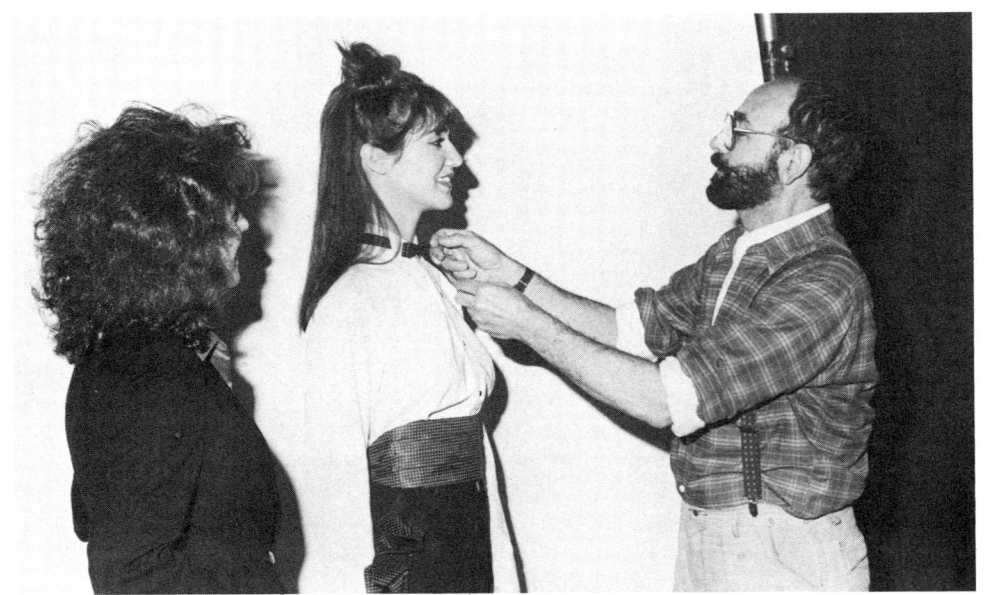

6-1a. *PR/publicity photography session. PR/publicist Sue Hartman, a model, and a photo stylist discuss the look desired in the photograph which is intended to highlight the matching bow tie, cummerbund, and pocket scarf worn by the model.*

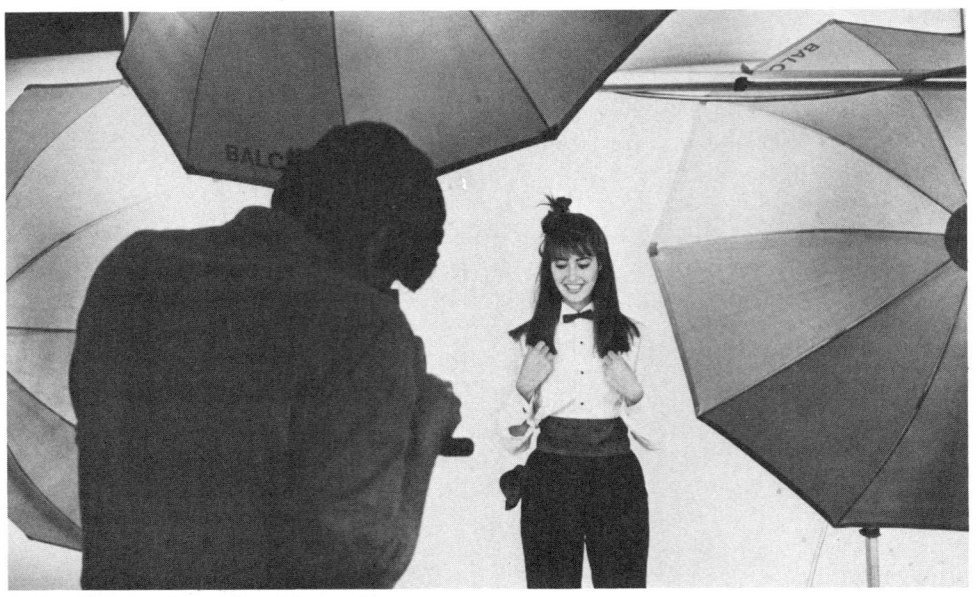

6-1b. *Photographer and model at work.*

83

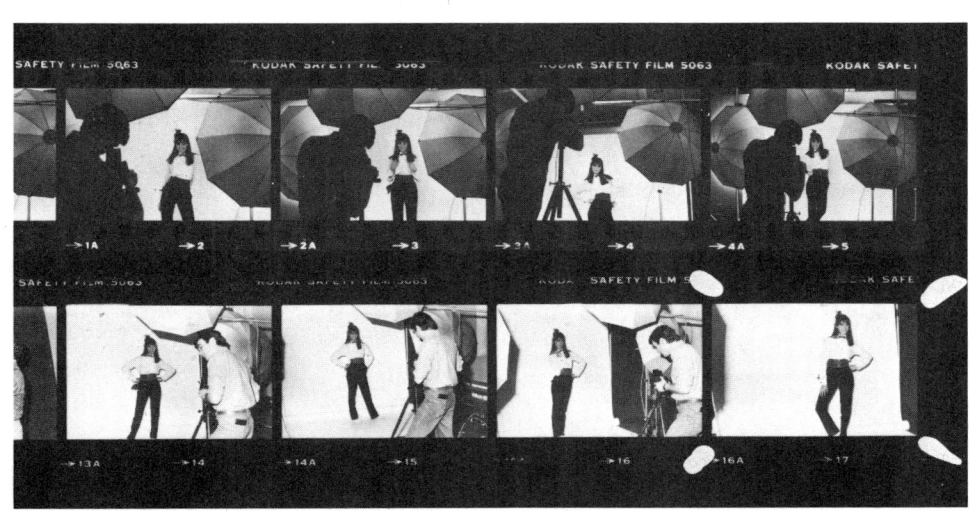

6-1c. Contact sheet of the various "takes" and how they were taken. Shot to be enlarged is marked.

6-1d. A proof print of the selected "take," enlarged from the contact sheet and marked for cropping to the desired proportions. This will serve as the guide for the printing and enlarging of the actual photo from the negative.

EXECUTIVE AND PERSONALITY

Executive and personality photos should express the individual. If possible, some familiar expression, mannerism, or gesture should be part of the portrait. Head-on, looking-into-the-camera shots should be avoided at all costs. These "mug shots," while easy to do, usually make the subject look lifeless and harsh.

Posing a person in natural surroundings, such as office or home, usually produces the most flattering and appealing results. Clothing for both women and men should reveal personal style and position. If the subject is a male executive who always wears a sweater and tie, it is best to photograph him that way rather than dressing him up in a more formal looking jacket and vest. If the subject is not wearing his or her customary apparel, he or she is bound to look awkward. A man should be freshly shaven to avoid a facial shadow which can be very unflattering and make an otherwise pleasant face look sinister.

It takes considerable skill to produce a flattering, realistic, and appealing photo that captures the essence of an individual's personality. Experienced professional photographers who specialize in this type of work should be used. In addition, the PR/publicist should prepare the subject for the photo session by discussing what aspects of his or her personality the photograph will try to capture. Needless to say, this should also be discussed with the photographer in advance of the photo session.

Sometimes, the most aggressive and dynamic personality becomes shy and retiring in front of a camera. Prior planning and even rehearsal before the photo session will make the subject feel more confident and less apt to appear awkward.

Once a good portrait is available, it should be used consistently in the company's or individual's contact with the media rather than alternating a variety of shots. Unless the person is a celebrity who will be recognized under any circumstances, repetition of the same photo will help build individual and company identity.

Unless a person has undergone changes in appearance, such as a dramatic weight loss or gain, most portraits should last five years. Used for a longer period of time, the picture is apt to look dated. Showing a person as he or she used to look rather than current appearance can reflect badly on the individual and the company.

PRODUCT

Products featured in PR/publicity pictures should be shown in a natural setting, sharp and clear. For example, a frying pan would work well on a kitchen counter, a car on a street corner. These backgrounds add believability to a product picture. However, care should be exercised that the background does not overpower the product itself.

Sometimes, the use of props, such as models, company personnel, and cute animals can add life to product photographs. An attractive model holding a tray upon which sits a featured tea set, an over-the-shoulder shot of a secretary using a new word processor, a kitten looking at a new glass bowl—these are examples of props that can add visual appeal and interest to items that might otherwise have little news value.

The angle at which a product picture is taken is also an important consideration. Highlighting a product's special feature without having the result look like a catalogue shot or a diagram is often a necessity. For example, showing a new, double-blade blender from the top, with the cover open, can spotlight the two blades—a feature that distinguishes it from an older model—in a manner no side-by-side comparison photos of the two models could accomplish.

Another way of handling a product shot is to treat the product as art. That is, use dramatic lighting to bring out line and texture, accentuating those qualities that distinguish it from its competition.

FASHION AND BEAUTY

Producing appealing fashion and beauty photographs requires special skills and techniques. It is important to work with an experienced photographer who knows how to capture the essence of a beauty or fashion message in a photo. Unlike advertising, the scene must seem real and natural and not staged, yet the product message or beauty concept must be apparent.

Most fashion and beauty PR/publicity photographs are action shots involving people. It is best to use professional models from a recognized agency because they are experienced in projecting a fashion statement to a camera. Also, the camera adds at least ten pounds to the appearance of the subject photographed, so the thin, angular model is more apt to flatter clothes or cosmetics. Occasionally, nonprofessional models, such as celebrities or well-known local personalities, are used but, in general, effective fashion and beauty shots need the look and grace provided by experienced models.

The PR/publicist and the photographer usually work together to select models for a project. They consider whether the model's appearance and proportions are right for the project, and they will often call a few models in for a "go-see" interview before making the final choice.

Models are initially selected through "head sheets" from agencies. These show heads and faces. Also indicated are models' sizes and daily and hourly rates. Additionally, model agencies supply composites for each of the models they represent. These show the various looks the models can achieve and give detailed size, height, weight, and coloring information. Models for fashion shots are called in for a clothes fitting after the final selection has been made.

Models usually charge an hourly rate to do PR/publicity work. They bill at one-half their hourly rate for fitting sessions, but "go-see" interviews are free. There are usually special rates plus expenses for shootings that involve travel.

6-2. *Executive/personality photo. Consider the earnest, natural expression in this photograph of a young executive. The position of her hands on the papers on the desk implies she is at work. The crisp focus on her face is highlighted by the less distinct focus of the background.*

6-3. *Product photo. The use of sharp contrast and the pattern made by the shadows contribute to make these small ceramic sculptures almost lifelike. Through careful composition, the photographer has used the complicated shadow pattern to lead the eye to the figures which then appear distinctive against the darker background.*

6-4. Two fashion photos. The figure on the stool (top) stands out against a plain background. Her pose is flattering to the clothes she is wearing. Even though she is not in a realistic setting, one senses that she is at ease.

In contrast, the model seated at the table (bottom) seems uncomfortably strained in her pose, the clothes do not flatter her, and she seems almost "caught" in them. In addition, the patterns and dark areas of the background fight the figure. There is nothing wrong with photographing a fashion figure in a realistic setting, but it is vital to avoid an awkward composition and an overpowering background as is the case here.

Because achieving the "right" look is so important in PR/publicity fashion and beauty photography, a stylist is often used to make certain that every aspect of the fashion statement is correct. In some instances, the photographer may have a stylist with whom he or she regularly works. Sometimes, the PR/publicist assumes the responsiblitiy of providing the stylist; at other times, the photographer and PR/publicist handle the styling themselves.

In shooting fashion and beauty photos, styling is critical. It involves shopping for or borrowing the right accessories for a sitting, making sure that the clothes fit exactly, that the model's hair style and makeup are in keeping with the desired look. In a shooting that involves only one or two takes, a stylist may not be necessary, but if one is working with more than one model over a period of several days, working without one becomes quite burdensome. Stylists bill at an hourly or daily rate.

Depending on the kind of photo called for, a beauty preparation, for example, a hair stylist and a makeup artist, in addition to the fashion stylist, are sometimes used. In those instances when they are not available, it is the responsibility of the models to do their own hair and makeup.

Photography sessions may be held in a studio or on location, depending on the nature of the project. These sessions require much patience and attention to detail. Sometimes, the rapport between the model and the photographer is the essential ingredient in getting a flattering and attractive shot. Often, the two will joke with each other as they work or the model may move to background music in order to be caught in a relaxed and natural stance by the camera's eye.

In evaluating the takes, the PR/publicist looks for a photograph that flatters the apparel or makes the beauty statement apparent. For example, a shot may be beautiful and dramatic with the swing of a skirt caught in a graceful swirl, but if it does not show the merchandise clearly, it must be rejected. The PR/publicist and the fashion/beauty photographer must achieve a delicate balance between an eye-catching picture and a clear representation of the product.

Fashion shows frequently provide PR/publicists with opportunities for picture placement in media. Here again, the services of a professional photographer, one who knows how to capture "a look" off a runway, is a must. There are so many elements of lighting and angles to be considered. Also, in most fashion shows, there is no possibility of a second chance. The first take must get the picture, and it must have detail as well as movement.

SPECIAL NEWS EVENTS

News events about a person or company can command more space in the media if there are good human interest pictures documenting what happened. For example, a ground-breaking for a new store might only receive a one or two sentence item in a local paper, but with a photo showing the spade breaking the ground from an interesting angle, the story would receive more attention from the press and the reader.

News-event photography requires special techniques. Most individuals doing this type of work have had professional experience. Sometimes, a photographer currently employed on a newspaper will do such work on a free-lance basis.

In planning pictures to be taken at an event, the PR/publicist and the photographer should discuss the possible takes beforehand. These should include ones that are part of the planned presentation as well as those that it might be desirable to stage, such as a group shot of the company president, the mayor, and the oldest employee at the ground-breaking ceremonies for a new factory. The human interest inherent in such a photograph, particularly if it is taken in such a way as to appear real and candid, greatly increases its news value.

OFFICES, FACTORIES, AND STORES

PR/publicists are often called upon to send out material in which pictures of various buildings and structures play an important part. Stories about the opening of a new store or plant or the moving to new quarters are instances where the use of an interesting photograph would greatly increase the news value of the information.

Here again, the use of an experienced professional photographer will more than pay for itself. In dealing with structures, the photographer has all sorts of technical problems to worry about—converging lines, angles of view, parallax. In some instances, special types of equipment are needed. Again, the injection of some kind of human interest will make the photo more desirable.

TRANSPORTATION

An important aspect of any picture showing a car, a bus, or any kind of vehicle is to show it in action and in a natural setting. A plane caught in flight against a cloud-filled sky, a boat tied to a dock, a bus stopped, but with real traffic behind it—scenes such as these provide "stopper" quality to a PR/publicity photograph.

Again, the presence of some animated objects—people in the act of getting off the boat or on the bus—will heighten interest in the picture. However, caution should be exercised that the human interest elements do not appear "stuck-in" as if they were afterthoughts. Rather, they should seem directly involved, but not to such an extent that they overpower the central message.

6-5. Special news event. This photo taken at a bookstore opening seems natural and suggests that the two celebrities are enjoying themselves. The book display in the background is an instant reminder of where they are.

6-6. Offices, factories, stores. These buildings house offices and an exhibition gallery at the Fashion Institute of Technology in New York. Note how the angle of the shot, the shadow of the tree, and the contrasting softness of the clouds contribute to the dramatic and appealing depiction of this urban college campus.

6-7. *Transportation. This photograph of the Goodyear blimp* America *has all the elements of a good transportation photo. It is clear, the angle at which the shot is taken suggests the forward motion of the blimp, and the view of the ground gives a sense of perspective and suggests its large size.*

6-8. *Local and scenic. The eighteenth century charm of these old buildings in Denmark is captured by this photograph. The perspective of the shot invites the viewer to continue exploring down the street and see what else it offers.*

LOCALE AND SCENIC

Many times, a locale will add authority to a photograph and provide it with a special dimension. Famous places that provide instant recognition can add memorability to the message being conveyed. Famous buildings or landmarks or recognizable parts of them can enhance certain aspects of a product; e.g., shooting sophisticated fashion with the Eiffel Tower in the background or college clothes on the steps of Columbia University's Low Library. A photograph of western wear seems more realistic if set against the background of the Grand Canyon.

It is helpful to find the unique character of a place and utilize it so as to put a distinctive stamp on the person or product you are publicizing.

Cropping and Retouching

Most photographs can be improved by judicious cropping—coming in close to the center of interest and cutting out extraneous material, both in the foreground and background. Cropping should start at the early stages—when viewing the contact sheets. This will improve the chances of getting a better picture later on in the blowup or enlargement.

Cropping can, in a sense, also start before the photograph is actually taken. For example, consider a situation in which the PR/publicist wants to highlight a politician standing in a crowd of supporters, but the crowded conditions make this difficult. The photographer can get as close as possible to take the photo. Then, in the enlargement, a blowup of the central figures and the cropping of unwanted individuals can be made.

Similarly, if a PR/publicist is forced to take a group shot at an event and he or she does not want to include the entire group, the photo can be set up in such a way that the "unwanteds" are on either end; then, they can be cropped off in the eventual blowup.

While cropping is done in the darkroom when the photo is being enlarged, setting guidelines as to what areas should be cropped is usually done on the contact print before the work goes into the darkroom. Using a grease pencil (also called a China marker), the practitioner, sometimes in consultation with the photographer, either puts guidelines in the margins of the contact print or more frequently draws a rectangle or a box indicating which areas should be included.

No matter how hard the photographer tries, there are times when pictures do not come exactly as intended. A tree, which seemed not to be in the picture when taken, suddenly emerges from the head of a subject in the enlargment. Under those circumstances, the photographer has little recourse but to retouch the photo—that is, to correct the error through the use of an airbrush or paintbrush. While some photographers are competent to do this, best results can be obtained by sending the photograph to a professional photo retoucher.

Photo Releases

A signed authorization form giving the rights to the use of the photograph should generally be obtained from any person whose picture appears in a PR/publicity photograph. This is required by professional modeling agencies and is a "must" if there is any chance that the picture will be used in promotion or advertising. The same is true for any quoted testimonial statements or endorsements. Figure 6–9 is a standardized form that can be used with either a photograph or a testimonial.

Photo Do's and Don'ts

As has been stated previously in this chapter, the submission of interesting, definitive, technically correct photographs is extremely helpful in the media placement of news and information. However, because there are many aspects to PR/publicity photography, some more technical than others, the following list of do's and don'ts is presented as a summary aid to the beginning PR/publicist:

- Photos should be planned.
- Each photo should tell a story.
- Make sure the picture is sharp, has detail and contrast.
- Do not have people looking into the camera. They should be doing something.
- Make sure the subject does not look down when picture is taken. If so, his or her eyes will appear closed.
- Keep backgrounds simple. To avoid clutter, a safe background is a bare wall, open sky, etc.
- Sometimes, backgrounds can help tell the story, but they must relate directly to the subject.
- Watch out for "point mergers"—telephone poles growing out of heads, for example.
- Close-ups of speakers at meetings are commonplace. Vary the approach by asking the photographer to shoot the speaker so that some of the audience can be seen.
- News pictures generally do not need a release, but if you want to be safe, get one.
- Keep borders on your prints. Use them to indicate crop marks.
- Crop close to add impact. Use long shots sparingly.
- Do not write on the back of photos. It will crack surface emulsion. Use a soft-point writing tool.

- Most newspapers prefer glossy prints. Television and magazines like a semi-matte or matte finish.
- Do not use paper clips on photos. Use a scrap of paper as a buffer.
- Headgear in outdoor pictures produces shadows. Ask people to take off their hats.
- Watch out for sunglasses on subjects. They will appear as dark spots.
- Break up large groups into smaller groups. They are easier to photograph.
- Put less desirable subjects at the ends of your groups. They can be cropped in the enlargement.
- Use two pieces of cardboard to "sandwich" your photos or artwork when forwarding them by mail. Also label the envelope "Photographs" or "Fragile." "Do not bend" or "Handstamp" are sometimes added as well.
- 8-inch x 10-inch photos may be too large for the smaller dailies and weeklies who do not have facilities for changing the size of the photo in the production process. A good idea is to check with the publication beforehand to see what size print it needs.

The following comments about photography from a newspaper fashion editor support some of these points:

I will not look at a formally posed picture twice. One glance, and then the picture is promply deposited into the proverbial "circular file." A posed picture is a cold picture, and if I don't like to look at it, you can be sure my readers won't either....

Some background is needed to give the picture proper mood. Even a relaxed model tends to look frozen against a cold, blank wall.

The perfect picture, of course, would combine both action and detail, and that's a good goal to aim for. But, if a compromise must be made, it's better—in order to get your fashion picture accepted by an editor and placed before a newspaper's readers—to favor action.

Jeanne Albers, Men's Fashion Editor,
The Cleveland Plain Dealer

Sketches, Diagrams, and Charts

Editors like to use sketches, diagrams, and charts as well as photographs on their pages. These can add "life" to a page as well as provide detailed information.

Surveys show an increasing number of publications opting to use drawings of all types as a counterpoint to photographic treatment. Such a trend should be recognized by the PR/publicist as an opportunity to provide additional and dramatic information sources to the media. As with photographs, however, there are some restrictions and requirements about which the PR/publicist should know in order to prepare material that has the best chance of being used.

PHOTOGRAPH AND/OR TESTIMONIAL AUTHORIZATION FORM

For good and valuable consideration, receipt of which is hereby acknowledged, I hereby irrevocably authorize_____
and_____
their successors and assigns, in its or their discretion, for its or their own account and without control of any kind by me, to use, display, sell, publish, reproduce, modify, televise, alter, combine with others, and otherwise treat or deal with any and all photographs and motion pictures taken of me and any and all plates, films, prints, copies, enlargements, etchings, modifications, alterations, combinations, and other treatments thereof. I hereby convey to_____,
and_____
their successors and assigns, all property rights and privileges in connection with said photographs and motion pictures, together with the right to confer any or all such rights and privileges upon others, without obligation of any kind by _____
and_____,
or anyone else to whom such rights may be conveyed.

It is further understood and agreed that the above includes the right to use my statement:

_____

_____

_____

_____

In any manner set forth in the above authorization for the use of my photograph.

Signature:_____

Address:_____

_____

Date:_____

6-9. *Authorization form for the use of a photograph and/or testimonial. Although the actual wording varies, individuals are required to sign forms similar to this to disclaim any rights to further payment when their photographs or testimonials are reprinted. Such forms are also commonly called* model releases, *or* photo releases—*reflecting that they "release" the client from further obligation to pay the individual.*

Diagrams are especially useful to illustrate how complicated machinery is constructed or to show the steps in an involved manufacturing process. Charts offer a quick graphic summation of figures and trends. It is important that they both be rendered with clean line drawing and lots of white space so that they are easy to read and understand.

Most sketches, diagrams, and charts are distributed to print media as 8-inch x 10-inch black-and-white glossies with descriptive captions affixed to the print. High contrast line drawing is desired because of the dulling effect of print reproduction, especially in newspapers.

For broadcast, however, actual poster-size (20-inch x 30-inch or 30-inch x 40-inch) pieces can be used. And in some cases, the show's format may lend itself to having someone hold or display the sketch or chart during the program. Often an 8-inch x 10-inch black-and-white glossy is used to "sell" the PR/publicity to the program's producers; the full-size artwork is later submitted for actual airtime use.

In the majority of cases, a professional artist is required to create sketches and diagrams for PR/publicity use. The artist works under the direction of the PR/publicist and strives to create a visual which is clear and simple to understand. As in photography, the PR/publicist may use different artists for different projects. There are illustrators who specialize in graphs and charts; others who are strong on drawing buildings and other architectural details; some with strong fashion experience. The PR/publicist picks the artist with the best style and the most thorough understanding of the subject to be publicized.

The procedure for working with an illustrator goes something like this: The PR/publicist selects the artist to be used, calls him or her to view the merchandise or, if it is outside the office, to look over the site or situation. A general discussion follows in which the PR/publicist describes the effects wanted as well as the target medium. The artist then does a "rough" of the concept and shows it to the PR/publicist for approval. If given the go-ahead, he or she completes the art.

The approved artwork is then sent to a photographic reproduction house to be converted into glossies, captions are affixed, and so on.

SKETCHES COMPARED TO PHOTOS

There are some distinct advantages to using sketches instead of photographs for PR/publicity. An artist with the right feel for the situation is not restricted to the actual likeness as the camera sees it. This provides more flexibility and the freedom to emphasize or even glamorize the most newsworthy aspects of the subject or product. Also, the problems associated with hiring models, renting props, or traveling out to a location can be eliminated—all taken care of by the artist working under the direction of the PR/publicist.

In beauty and fashion assignments, particularly, the use of sketches can save time and money. There is no need for samples and accessories in the model's size

6-10. *Example of a PR/publicity sketch. The shoe fashion sketch shows three related styles and tells a visual story of how they each would complement the dress shown. It would be difficult to include all of this in a photograph. Clean, sharp line drawings, such as this and the one in Figure 6-11, both of which have a great deal of white space, serve to highlight the subject, reprint clearly, and are often selected for use by editors.*

and no need to hire a stylist. One is dealing solely with the artist whose fee is roughly comparable to that charged by the photographer, and sometimes less.

USING SKETCHES AND ILLUSTRATIONS

Although sketches and illustrations have a number of advantages over the use of photos, their rendition has to be carefully monitored. Here are some pointers of which the PR/publicist should be aware:

- The illustrative feeling should be paramount; nothing too "jazzy" or with too much "mood." (A certain amount, depending upon the subject matter, is permissible). Overall, the impression should be one of a "graphic report."

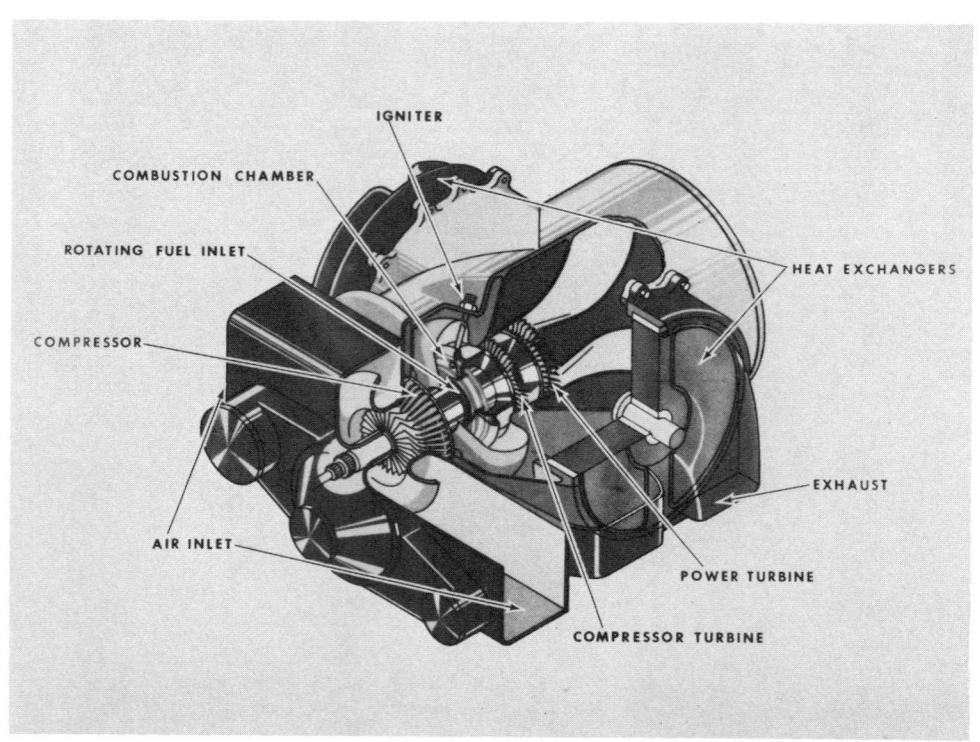

6-11. *This reproduction of a diagram of a motor illustrates the components in a clearer and more understandable way than could be accomplished with a photograph.*

- Line drawings, with little or no shading, are particularly good for use with print media.
- If wash or gray tones are used, they should contrast with the black and white areas to give good contrast.
- In all instances, sketches and illustrations must be easy to follow and simple to understand.
- A great deal of white space should be used. White space will make the drawing or sketch stand out.
- Illustrations should be clear and tell a story. They should illustrate the points made in the caption.
- The style of drawing should not overpower the person, merchandise, or place being publicized.
- Drawn-in props should be subtle, not overdone.
- Charts and diagrams should be clearly labeled and easy to read.
- The visual must have an objective, editorial impact; it should not be overly stylized.
- For print media, diagrams and sketches should be submitted as 8-inch x 10-inch glossy prints.
- Type all instructions and information (but not including captions) relative to the source or handling of the visual on a separate piece of paper. Apply it with rubber cement to the back of the material.
- Do not use colored inks on drawings. Use black and white only in order to achieve better reproduction.
- Do not use dated, old-fashioned-looking art unless it serves a purpose. An up-to-date visual look is best. Use a style of drawing and type that is appropriate to the subject and is currently in style.

Captions

Captions, sometimes called *cutlines* by newspaper people, are words that identify the publicity photo, diagram, or illustration that they accompany, and give specific facts about the product, service, or idea shown.

Captions should be carefully written. Like releases, they require time and attention to detail. In a few words, they must explain the visual and summarize its news value.

Captions should be able to stand alone and provide sufficient information about the photograph, diagram, or illustration should the editor decide not to run the press release that normally accompanies the visual and caption. In a sense, then, the information that the caption contains gives the PR/publicist a second shot at getting the story into print.

Captions for product visuals, particularly fashion shots, usually contain such specifics as style, description, price, style numbers, store and/or manufacturer,

Contact: Sue Hartman　　　　　　For Immediate Release
　　　　　Jackson/Hartman
　　　　　635 Madison Avenue
　　　　　New York, N.Y. 10021
　　　　　212/ 888-7575

<u>ROSIER</u>

FROM WAMSUTTA'S NEW CAPITAL STYLE COLLECTION

Rosier is bed dressing elegance personified in 50% Cotton/50% Fortrel Ultracale. Formal rose nosegays are garlanded with green leaves on an ecru ground. Available with matching comforter and pillow shams.

Photographed in a restored town house in the Capitol Hill District.

6-12. *Captions printed on a separate sheet of paper are used when a considerable amount of information is needed about the photograph. The top of the sheet is taped or pasted to the back of the photograph so that it will not separate from the photo and can be folded over for mailing convenience.*

A farm vacation in Denmark offers fun for the whole family. Here is a scene from the Fairytale Island of Funen.
Photo: Danish National Tourist Office, 75 Rockefeller Plaza, New York, N.Y. 10019.

6-13. *Captions that are printed right on the border of a photograph are most often used when the information is brief and the photo tells the story, as is the case in this picture of a Danish farm.*

and availability information. Sometimes, a reference to style trends is noted. However, captions are only going to be read if the visuals they accompany are of interest to an editor. A well-written caption cannot help a poor visual.

Photographers or illustrators are sometimes credited in a caption, especially if the visual is outstanding or the photographer's or illustrator's reputation is such that it will enhance the chances of the material being used.

There are two forms of captions: the long form and the short form.

The long form of a caption is set up like a press release with the name of the news-seeking organization, the contact, etc. It also has a headline in capital letters and underlined. Most fashion and product PR/publicity photos and sketches require the long caption form because it gives maximum backup to the visual and, thus, the best chance of presenting a complete story. The caption is taped or pasted to the back of the photo or sketch in such a way that it overhangs the visual.

The short form of a caption is typed or printed onto the bottom border of the original photograph and reproduced right on the prints to be distributed for PR/publicity purposes. It is most often used when the visual requires little identifying information, as in the case of photographs of well-known places, such as the Empire State Building or the Eiffel Tower, or easily recognizable personalities and celebrities.

CAPTION DO'S AND DON'TS

Writing a good caption can take almost as much time as writing a good press release. Form, as well as content, is important. The following are some guidelines:

- All copy for the long-form caption should be typewritten on regular size 8½-inch x 11-inch white bond paper. Do not use onion skin or tissue. (Some publicists use a half sheet of paper. Some use a whole sheet. The latter, when folded back, provides protection to the whole visual.)
- Begin all written material at least ½-inch down the page. The empty ½-inch at the top is used to affix the caption to the bottom of the back of the visual. Only rubber cement or transparent tape should be used. Do not staple.
- Double space with 1-inch margins on the left and right.
- Write on one side of the paper only. Use a separate page for each visual.
- Use release date information: either "For Immediate Release" or specify date.
- The caption should have a one-line summary headline.
- Include necessary information in the same placement as in a release: company, address, phone number, contact. Also, if appropriate, include "Special" or "Exclusive."
- In the body of the caption include, where applicable, product information (manufacturer or producer name, style number, material, sizes, colors, suggested retail price, etc.) and the store(s) where the product is available in the city.
- Capitalize or underscore the name of the client or product.
- Leave about four spaces between the end of identifying information and the body of the caption.

7
Presentation Strategy and Placement Techniques

A large factor in the success of any PR/publicity effort is the practitioner's ability to communicate story ideas clearly and present materials effectively. It is essential, then, that the PR/publicist pay particular attention to the communication of his or her ideas to the press—whether they be presented by phone, in person, or in writing.

As good as a story idea may be, poor "packaging" can vitiate it. With competition the way it is, presentation often makes the difference between one story that ends up in print or on the air, and another in the trash can.

More specifically, if a PR/publicist has a likeable telephone personality, a good presence in a person-to-person meeting, and a sense for visual presentation, he or she is way ahead because first impressions often determine whether the PR/practitioner or the material is even considered.

In essence, PR/publicists must know how to approach an editor. To do so, they must be well aware of the style of the medium they are approaching and, even more so, the style and responsibilities of their contact person. In all such meetings, it is important for practitioners to show evidence of being reliable, punctual, and well organized. It is equally important for them to respect editors' deadlines and working routines and not exert pressure at inappropriate times. Finally, PR/publicists must be resilient and professional. If an editor does not "buy" an idea, they can find out why, but practitioners should never protest or try to "strong arm" a contact to use a story no matter how good they think it is.

The Spoken Word

The ability to speak, as to write, is vital to the success of the PR/publicist. To be a good and persuasive speaker, whether person-to-person, over the phone, from the corner of the client's conference table, or from behind a rostrum, is no easy undertaking. Speaking, like writing, requires constant practice. Here are some general guidelines to effective oral communication which a PR/publicist can follow:

- Have a firm idea of what you are going to say.
- Look the person or persons you are talking to in the eye. If it is a group you are addressing, make sure you establish eye contact with more than one individual.
- Try to be aware of audience reaction to your words. Keep your antenna flying to determine feedback.
- In a conversation, listen intently before you reply. Make sure you understand the point the other person is making before you agree with it, question it, supplant it, or praise it.
- If you are trying to sell a concept, empathize. Phrase your thoughts with the interests of your audience in mind. Avoid an antagonistic attitude even if an editor does not want to use your idea.
- Make sure your terminology is understood by all parties involved. Avoid being on different "wavelengths."
- Stay away from jargon and gobbledygook.
- Do not repeat the same words and terms too often. Seek variety.
- Persuasion is most successful when the points that are being made do not depart too far from what has been done before.
- If there is a group of people making a "pitch," try to go last. When arguments of the same relative value are presented, the audience will probably opt to go for the last one made.
- If you are trying to change an opinion, a mild statement challenging that opinion is generally more effective than a strong one.
- If you think that your audience is going to object to what you propose, explain the positive as well as negative aspects. It is better that the shortcomings in your program be explained by you rather than someone else.
- Do not sell too hard. Express your ideas with enthusiasm, but do not overdo it.
- If you are making a speech, remember that it is really a conversation in expanded form. All you are doing is extending your audience. So talk *to* the people, not at them.
- Before a speech, practice aloud. Make your business associates or family listen.

- Do not be afraid to gesture—even in conversation. Use your hands to emphasize and clarify the points you are making.
- Do not explain too much. If you have made your case, move along and do not burden the listener with tedious repetition.
- Try to be believable and friendly.
- Use your instincts. Only make press contacts when you feel positive about what you are "selling." And quit when you are ahead.

The Written Word—With Eye Appeal

Another important aspect of effective communication with the press is the physical manner in which PR/publicity material is furnished to them. Among these transmitted materials are press kits and their ingredients: publicity releases, fact sheets, bios, captions, and so on.

While it is the information that these materials contain which is the deciding factor in their being used, often it is their visual attraction that will pique an editor's interest. Consequently, the design motif used on PR/publicity materials is an important component in their presentaion and potential effectiveness. Such materials should be designed to be eye-catching and appealing. They should strive to stand out among the competition. Everything in the design scheme comes into play: colors, typography, graphics. Like shopping bags, those materials with an attractive design and visual appeal suggest that the matter they contain is of fine quality.

The Press Kit

Of all the materials used in PR/publicity, the press kit is the one in which graphic design plays the most important role. The press kit folder is the "gift wrap" for the story ideas and facts it holds. Consequently, it depends on visual effectiveness to interest an editor.

Press kits are usually file-sized folders with pockets inside the covers to hold the releases, fact sheets, and photographs that are given or mailed to the press. To attract attention and to give an indication of the central theme of the material they contain, their covers are often decorated with artwork and distinctive graphics. Free-lance artists are usually employed to design the covers.

Graphic design, then, serves an important function in the presentation of PR/publicity materials. Professional designers, working with PR/publicists, seek to arrange the elements of an image within a cover format to reflect the full meaning intended. Graphics can communicate any type of message from rock-and-roll loud to whispering soft, from protesting to selling, from pristine to earthy. Just as

7-1. Two press kit covers. The press kit cover depicting the foot and the three-dimensional posies (top) is a creative concept that was used for a shoe company's spring fashion mailing. No company name appears on the cover. It is intended to surprise and amuse the receiver by its greeting card quality.

The more dignified press kit cover (bottom), used by Eastern Airlines, is immediately recognizable because of the wing motif printed in the lower right corner. The simple design works because the airline and its symbol are so well known, and the understated placement of the printing suggests that there is serious business news inside.

record covers help sell records, and book jackets help sell books, the art on press kit covers can help sell the material they hold.

Good design can communicate the essence of the message and move the reader to visual participation and interest in the information enclosed. Well-designed press kit covers, besides being a means of identification, are mood-setters and attention-grabbers. The same applies to the paper on which press releases are run off and the envelopes that enclose them.

Sometimes, press kits can become very elaborate, assuming the proportions of an over-sized box or portfolio. This is frequently done when kits are to be delivered in person at a show or special event. Most editors consider this practice a waste of money because such containers are bulky and hard to file.

While "art" press kits have their adherents, ordinary file folders of the office variety, with a neatly typed label already affixed, can also handle the situation.

Press kits are most often used as the repository for a large variety of press materials. It is considered uneconomical to use them for only one release and a photograph.

PREPARING A PRESS KIT

The specific material included in a press kit will depend on the goals of the PR/publicist and the occasion for which the kit was prepared. Before starting to assemble the kit, the practitioner should think through the PR/publicity objectives. What should the kit do? Announce a new product line? Present a change in corporate strategy? Provide the background for a selling spectacular?

If the PR/publicist is working for a large organization, and there is a specific occasion for which a press kit is planned, he or she might distribute a memo to all departments whose material could be used in the kit, asking for their thinking and samples.

The next step would be to sift through the samples and suggestions, eliminating those that are duplicated and those that instinct and experience tell would not be of interest to the press. The next step would be to make up a list of "haves" and "have-to-go-afters." Then, these should be collected. The writing of press releases and the assignment of taking photographs should be started. One must be sure to clear all copy, both releases and bios, in addition to any other material, with management.

The final step is duplicating the material. While one can reproduce and distribute press kits through an in-house arrangement, there are mailing houses that will handle the entire operation, including running off all the written material; reproducing any photos, diagrams, charts; collating; inserting; and mailing to any specified list of media.

The practitioner working for a PR/publicity agency or for a smaller organization goes through roughly the same procedure in preparing a press kit.

7-2. *The Canon Snappy 20/50 press kit. The various releases and promotional materials included in the kit resulted in the consumer and trade newspaper coverage of the new camera introduction which is shown in Figure 7-3.*

Elements of a press kit

Press kit cover

Individual product photo

Action photo with caption

Three press releases about the Snappy 50/20

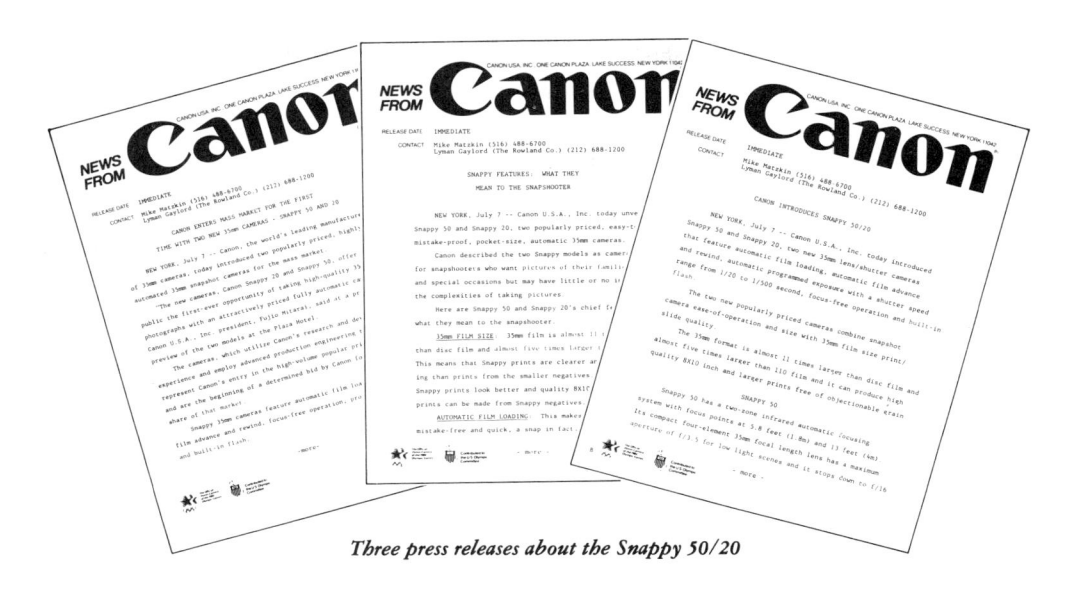

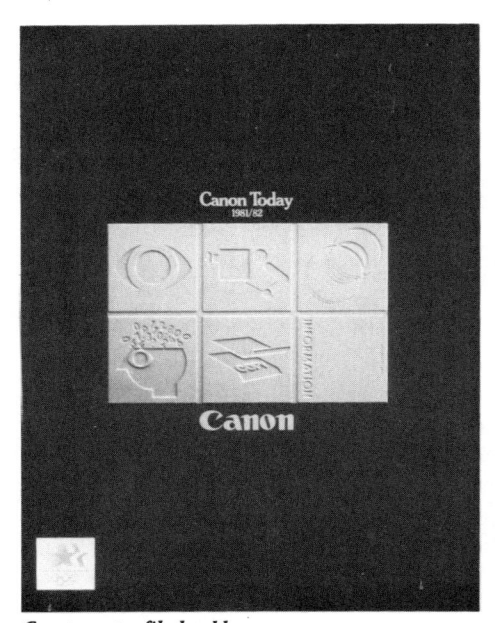

Company profile booklet

Sales booklet

THE PRESS KIT MIX

Press kit contents can vary considerably. Here are some sample contents tied to a specific need or occasion:

- *A dinner for a community fund drive for a hospital.* News release announcing the fund drive, bio of the featured speaker, drawing of the proposed building, a location map, a fact sheet on hospital and health needs in the community. Kit cover is serious and dignified.
- *Announcement of a new line by a fashion manufacturer.* News release on the fashion trend and philosophy reflected in the new line, profile of the company, photos and sketches of the new fashions, a list of stores where the items featured could be purchased, a price list. Kit cover is a stylized design motif.
- *Updating of background information on an industrial firm.* News releases on corporation's growth, chart of corporate structure, copy of annual report, aerial photos of the plant, pictures and description sheets showing new equipment, a map showing worldwide offices. Kit cover could include company trademark or photo of a major product it produces.

While press kits are produced primarily for use by the media, some companies make other uses of them. A press kit, for example, makes an excellent package to put into the hands of salespeople and customers because it gives them the feeling of having been provided with advance and inside information. The background material, which is often included, could be used to recruit distributors. Properly prepared, the press kit gives a fast, up-to-date picture of a company or an institution and its attributes.

Placement Techniques

Although each PR/publicity project requires a unique presentation strategy and series of placement techniques, there are some general routines that apply to all efforts. The following case studies illustrate the typical course of events in generating PR/publicity in a magazine, newspapers, and a television show.

CASE STUDY: GETTING A STORY INTO A MAGAZINE

The placement of a story in a particular medium often requires the expenditure of much time and energy. For example, take the possible placement of a bathing suit in a special fashion section of the May issue of a women's magazine. The process by which it is selected, photographed, and written up is complex and involves the interaction among various members of the magazine, the company whose merchandise is being featured, and the PR/publicist working for that company.

In the timetable that follows, it is to be noted that the sequence of events involves only *one* item. Almost every other item so featured in the special section would go through the same process at approximately the *same* time. To make the situation more complex, the editor and the PR/publicist involved may each be working on other such projects with other contacts simultaneously.

October
- Fashion editor meets with editor-in-chief to discuss theme of May issue.
- Fashion editor meets with magazine art director to discuss tentative page count and layout of May issue.
- Fashion editor meets with assistants to discuss merchandise they should look for in the wholesale market that might work in the May issue.
- Fashion editor selects and books time of photographer whose style is appropriate for the merchandise to be featured in the May issue.

At the same time
- PR/publicist previews new line of bathing suits with company designer and other executives.
- PR/publicist develops news angles and ideas to use to "pitch" or "sell" the new line to the press.

November
- PR/publicist contacts or receives call from fashion editor or assistant to see and discuss the new line. Date is set.
- PR/publicist shows the new line of swimsuits to editor. May take editor to lunch afterwards. Designer or company president may join them. *Or,* if fashion editor's time is tight, PR/publicist will send samples that might work for the fashion editor's story concept to the magazine office.
- Editor calls in samples under consideration for the May story and discusses this with staff, art director and, sometimes, photographer. PR/publicist is responsible for getting samples for this meeting to the editor on time.
- Editor calls PR/publicist to say whether merchandise submitted can be used. If it can be, date in future is set for photo session using sample.
- PR/publicist arranges pick-up of sample so it can be used to show to buyers and other editors in the showroom in the interim. Checks as to whether a duplicate sample can be used for actual photo session or reserves the original sample.
- Models "go see" editor and, sometimes, photographer, too. Selection is based on the right look, size, and with whom the photographer prefers to work.

- Editor contacts photographer and they plan the place for photo session or "sitting," discuss the desired look of the photos, special effects, props, etc.
- Editor calls PR/publicist and confirms arrangements for borrowing merchandise for the shooting. Decision made as to whether it is to be sent to the magazine's offices or the photographer's studio.

December
- A day or two before the shooting, PR/publicist confirms delivery place and time of the samples.
- A day or two before the shooting, editor "packs" merchandise (together with accessories, props, etc.) so it is ready early on the day of photography. Extra items are usually taken in case of last minute model changes, and to provide enough shots if one or two do not come out as expected.
- During the shooting, the editor and assistants usually work along with the photographer, model(s), and stylist, if not during the whole session, at least part of the time.
- PR/publicist waits for call from editor to see if borrowed sample will actually appear in the magazine.
- PR/publicist informs company management that merchandise will be used, and gets price and style information as well as a list of stores that will have the item at the time of the magazine's publication.
- PR/publicist passes this information onto editor and arranges pickup of the samples.

January
- PR/publicist informs sales force that the item will appear in the magazine. If possible, PR/publicist shows the sales manager a rejected version of the photo that is scheduled to appear. If the shot is very good, black-and-white copies may be made for salespersons to show to their customers (store buyers).

At the same time
- PR/publicist is working on other projects.
- Editor is working on other projects after approving final layout and copy for this feature.
- May issue is "put to bed" (finalized) and the production process begins.

February to April
- Magazine in production.
- Editor and PR/publicist working separately on other projects.

May
- Magazine is out with PR/publicity in it.
- PR/publicist is sent copies of the issue and tear sheets of the feature with company identification; can be used as sales promotion mailers or posters and recorded in the company's PR/publicity scrapbook.

- PR/publicist calls and/or writes to thank editor for the PR/publicity.

CASE STUDY: GETTING A STORY INTO NEWSPAPERS

The procedure involved in the possible placement of a story in newspapers throughout the country varies somewhat from the sequence just described. To illustrate, let us take the introduction of a new drug product for which the PR/publicist is attempting to place a story in as many newspapers as possible coordinated with the introduction of the drug in May. An important consideration is that while the practitioner was previously dealing with one magazine, in the following sequence he or she is dealing with many newspapers, all in competition with each other. Consequently, care has to be taken not to send the same story with the same visual materials to two newspapers in the same city. There is a better chance of a "pickup" if the story is sent to them early so as to ensure space for coverage and as an "exclusive" in their readership area.

It is important to note that in a case such as the one illustrated in the timetable below, other mailings probably would have been prepared and mailed to another "exclusive" set of papers at the same time, to ensure the maximum chance of coverage in each city contacted.

January
- PR/publicist meets with management and gets background information about the new drug product and the goals of a PR/publicity effort related to it.
- PR/publicist researches the product and develops a series of relevant news angles and story ideas appropriate for various kinds of media.
- PR/publicist writes or hires a writer to write releases, fact sheets, and any other relevant materials to make news about the drug product.
- PR/publicist hires artist and/or photographer to prepare visual materials to accompany releases and fact sheets. Such materials might illustrate how the product is taken and how it works in the body.

February
- Releases and visual materials are completed and submitted to the company for management approval.
- After any necessary adjustments and corrections are made, the PR/publicist has the materials reproduced in the proper size and form for PR/publicity mailing to the papers. A special press kit folder may be designed and all material assembled into the number of sets required.
- Simultaneously, a mailing list of contacts at newspapers that include news about drug products is established.
- PR/publicist is responsible for mailing out the press materials at a predetermined date. PR/publicist may direct mailing procedure personally or may hire a mailing house to follow through.

March

- PR/publicity materials are mailed out with an advance date in order to give editors time to plan space and to edit or rewrite parts of the story.
- Editors may contact PR/publicist to clarify points and request more information if necessary.
- PR/publicist sends copy of the press kit and a list of papers to which it has been distributed to press clipping service so they can assign their readers to look for stories as they appear.

April

- PR/publicist awaits results.
- Articles based on the press kit usually start to run in the newspapers sometime during this month unless there is a more specific release date issued by the company.
- Editors may send some clippings directly to the PR/publicist, but the majority assume the company has a clipping service and do not take the time to do so unless specifically asked and are provided with a postage-paid self-addressed envelope.

May

- PR/publicist usually thanks the editor who has run a good-sized story by writing a note or, if he or she has met the editor, making a phone call. If there is a vast amount of pickup, the PR/publicist may not do thank-yous.
- PR/publicist compiles clippings of the various versions of the story.
- PR/publicist may analyze the results the press mailing has produced in various ways, including: (1) counting the number of articles picked up and used; (2) computing the equivalent value of advertising space of the same scope and size; (3) calculating the number of people in a selected public reached, based on the circulation figures of the media outlets that used the story; (4) seeking to have stories analyzed in terms of their ability to influence the reader (content analysis).
- PR/publicist retains the clips and analysis for report to company management and/or mailing piece for sales force or customer sales promotion.

CASE STUDY: GETTING A GUEST ON A TV INTERVIEW SHOW

In order to arrange for an interview to take place on a television or radio broadcast show, the PR/publicist must work well in advance of the actual date the interview is to take place. Whether the show is aired live or pretaped, the PR/publicist usually has been in contact with the show producers at least a month and, in some cases, many months before the actual interview date. (Television is discussed in Chapter 11.)

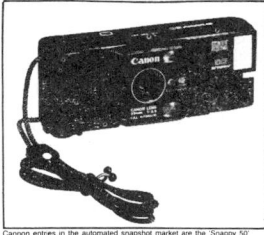

7-3. *A selection of results from the Canon press kit placement (see Figure 7-2). Consider the variety of stories, news angles projected, and use of materials. Also note the dulling effect of the newspaper reproduction of the originally sharp photograph.*

Broadcast shows are interested in timely subjects and lively individuals. Many times, the PR/publicist's role in the broadcast interview involves script writing and interviewee preparation as well as the preparation of releases.

The following timetable suggests the typical month-by-month routine a PR/publicist would follow to secure a broadcast interview for a client. Often such interviews are strung together as a city-by-city tour. In those situations, several preparations would be taking place almost simultaneously.

The schedule that follows is based on a series of TV interviews for an author of a controversial book about the author's youth.

Three months prior to publication of the book
- PR/publicist receives and reads an advance copy of the book from the publisher.
- PR/publicist meets the author and evaluates the author's potential as an interviewee on a broadcast show.
- PR/publicist works with the publisher and author and establishes news angles and subjects that will be suitable to discuss on a broadcast TV interview.

Two months prior to publication
- PR/publicist writes a general news release about the book and author, submits it to the publisher and author for approval, and then has it reproduced for distribution.
- PR/publicist draws up a list of possible broadcast shows on which the author can appear, shows that are in the markets of interest to the publisher. A series of shows is then selected from the list.
- PR/publicist secures and reproduces a photograph and biography of the author.
- PR/publicist writes a suggested script for the interview based on the information and goals worked out with the publisher as well as on a knowledge of the typical talk show format.
- PR/publicist writes a query letter to the producers of the desired shows, presenting the guest, the subject to be discussed, and asking if they have an interest in interviewing the author during a specific week. TV show producer responds and, if there is interest, PR/publicist sends the release, a photo of the guest, bio, and a copy of a suggested script.
- A sample copy of the book is sent when available.

One month prior to publication
- Interview dates and arrangements are confirmed.
- PR/publicist works with author, conducting training and practice sessions for the interview, including a series of difficult questions to answer. Sometimes, these practice sessions are taped and reviewed by the PR/publicist and author. Author is advised on how to dress for interview.

At the same time
- Show staff reviews PR/publicity materials and the book. Simultaneously, they edit the script for the interview, determine its length, and choose a set.

On the days of the interviews
- PR/publicist accompanies author to the studio. Sits through the run-through with show hosts, author, and show director and staff. Watches the actual interview.

Following the interviews
- PR/publicist writes thank-you note to the show for using the guest.

8
Making Contact with the Media

Reaching the media means more than simply mailing materials to all the names on a list of outlets. It means determining what type of story will be appropriate and appealing; then conducting research, concept development, planning, and identifying news angles; selling either in person, by phone, or by cover letter; and, finally, following through to make sure the material is delivered on time.

Each particular PR/publicity effort, whether print or broadcast, requires a unique combination of materials and contact techniques. In every case, the practitioner must make sure that each step in the effort to reach the media is the best of all possible choices. Common sense and professional experience determine which combination of materials and techniques is used.

Contact Techniques

Telephone and Person-to-Person. Whenever possible, a PR/publicist uses telephone or person-to-person contact. This permits an individual "sell" or "pitch" of the story and can establish a good working rapport for the future. The correct timing of such calls or meetings is essential. The PR/publicist must respect how busy editors can be around deadline time, planning meetings accordingly. Press releases and other written materials can be used as a follow-up.

Mail. This is the contact method PR/publicists use most often because it allows them to reach the maximum number of press contacts with the minimum expenditure of time and money. An individual newspaper receives thousands of releases each week, and of these only a small percentage (about 10 percent) are actually used. Such odds make it essential that all mailed materials be in correct form and impressively neat. Although the actual work of making a mailing may be done outside or at the client's office, it is always the responsibility of the PR/publicist to arrange for photo reproduction and art work, and to determine the appropriate press list for the materials.

Local PR/Publicists. When the placement of a story away from the organization's home base is important (for example, when a company executive is scheduled to make an important appearance in a selected city), local PR/publicists can be hired to work with the press. These individuals are usually engaged through a national agency and charge an hourly rate. Sometimes, these local PR/publicists will even appear on a television or radio program on behalf of the company.

Hand Delivery. Hand delivery is used when an editor, located in the same city as the PR/publicist, needs written materials or product samples quickly. Many PR/publicists try to make the packaging of hand-delivered materials eye-catching and attractive, and in the fashion industry, some even go as far as using colorful shopping bags, tissues, and ribbons.

Interviews and Meetings. When it is necessary for an editor to meet with a company representative, the PR/publicist sets up the time and place, gives the editor some idea of the story to be discussed, and briefs the representative(s). During such meetings, PR/publicists act as liaisons or arbiters. Their involvement in the conversation should not be dominant, although they may be subtly directing the meeting. Often, such meetings will start in the client's office and continue over lunch in a restaurant.

Establishing a Contact List

Every PR/publicity project requires a different kind of research to establish the most accurate and complete contact list. In some industries, the trade and consumer publications available are well known and easy to find. In others, the relevant media outlets are more specialized and difficult to identify. If the PR/publicist and the editorial contacts are in the same location, the "Yellow Pages" is a good place to start for names and addresses of media. A basic list can be drawn up and, then, phone inquiries made to establish who at each outlet has responsibility to cover the news in the area in which the PR/publicist is working. In addition, the mastheads of certain magazines and trade publications list this information, and a PR/publicist can develop a list by using them.

No matter where the initial information comes from, it is a good idea to clarify whom to contact by telephone. In addition, for a PR/publicist just beginning to work in a new area, a phone clarification of whom to contact can serve as graceful way to introduce oneself and establish a relationship, inquire as to

> **Four Basic Questions to Ask Before Contacting Media**
>
> 1. *Who reads, watches, or listens?* (Or what is the circulation and audience?) Are they young/old? Male/female? Married/single? High income/low income? With children/without children?
> 2. *What are the deadlines?* (Or when does the material have to be submitted?) How early for the afternoon edition of a newspaper? How far in advance of the on-sale date of a monthly magazine? How much time before an interview on radio?
> 3. *Who gets the information?* (Or to whom should it be sent?) Does the story go to the city editor, news editor, style editor or business editor of the newspaper? To the producer, director, or commentator of a television show?
> 4. *What PR/publicity technique is required?* (Or how should the story information be presented?) Should the story be written as a release, outlined in a fact sheet, described in a query letter, or explained on the telephone?

deadlines, working routine preferences, etc. If one is going to use this telephone technique to establish contact, it is a good idea to read current issues of the publication or view or listen to current broadcast programs before calling. In this way, the PR/publicist can develop a sense of the media's working style and can also avoid the embarrassing possibility of approaching editors with a concept they have already run.

Phone and phonebook research is possible when PR/publicists are in the same location as the editorial offices of the outlets in which they have an interest in establishing contact. In no place is this more in evidence than in New York City, where many important print and broadcast outlets as well as some of the country's major corporations are located. As a result, much of the contact work in New York is done by phone and on a person-to-person basis. There are, however, many publicists working in New York who need to work with publications whose editorial offices are located outside the city. Also, many PR/publicists working around the nation do not have the luxury of easy phonebook and phone confirmation work to establish a contact list. Consequently, there are references available to professionals in the PR/publicity business which are used to develop a basic contact list for a project.

PROFESSIONAL SOURCE BOOKS

Professional source books that list media contacts are available by subscription. Updates are mailed to subscribers at regular intervals.

One of the most commonly used is the *Editor and Publisher Yearbook*, which lists names of editors and reporters and their addresses and phone numbers

Contact List

San Francisco Gourmet Project

Local Newspapers	Radio/Local	Gourmet Magazines
Ms. Ruth Miller Style Page Editor SAN FRANCISCO CHRONICLE 5th & Mission Sts. San Francisco, CA 94119 (415) 777-1111	Mrs. Betty Bee San Francisco Day KBAY Radio 8th & Mason Sts. San Francisco, CA 94108 (415) 983-2700	Ms. Barbara Varnum Associate Editor BON APPETIT 5900 Wilshire Blvd. Los Angeles, CA 90010 (213) 557-3800
Ms. Mary Stanyan Food Editor SAN FRANCISCO EXAMINER 110 Fifth St. San Francisco, CA 94102 (415) 442-3300	Mr. Melvin Marsh Restaurant Reviews KALW Radio 21st & Harrison Sts. San Francisco, CA 94110 (415) 663-2900	Miss Bonnie Lee Pease Associate Food Editor GOURMET MAGAZINE 560 Lexington Ave. New York, NY 10022 (212) 371-1300

T.V./Local	West Coast Magazines	National Newspapers
Mrs. Sally Smith Producer THE BAY GOURMET KEMO-TV, CH 20 2500 Marin St. San Francisco, CA 94124 (415) 777-1600	Mrs. Ruth Williams Best Choices Editor CALIFORNIA MAGAZINE 5000 Wilshire Blvd. Los Angeles, CA 90010 (213) 444-6800	Mimi Sheraton Food Reporter THE NEW YORK TIMES 224 West 43rd St. New York, NY 10036 (212) 556-1234
Mr. James Johnson Women's Interest Editor KBHK-TV, CH 44 420 Taylor St. San Francisco, CA 94102 (415) 442-6500	Mr. Joseph Price Restaurant/Food Editor WHERE-WEST COAST 1 Market Plaza San Francisco, CA 94105 (415) 442-8000	Mrs. James Smith Marketing Editor THE WALL STREET JOURNAL 22 Cortland St. New York, NY 10006 (212) 285-5000

T.V./National	General Interest Magazines	Business Publications
Mr. Walter Felix Program Coordinator GOOD MORNING AMERICA WABC-TV Lincoln Square New York, NY 10023 (212) 887-7777	Mr. Robin Ward Researcher PEOPLE 3435 Wilshire Blvd. Los Angeles, CA 90010 (213) 683-3000	Mr. Brian O'Reilly Reporter--New Trends FORTUNE MAGAZINE Time/Life Bldg. Rockefeller Center New York, NY 10020 (212) 586-1212
Miss Sally Rice Production Associate THE TONIGHT SHOW WNBC-TV Rockefeller Center New York, NY 10022 (212) 751-6000	Mr. Jerry Eitelberg Assistant Editor, Leisure NEWSWEEK MAGAZINE 444 Madison Ave. New York, NY 10022 (212) 666-4800	Miss Sandra Rifkin Marketing Editor BUSINESS WEEK 1221 Avenue of Americas New York, NY 10020 (212) 997-2511

8-1. *Abbreviated contact list. Note the various categories of press contacts on this list for a PR/publicity project for a natural foods, gourmet catering service in San Francisco, California. Such lists are compiled to include the broadest selection of media outlets that might reasonably write or broadcast news about the service. Ordinarily, such a contact list would be many pages long. In this case, however, only two entries appear under each category in order to illustrate on one page the range of outlet classifications.*

at all U.S. newspapers. In addition, there are references for PR/publicists who specialize in a particular kind of news, such as *The Style Page Directory,* which gives information for the style pages only.

A reference book helpful in identifying news service correspondents is *New York Publicity Outlets,* which breaks down supplementary news services into categories, i.e., AP, UPI, special interest news, foreign news, news photos, feature syndicates, syndicated Sunday magazines. *New York Publicity Outlets* also lists virtually all New York City based outlets, magazines, foreign correspondents, broadcast talk shows, and so on.

Directories, such as *Broadcasting Yearbook* and *International Television Almanac,* can be used to find broadcast contacts; but the directories that are most useful to the PR/publicist in selecting shows and developing appropriate story ideas are *TV Publicity Outlets—Nationwide* and *National Radio Publicity Directory.* These offer show-by-show listings, including audience size, type of PR/publicity materials accepted, station affiliations, etc., as well as contact names and addresses.

Bacon's Publicity Checker, another aid, comes out yearly and is regularly updated. It gives names, responsibilities, and editorial profiles, by industry, of a wide variety of media outlets. These are helpful to the PR/publicist just starting to work in a new, specialized area, and can be used to compile complete lists of relevant specialty publications and to plan large mailings to out-of-town special interest publications.

Ayer's Directory of Newspapers and Periodicals is an annual that contains a listing of most of the publications issued in the United States. These are broken down first by states, then listed alphabetically by cities. For quick reference there is an alphabetical index of all the publications in the rear of the directory.

The Membership List of the Society of Magazine Writers contains the names and addresses of the country's top magazine writers, most of whom work on a free-lance basis. These writers often take on publicity assignments in addition to their magazine work. When this occurs, however, the magazine involved must know that the writer is representing the PR/publicist.

The Working Press of the Nation comes in several volumes and lists key personnel under more than one hundred different news categories. Newspapers, magazines, television and radio stations are covered.

Burrelle's, Livingston, New Jersey, a well-known news clipping service, issues a number of state media directories, comprehensive listings of newspapers, periodicals, radio and television stations, cable television and college publications on a state-by-state basis. Information is updated every six months.

For PR/publicists who want to contact editors of house magazines, the Gebbie Press, New Paltz, New York, publishes *The Gebbie House Magazine Directory* which lists more than four thousand of the country's most outstanding company and organizational in-house publications. The company also publishes the *Gebbie Press All-in-One Directory* which lists separate categories of contact,

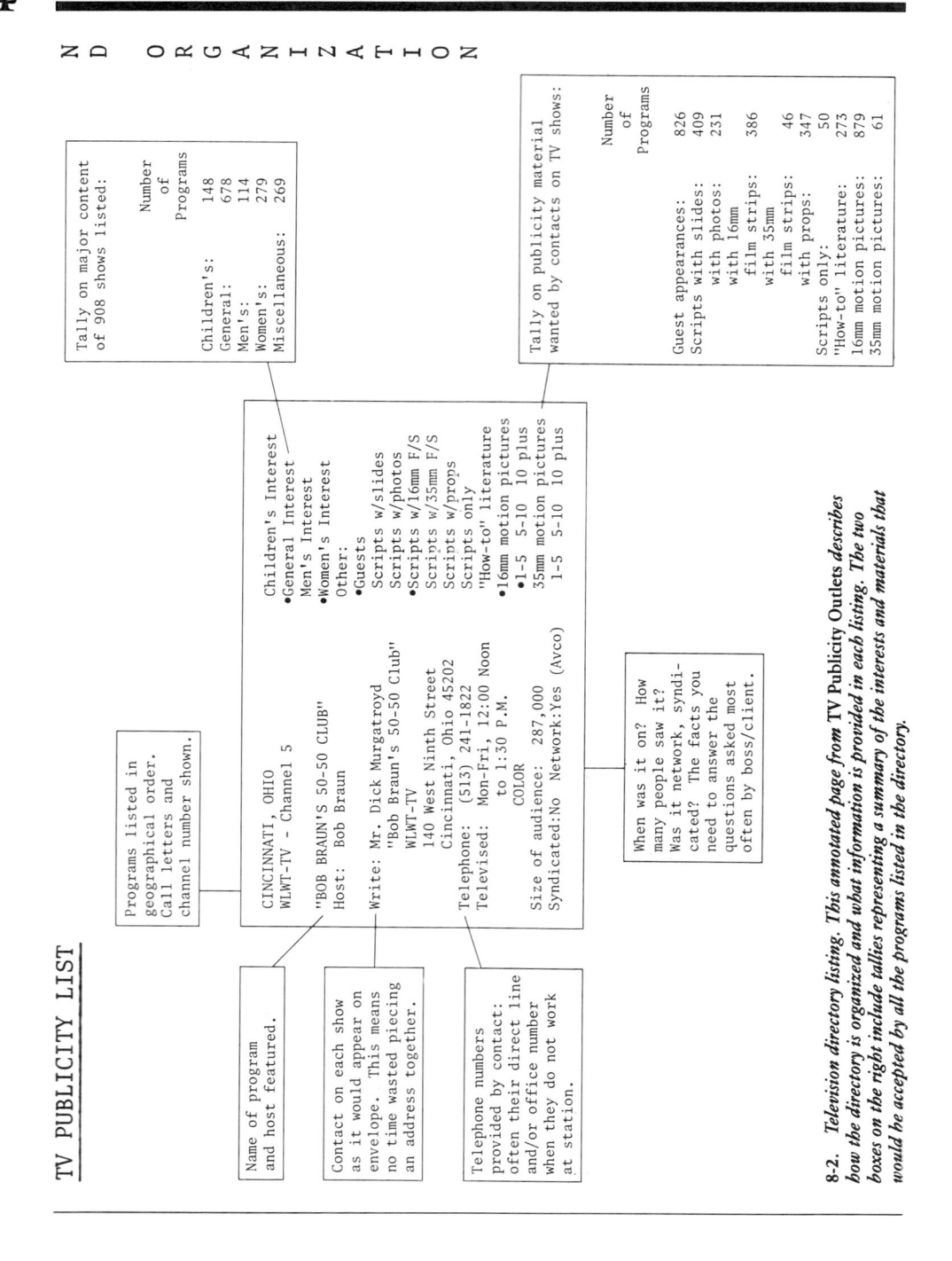

AND ORGANIZATION

TV PUBLICITY LIST

Programs listed in geographical order. Call letters and channel number shown.

CINCINNATI, OHIO
WLWT-TV - Channel 5

"BOB BRAUN'S 50-50 CLUB"
Host: Bob Braun

Write: Mr. Dick Murgatroyd
"Bob Braun's 50-50 Club"
WLWT-TV
140 West Ninth Street
Cincinnati, Ohio 45202
Telephone: (513) 241-1822
Televised: Mon-Fri, 12:00 Noon
to 1:30 P.M.
COLOR
Size of audience: 287,000
Syndicated:No Network:Yes (Avco)

Children's Interest
•General Interest
Men's Interest
•Women's Interest
Other:
•Guests
Scripts w/slides
Scripts w/photos
•Scripts w/16mm F/S
Scripts w/35mm F/S
Scripts w/props
Scripts only
"How-to" literature
•16mm motion pictures
•1-5 5-10 10 plus
35mm motion pictures
1-5 5-10 10 plus

Name of program and host featured.

Contact on each show as it would appear on envelope. This means no time wasted piecing an address together.

Telephone numbers provided by contact: often their direct line and/or office number when they do not work at station.

When was it on? How many people saw it? Was it network, syndicated? The facts you need to answer the questions asked most often by boss/client.

Tally on major content of 908 shows listed:

	Number of Programs
Children's:	148
General:	678
Men's:	114
Women's:	279
Miscellaneous:	269

Tally on publicity material wanted by contacts on TV shows:

	Number of Programs
Guest appearances:	826
Scripts with slides:	409
with photos:	231
with 16mm film strips:	386
with 35mm film strips:	46
with props:	347
Scripts only:	50
"How-to" literature:	273
16mm motion pictures:	879
35mm motion pictures:	61

8-2. *Television directory listing. This annotated page from TV Publicity Outlets describes how the directory is organized and what information is provided in each listing. The two boxes on the right include tallies representing a summary of the interests and materials that would be accepted by all the programs listed in the directory.*

including: newspapers, magazines, radio, television, news syndicates, black press, and business press.

THE IMPORTANCE OF THE RIGHT CONTACT

While preferences may develop for working with individual reporters, these should not interfere with sending stories to the right department and the right person. For example, information on a fashion show by a department store should be sent to the style page editor despite any relationship the PR/publicist might have developed with the sports editor.

At any media outlet, a good idea for a story can be rejected by the wrong department when it would have worked in another division. In some cases, materials will be referred to the right editor, but all too often they are not. Most editors assume that it is part of the PR/publicist's job to know the right contact and are often annoyed by misdirected stories.

Sometimes, more than one department might be legitimately interested in a story. In such a situation, information is directed to both editors and each is told that the other has received the story. The decision as to how the story will be used is worked out between them.

Media Mailing Services

Many PR/publicists use services to collate, assemble, and mail materials. These services maintain lists of press contacts which are cross-referenced by location, circulation, readership statistics, and area of news interest. When utilized, they relieve the PR/publicist and the client of the problems of maintaining a contact list, as well as the mechanics of assembling a mailing. Examples of companies that provide such services are PR Aids (Public Relations Aids, Inc.) and Media Distribution Services.

MAILING IN-HOUSE AS COMPARED TO MAILING HOUSES

It is usually less expensive to process PR/publicity mailings in-house or at a PR/publicity agency. In these instances, the appropriate lists for each project must be maintained and updated by the in-house or PR/publicist's staff and help must be available to collate materials, affix labels, stuff envelopes, etc.

There are, however, some distinct advantages to using professional PR/publicity mailing services. These services maintain and constantly update mailing lists and can take the PR/publicist's materials in the "rough" and do all the typing, printing, and mail processing in a relatively brief period of time. They have evolved fairly sophisticated systems for defining a mailing list; these systems offer the PR/publicist a lot of flexibility. These companies have account representatives who can help a PR/publicist plan a story and give mailing list advice. Such services also provide clippings of any stories that run. Although quite expensive, they are used by many professionals, especially those working at companies and agencies issuing a large volume of press material on a regular basis.

Other Means of Reaching the Media

Feature syndicates, mat services, photo syndicates, and PR wires are specialized means of reaching the media. PR/publicists use them to supplement other forms of contact. In the case of feature and photo syndicates, queries are often made in advance of preparation of materials. This is because competition for placement is keen and each has specific requirements for materials which entail extra time, effort, and expense.

FEATURE SYNDICATES AND MAT SERVICES

If a PR/publicist is seeking a broad pickup of a story, he or she can approach feature syndicates or hire the newspaper mat mailing services. Syndicates are organizations that send out all sorts of features on subjects from beauty to home repair as well as bylined columns and comics. These features are sent to editors for consideration as fillers in their publications. The services offered by the syndicates are bought and paid for by the newspapers that subscribe to them. Some of the best known syndicates are NEA (Newspaper Enterprise Association), King Features Syndicate, and the Chicago Tribune—New York News Syndicate.

Contacts at syndicates should be made in the same way one would approach an editor of a single publication. If it is practical, it is best to make phone or person-to-person contact, but some placements can be made by mail. Syndicates require special feature material that is solely for their use. Competition for story placement with them is keen because of the simultaneous national pickup and potential coverage they offer.

Mat services, such as Derus Media and North American Press, will set a client's story in type as a feature column and offer it to interested newspapers in a ready-to-print cardboard mat. Mat services differ from feature syndicates in that they are free to the newspapers and are paid for by the companies that place stories in them. Mat services are easier to work with than syndicates because they are selling their services to the PR/publicist. These companies also produce novelty features, such as crossword puzzles and quizzes which highlight a client's name or cause. Some will develop narrative concepts and scripts for broadcast use and distribute them with a postage-free reply card on which an editor's interest can be indicated.

PERSON-TO-PERSON LINE

HOME HEALTH HOTLINE

"At what age should my child start brushing his teeth?"

"What is the correct way to tape a bandage."

"What can I expect at a gynecological examination?"

Consumers wishing to learn the answers to these and other questions about home health care can now call the new toll-free Person-to-Person Line provided as a public service by Johnson & Johnson Products, Inc.

The types of questions which the Person-to-Person Line is prepared to handle include the care of minor wounds in the home, use of consumer wound care and dental care products, general oral health, and feminine hygiene.

Calls are answered in person by trained consumer information specialists. In addition, experts from various medical specialties—including dentistry, pharmacology, gynecology—are ready to assist callers by means of a taped library of replies to common concerns.

The toll-free number is 800-526-2433 (in New Jersey call 800-352-4777). The Person-to-Person Line serves the continental United States and is open from 10 a.m. to 5 p.m. (Eastern time) Monday through Friday, and from noon to 4 p.m. on Saturday. The number is on or in most of the company's packages now and will be appearing on the rest.

Treat The Tree Trimmers

Neither Santa nor elusive elves decorate the Christmas tree—unless you live in the land of make-believe. Launch holiday festivities with a tree-trimming party ending with delicious Easy Chocolate Cheese Pie and a pitcher of cold milk. The pie is made to order for this busy time of year and can be prepared early in the day or the night before. Semi-sweet chocolate squares and cream cheese provide a rich creamy mixture; the addition of thawed frozen whipped topping lends a light, fluffy quality to this holiday pie. Chill or freeze the pie until firm. Garnish with grated chocolate and take it to the trimming party.

EASY CHOCOLATE CHEESE PIE

3 squares Baker's semi-sweet chocolate	1 container (8 oz.) Cool Whip non-dairy whipped topping, thawed
¼ cup water	
1 package (3 oz.) cream cheese, softened	1 baked 8- or 9-inch graham cracker crumb crust, cooled

Heat chocolate with water in saucepan over low heat, stirring constantly until melted and smooth. Beat cheese until smooth and fluffy; gradually beat in chocolate. Fold in whipped topping. Spoon into crust. Chill 2 to 3 hours or freeze until firm. Garnish with grated chocolate or chocolate curls, if desired.

8-3. *These typeset columns are typical examples of features distributed to the press by mat services in a printed, multipage circular. PR/publicists pay to have their materials circulated by the service to subscribing newspapers. If a paper wishes to use a particular piece, they can use a reply card to order a ready-for-print mat. Features such as the health hotline and recipes offered in these examples are typical of the noncontroversial, public service-oriented materials that are most often used for mat mailings. Mat services are advantageous to PR/publicists because the stories run as they have written them, and there is generally a high percentage of pickup because these pieces are ready-to-print fillers. In addition, the mat service will work with the PR/publicist to edit and prepare the story in the most appealing way for no extra charge.*

These media mailing services are quite expensive and are utilized in extensive, on-going PR/publicity efforts. Usually, results are good because the services know their outlets well and can guide the PR/publicist in determining the most appropriate news angles and story forms.

PHOTO SYNDICATES AND PR WIRES

While many of the news services (e.g., Associated Press, United Press International) and feature services have divisions that distribute news photos, there are syndicates that concentrate on pictures alone. PR/publicists submit special photos to them for possible distribution just as they do with feature syndicates. Among the best known photo syndicates are Wide World Photos, Inc., Globe Photo, Inc., and Black Star.

There are wire services that provide PR/publicity organizations immediate access to the newsrooms of newspapers, magazines, and radio and television stations by direct teletype communication between the offices of that wire organization and the media. The cost of these services is borne by the originating source—the PR/publicist—in order to get news and information to important outlets in the shortest possible time. Examples of PR wires are Public Relations Newswire and Business Wire.

Successful Placement in Media

To place PR/publicity material consistently in media requires a combination of knowledge, skill, tact, assertiveness, and just plain hard work. Moreover, there is no substitute for experience. There are, however, certain precepts that all practitioners should follow to make their task easier.

NEWSPAPER PLACEMENT

To place a straight news story locally, the city editor is the most important person to contact. Since city editors supervise reporters and give out most of the assignments involving general news within the community, their approval or veto means life or death for a PR/publicity story.

For the most part, city editors do not respond well to outside hard sell. They are professional news evaluators and are quick to recognize the difference between a story that is "hard-news" oriented and one that is not. They will most often opt for the factual, hard-news item, but will sometimes accept a human interest concept, or "soft" news. In any case, if there is any chance that the story will appeal to them, they are worth a try.

Financial editors are major users of written releases because they cover business personnel changes and business trends on a daily basis. The editors of the "Style Page" or "Women's Page" are usually even more receptive to PR/publicity efforts because they use news and photos of fashion and products on a regular basis.

Other special editors—sports, entertainment, science, medicine, and so on—are receptive to exclusive product and company stories.

MAGAZINE PLACEMENT

Picking a magazine for possible placement should be done with great care. It is important that the PR/publicist's story matches the magazine's audience, that it coincides with its demographic characteristics.

In addition, it is important that the PR/publicist know the style of a magazine's editorial sections and understand what information they cover in each issue and what they cover only in certain issues. For example, some men's wear magazines run gift columns near the Christmas season and not at any other time, and some business publications run major national reports only once a year. If a PR/publicist misses one of these issues, the opportunity for placement may be lost for a whole year. Therefore, it is important to know the yearly schedules well. This knowledge can be acquired by reading issues over a year's time or by asking a contact at each media outlet.

Most magazines pride themselves on their individuality and creativeness and are responsive to new approaches and special stories developed just for them. When placing an article, the PR/publicist works along with the editors from the beginning in order to best satisfy their style and length requirements. The practitioner should avoid sending a finished article for evaluation, asking for further suggestions instead. This will involve editors in the story concept and help the practitioner to tailor it to their interests and style. Such an approach can avoid wasting time, and gives the PR/publicist the best chance of making a placement.

When lending merchandise for the magazine to photograph in their editorial product sections, make sure that the samples arrive on time, are clean and undamaged, and that style and price information is accurate and neatly presented. Obviously, this is true of merchandise lent to newspapers and broadcast media as well.

TELEVISION AND RADIO PLACEMENT

Working with broadcast personnel is a different situation than working with print personnel. Somehow, the pace is quicker, possibly because television and radio ride on split-second timing.

Television and radio depend on their ability to report on trends immediately. When PR/publicists see opportunities to relate stories to an item or event of

130 PUBLIC RELATIONS/PUBLICITY

> **Inquiry and Contact Procedure for Broadcast Placement**
>
> 1. The PR/publicist inquires by *mail* (query letter) or *phone* as to whether the producer of a given show might be interested in a projected story idea.
> 2. If there is an interest, a packet of more detailed information on the person or subject to be aired is mailed.
> 3. If the producer is positively interested, tentative scheduling of the appearance or airing is then confirmed by *mail* or *phone*.
> 4. A tentative script is written and mailed to the station.
> 5. A week prior to the scheduled date, scheduling is confirmed by *phone*.
> 6. If there is to be a guest appearance, the guest is briefed as to show format, what to wear, tentative script, etc., *in person*.
> 7. If there is an airing of prerecorded materials or advance demonstrations, these are forwarded to the station by *mail*.

current significance, they must react quickly to make a broadcast placement. In such situations, the practitioner must prepare materials and deliver them to the station within hours. Also, once time has been allocated, it is essential to deliver, or the station could be left with a programming gap and the PR/publicist with a "bad" reputation!

For national network shows, the PR/publicist generally should call, not write. Broadcast contacts tend to be telephone oriented, but most will request a follow-up letter summarizing the ideas discussed if they have interest. Local shows will respond to a query letter. In general, arrangements for live interviews necessitate more phone discussion than the placement of prerecorded materials or a suggested script for use by the show without a guest appearance.

Stories for broadcast should be kept brief. Television and radio programs do not have the editorial space of newspapers and magazines. A one-minute story on radio is equal to one and one-half pages of triple-spaced, typed copy, and most stories only last a fraction of a minute. In television, time given to copy (audio) is even less because of the additional impact and news value of the visual.

Deadlines are tighter than in print. Materials for an evening TV news program must be taped/filmed by mid-morning. Radio offers greater flexibility because there is no film editing needed.

Broadcast placement will be discussed in greater detail in Chapter 11.

Editors Want News, Not Gifts

A point of view sometimes advanced is that entertaining the press and providing them with "freebies" and gifts ensures the favorable reception of a story or an idea that the PR/publicist is trying to package. This view has been much overplayed. Most reporters and editors judge a story on its individual merits. The more professional the editor or reporter, the less he or she will be influenced by outside factors.

Most newspapers and broadcast media have a stated policy of not wanting gifts, and many have a policy of returning them to the donor. When a gift cannot be easily returned, such as the case with candy, baked goods, flowers, and fruit baskets, the policy is usually to share these items with others in the office and politely to discourage future giving. Magazines also discourage gifts, but market editors usually welcome a discount on merchandise. News and feature syndicates, too, discourage their staffs from accepting gifts from PR/publicists and their clients. However, there are always some people who will look for gifts, no matter what. Gift-giving is a matter of the PR/publicist's personal philosophy. In general, a token gift can be a friendly reminder that you are around. However, gifts that are too lavish can offend the recipients, making them feel that they are taking "payola."

In contrast, all editors really appreciate a "thank you" note or call if they have run a PR/publicity story. This is especially important if the story is a major feature. Sometimes, professional friendships develop between editors and PR/publicists, and then the two may enjoy lunch or a drink together as part of the working relationship, but many prefer to keep business strictly "business" and avoid such socialization.

9
Events, Press Conferences, and Press Parties

PR/publicity events—sometimes called "special events"—press conferences, and press parties, are created to bring attention to a specific product or idea. They can, in themselves, generate news or they can be used to focus extra attention on an ongoing project.

Events

The best events are those that reflect the "personality" of the person or organization seeking to make news and are consistent with the long-term PR/publicity objectives. Because successful events can generate a lot of news and goodwill in a relatively short time, they have become quite popular among PR/publicists. Many companies, too, favor the event as a PR/publicity technique since it does not ordinarily call for a continuing long-term expenditure of funds. Consequently, there are a growing number of individuals and companies that specialize in creating, staging, and publicizing events.

PR/publicity events are usually planned much in advance of their occurrence. This planning can be simple or elaborate. Sometimes, a PR/publicist does not create or plan an event, but finds one that is part of the normal routine and adapts it to attract media attention.

Events can be anything from a "Mother's March for Salt-free Baby Foods" to a rock singer performing on a float in a Thanksgiving Day parade to an executive holding a press conference to explain his company's annual report. There is no limit to the directions in which one can go, restricted only by what is appropriate for the client and likely to make news at the time.

CLASSIFICATION OF EVENTS

One way to look at PR/publicity events is to classify them in terms of promoting merchandise, institutions, personalities, or ideas.

Merchandise Events. Developed specifically to promote and sell more of a product. These events can be used to reach both the consumer and the trade public. Examples include the following:

- Holiday-related promotions, special sales periods, fairs, and fashion shows in retail stores
- Introduction of new car models at automobile manufacturer's showrooms
- Sales meetings to introduce a new product or line to a sales force
- Giveaways or special price weeks at supermarkets
- Trade show exhibits by manufacturers of appliances
- Fashion show for retail store buyers by textile manufacturers.

Institutional Events. Designed to enhance an image over the long term. They do not feature merchandise or services in a direct way. Examples include the following:

- Department-store sponsored Thanksgiving Day Parade
- Marathon sponsored by a beverage company
- Tennis tournament sponsored by a cigarette company
- Jewelry design contest for students sponsored by a large jewelry manufacturer
- Lecture series on home finances held at a department store
- Ground-breaking ceremonies
- Corporate and foundation-sponsored awards and scholarships
- Preparation for annual meeting of stockholders
- Birthdays, anniversaries, and holiday celebrations.

Personality Events. Used to build recognition and enhance the reputation of an individual or group. Examples include the following:

- Store appearances by a fashion designer
- "Free" performance by an entertainer at a charity benefit
- Press conference by a political candidate
- Speech by a corporate executive to a local civic group
- Stunts, such as climbing a skyscraper or swimming around Manhattan Island
- Gimmicks, such as a rock group performing in front of a major office building or at the zoo.

Idea Events. Developed to influence the way people think about a subject. Examples include the following:

- Seminars on safe driving given by the American Automobile Association

- Forums on community problems at town hall sponsored by local governments
- Open houses at plants, hospitals, or schools
- Lectures on health-related problems at medical centers
- Discussion groups on ethical concepts at churches or temples
- Day- or week- or month-long "happenings," such as Peach Day, Stop Smoking Week, National Secretary Day, Grandparents' Day, Black Solidarity Day, and so on.

SPECIAL EVENTS ARE IMPORTANT TO RETAILERS

Special events are especially useful to the large retail store. As large retailers face more competition from specialized boutiques and mail order catalogues, the event has gained importance as a way of attracting attention and maintaining or expanding market share and image.

Consequently, special events planning has become an important store function and can provide the contemporary retailer with the opportunity to establish a unique position in the marketplace. Special events, for example, can be used to dramatize the opening of a new branch store or the move into a new area; provide new services, such as seminars dealing with the problems of modern living—jobs, aging, crime prevention, managing money; establish the store as an entertainment and cultural center by bringing the customs and merchandise of other countries to the attention of its clientele; and, in general, add a different-from-competition character to the whole operation.

In essence, special events provide the store with an opportunity to mean more to its customers and reinforce their buying loyalty. The same customers who might stop shopping at a large retail store after discovering they can find the same merchandise in a catalogue or in a small boutique will continue to shop at the large retailer if intrigued by the excitement of its special events. In fact, not only do such customers maintain their purchasing level, they often increase it by buying the basic merchandise as well as special merchandise related to the particular event. From import fairs to exercise classes, from makeup demonstrations to formal charity galas, special events are transforming stores into community and service centers that outstrip the original concept of a place where only merchandise is sold. And special events make news!

Special events can also be used to provide an answer to a specific merchandising problem. For example, in a merchandise category where the competition is stiff, such as the jeans market, appearances by designers, or a fashion show of models of various ages wearing jeans, or a jean painting contest can help a store create more news and draw more customers than its competitors.

In addition, in a situation where a department in a remote location in the store needs a sales boost, a special event can bring traffic to the area. For example, consider a large store that is having problems drawing traffic through its furniture department to the table linens and decorative accessories department in a number of suburban branch stores all of the same design. Renovation of the store design concept could be considered, but that would probably be too costly. If a series of table decorating seminars for an audience of store customers were held instead, the resulting news stories and goodwill created by the events would highlight the department as a good source for table accessories and decorations, thereby solving the problem.

Today, there is a trend toward special events that are sponsored, and paid for, cooperatively by stores and manufacturers. Such cooperative ventures give the store more money to use in planning the event and the prestige of featuring the manufacturer's brand in a unique way. For the manufacturer, cooperative events provide an opportunity to reach the customer directly at the point of sale. Sometimes, more than one manufacturer will cooperate in such an event, and often a fiber producer or a major magazine will also be involved. These events usually travel from an important department store to important department store, from city to city, and take months of planning and quite a good deal of money to stage. If well planned, programs of this type can generate an impressive amount of news for all those involved and an increase in goodwill and sales, too.

Cosmetic companies were the first to initiate such cooperative special events programs, but today many makers of branded merchandise, in categories as diverse as cookware and tennis equipment, seek to sponsor such events. Cooperatively sponsored events can take place in the store or in another location in the community that the store serves. No matter what the location, the goal of all such events is to generate favorable news for the participants and that, in turn, should build sales and prestige.

An example of a cooperative event which generated excellent press coverage is shown in the photographs of a "painting party in the park" co-sponsored by a major store, a fiber manufacturer, and a magazine. (See Figure 9–1.) The event evolved from the store's need for clever display material to insert in windows featuring a collection of children's back-to-school clothes tied in with a magazine story on back-to-school. The windows were timed to coincide with the magazine's publication date. In working out the event, the store, in early July, contacted a local school and developed the concept of a painting party. The store, together with the fiber manufacturer, would provide the paints, the canvases, and the special lunch. The children would participate by painting their ideas of autumn scenes. The event was held. Press and contacts important to the school and the co-sponsors were invited to attend. The story ran in major newspapers, the trade press, and over local television and radio stations. Weeks later, after the windows had been installed, the children were invited to the store to view their artwork on display in the windows together with the clothes and copies of the magazine. Both group murals and smaller individual works done by the children were used. After the windows were dismantled, the murals were sold through the store's art department and proceeds from the sale were donated to the school. This fact was used to generate additional news stories for the store in the trade press.

9-1. *Lord & Taylor, Du Pont, and* Good Housekeeping *children's painting party. At right, children at work painting pictures of their favorite thing at the event in the park. Below, one of the four Lord & Taylor windows in which the paintings were displayed along with children's clothing. Note the photographs of the party along the bottom of the window.*

MANAGING THE EVENT

PR/publicists who plan and implement events must be resourceful, ingenious, and experts at organization. They must work on the philosophy that no matter how careful the planning, one should be prepared for the unforeseen problems—the custom-made tablecloths getting lost in the mail and not arriving for a restaurant opening, the major dinner speaker cancelling at the last moment. The experienced professional knows that "foul-ups" are inevitable and will proceed to deal with such problems in an expedient manner. For example, he or she could comb local stores for tablecloth replacements, have a back-up speaker on tap, and so on. In short, the plans of an experienced practitioner have plans.

The timing of invitations to the media for an event is very important. If PR/publicists wait and send out invitations a day or so before an event is to take place, they run the risk of reporters not being free to attend. If, on the other hand, invitations go out too far in advance, there is the risk of "being lost in the shuffle." A technique that is used to help solve this problem is to send out two invitations—one quite far in advance, perhaps three weeks ahead, with a "save the date" note attached; the second to go out about four days before the event. If the PR/publicist knows the press representative well, advance notice can also be communicated by telephone. Sometimes, a telegram is also used to indicate "save the date." No matter how the invitation is conveyed, it must call for a reply, an RSVP. If it is not forthcoming, follow-up is necessary. Media people have busy schedules and they expect PR/publicists to take the initiative in trying to tie down possible press coverage. Consequently, they are receptive to attendance inquiries as long as the PR/publicist is not too "pushy."

Many press contacts will request press kit materials before the event so they can plan their stories and concentrate on the flavor of the event itself when they arrive. Sending press materials in advance has an additional advantage should a reporter fail to attend because of another important assignment. The PR/publicist can, at a later date, follow up with this reporter, providing him or her with details as to what actually happened, supplying photos, samples, etc., so that the story could be written anyway.

The time of day for which an event is planned can affect its potential media placement. An event scheduled any time near deadline will mean less press coverage. Generally, the best time to schedule events is mid-morning or at lunch time. This gives reporters, working toward an afternoon deadline for the evening paper or broadcast news, and those working toward a later deadline for a morning paper or television show, ample time to write their stories or edit their filmed or taped segments.

Celebrities participating in an event can sometimes provide the practitioner with problems—particularly if they do not want to be disturbed by the media. In such instances, it is important that the PR/publicist restrict the media's access to them or set up a specific time and location for an interview. A celebrity can be easily alienated if the proper arrangements for his or her comfort and welfare are not made.

FACILITIES FOR THE PRESS

The news people who attend events often require special attention and facilities to conduct their business. While other guests may relax and enjoy the event in a leisurely fashion, some reporters may be "on deadline" or have just a brief period of time to handle the assignment. Consequently, experienced PR/publicity professionals will make sure that they and/or members of the staff are on hand to answer questions quickly and provide information. If the event is of major importance and is called close to deadlines, telephones ought to be provided for reporters to call in their stories.

If the event has a possible photo angle, a photographer should be available to take shots for those members of the press who do not have a staff photographer with them. For recordkeeping, a press sign-in book should be readily visible at the entrance. Press kits should also be placed there.

If a luncheon is involved, the press needs its own table near the speaker's table, one with easy access to an exit should a reporter have to leave early.

The Press Room. A separate press room (also called a *news room*) is necessary for major events where there are many participants and press coverage is expected to be heavy. Such an event might be an industrial trade show, a political convention, or—on the community level—a demonstration, parade, fair, or rally.

A press room can be a ballroom in a hotel, a parked bus in a park, or part of the lobby of a civic center. The size and location is determined by the event. The press room should be staffed by PR/publicity people who know exactly what is going on so they can answer any and all questions.

Any press room, large or small, should contain an ample supply of press kits and handouts about the event, writing supplies, desks, telephones, typing and recording facilities—in short, anything that the press might need. Usually, refreshments and toilet facilities are also provided.

In most cases, it is advisable that the room be reserved for the use of media people only. There are some events at which it may be useful to set aside a time for other attendees in the trade to visit the press room in order to pick up technical information. For the most part, however, an "open door policy" only serves to clutter the press area and prevent its function and service to the journalists.

At trade shows, exhibitor PR/publicity personnel should be welcome in the press room to meet editors and reporters and discuss stories with them, or even just to introduce themselves. It is essential, however, that the press room director guard against any undue badgering of the press by those exhibitor PR/publicists seeking to generate individual news stories.

One of the most common problems of the press room at major events is that competing PR/publicists can risk losing exclusive story ideas because their discussion is overheard by others in the trade. Consequently, there are some practitioners who prefer to work with press contacts before the event and avoid distributing materials and discussing story concepts in press rooms.

ORGANIZATION FOR SPECIAL EVENTS

Organization is the key to creating successful events. Every last detail must be anticipated from seating to equipment to pencils for note-taking. A checklist is essential:

1. Plan to the smallest detail. In this way, mistakes will be only incidents, not catastrophes.
2. Use a checklist from the start of your planning. Figure the time needed to accomplish work. Make up a day-by-day schedule. Keep folders of plans, details, letters.
3. If the event calls for it, set up an hour-by-hour program. Allow extra time for each segment or part, in case things do not start precisely.
4. Make sure that you have made adequate arrangements for restrooms, refreshments, seating, audiovisual equipment, first aid, etc.
5. Leave extra time. Most things take longer than anticipated. Leave some leeway.
6. In case of an outdoor event, be prepared to move indoors, if bad weather occurs.
7. Include recess periods in long programs.
8. On the day of the event, have available an assistant or group of people who can handle minor tasks. You may be busy making changes or handling emergencies.
9. Check on the need for insurance, depending on the type of event.
10. Do not work participating guests too hard.
11. If the event warrants it, make up copies of the guest list, in alphabetical order. Carry one or more.

DEVELOPING A THEME

Brainstorming and other creative idea development techniques are used to develop events. (See Chapter 2.) The best events are developed with specific PR/publicity and business goals in mind. There is no set formula that can be used in determining whether the theme of an event will work.

The following guidelines for the opening of a fashion shoe boutique were adapted from those actually developed for a company selling franchises for such boutiques and were created to help new store owners set up an exciting and

The Window

Volume 3, Number 1

The New York Hospital—Cornell Medical Center

Cabaret!—A Night to Remember for NYH-CMC and Friends

Benefit Is a Smashing Success

Over 1,000 generous supporters attended *Cabaret!*, the benefit to celebrate the 50th anniversary of The New York Hospital-Cornell Medical Center. These party-goers gathered on Monday, December 13, in the Waldorf Astoria's grand ballroom to dine on roast goose and see actress Racquel Welch.

The event, which had a holiday theme and was co-chaired by Mrs. Vincent Astor of Cornell University Medical College's board of overseers and Walter Wriston of The New York Hospital's board of governors, brought in one million dollars, giving a visible boost to the medical center's Capital Campaign, with its three-year goal of $125 million.

The dinner was traditional with pumpkin soup, roast goose, and plum pudding. Decorations included two large Christmas trees trimmed with glass icicles made from laboratory pipette tubing.

Entertainment was anything but traditional, with jugglers and trampoline artists from the *Big Apple Circus*, songs by Karen Akers of the hit Broadway show *Nine*, Clamma Dale, and Douglas Fairbanks Jr., who also served as master of ceremonies. Especially appropriate for the audience of doctors and medical center benefactors was Kitty Carlisle Hart's rendition of Cole Porter's song "The Physician." Mrs. Hart is especially closely connected with the medical center because her daughter, Dr. Katherine Hart, is a member of the house staff in the division of dermatology. Other performers with a special connection to New York Cornell were the Cornell University glee club, which sang to open the show and then quickly took a bus back to Ithaca to continue studying for exams, and the medical college chorus, which sang during the cocktail reception wearing green surgical scrub suits and again at the close of the program wearing white jackets.

In addition to funds, the benefit has generated many new friends for New York-Cornell among those individuals and corporations who attended or made contributions.

The evening ended festively with dancing on stage, and everyone left looking forward to next year, when Mrs. Astor and Mr. Wriston have agreed to co-chair another exciting event.

(See additional photographs on page 4.)

Mrs. Vincent Astor sings Christmas carols with the chorus of Cornell University Medical College.

Henry and Nancy Kissinger, Cabaret! committee members and guests.

Racquel Welch and Walter Wriston enjoy the holiday meal.

The Canestrellis, from the Big Apple Circus, amaze the guests with their acrobatics.

9-2. *The front page of "The Window," a publication sent to supporters of the New York Hospital-Cornell Medical Center, describes and shows photographs of a gala holiday season social event which raised over $1 million. The event generated extensive press coverage because of the celebrities who attended and the unique special attractions, such as circus tumblers and a chorus of medical staff who sang Christmas carols in surgical green garb.*

meaningful event. They provide a good outline of the type of thinking and organization that goes into developing an effective PR/publicity event.

CASE STUDY: OPENING ABC SHOPS

Each new ABC Shop should be attended by as much fanfare and publicity as can be generated. The name ABC is identified with status, style, fashion, and good taste. Fashion editors and radio and television personalities will have a natural interest in the opening of the shop. But these people's interest will not be translated into free publicity without some effort on your part.

There is a professional way to coordinate opening activities and to prepare materials for the press. You should use a local public relations expert to handle the opening. We can supply you with the name of a person in your area who is associated with a national network of PR pros who have worked with us successfully, opening ABC shops across the country.

In any event, make plans to open with a "bang." You will have only one chance to capitalize on the built-in excitement of a new store opening, so take advantage of it. If you can get a lot of key people interested in and excited about your shop at the very beginning, you will have the advantage of a momentum that you can continue to build upon.

The procedure for opening an ABC Shop should include the following:

1. *Make local contacts.* You and/or your publicity representative should meet with newspaper fashion and society editors; stars and producers of local radio and television shows; editors of local magazines, playbills, and house organs of large companies; and program chairpersons of civic, charity, and political organizations. Interest these contacts in your opening and take your cues from their suggestions.
2. *Prepare an impressive press kit.* Include a copy of the ABC Story booklet, plus releases, photographs of the interior and exterior of the shop, and photographs of current fashions. Deliver the kit in person. Be sure to highlight any unique aspects of your store's design, any interesting personalities working in the store, etc. The help of your professional PR expert will be valuable in selecting the most interesting approach to take.
3. *Plan a sensational store opening.* Your aim is to throw "The Event of the Season." Have a preopening affair for those people who could serve as the vital nucleus of an ever-expanding clientele. Invite socially prominent young people and some exciting "youngish" older people, who occupy the local spotlight or who occupy positions of prominence in the community and in clubs, organizations, charities, cultural groups, college campuses, etc. Invite exciting personalities who, by their presence, liven up the affair and make it the talk of the town. Invite these people, in person if possible, or by sending unique and interest-provoking invitations. Also invite the press, and make sure they have a guest list.

The opening party should be fun, sophisticated, and exciting. Whether you serve cocktails at five, have a wine-tasting at noon, or serve Irish coffee at dawn, do it with style and taste.

Then, all through the opening week, make sure there is a constant flow of publicity in the local media, and that you support the opening with well-planned advertisements. Mail announcements of the shop opening to as many potential customers as possible. Most important, make sure that the shop is ready for the opening and that all of your people are well trained. That first impression is going to be vitally important, so it had better be good.

4. *Determine a procedure and time schedule:*
   - Teaser mailing (four weeks prior to opening).
   - Post signs in public places in the community (four weeks prior to opening).
   - Mail invitations to opening party and first week's festivities (seven to ten days prior to opening).
   - Arrange for preopening publicity in local papers or on television.
   - Make follow-up calls to ensure local and press attendance at party (five days prior to party). Keep calling until you have more than your desired number of acceptances on the phone.
   - Provide bus or limousine transportation for important guests. (If bus transportation, have champagne party en route.)
   - Give opening party.
   - Continue festivities during opening week.
5. *The party is never over.* A good publicity job does not end when the party is over. That is just the beginning. You must continue to call attention to the shop throughout the year.

Supply fashion editors with ABC fashion photographs and news of interesting items on a seasonal basis.

Plan special events, such as charity art sales, fashion shows at benefit luncheons, and poetry readings in the store which will keep the public interested in seeing what is happening at ABC.

THE EVENT INSURANCE POLICY

There is no way the PR/publicist can prevent the planned event from being preempted by something more significant. The only insurance that the company's money and the PR/publicist's efforts will be well spent is to have the event serve a function in addition to that of generating news in the media.

It is important to make sure that an event has two audiences and two purposes. One audience is the media and the purpose is to get them to write or broadcast news about the client. The other audience could be employees, business contacts, or the general public, who could benefit from the event regardless of whether the press comes and covers it.

For example, consider a ground-breaking ceremony for a new cancer care and research building at a major medical center which is intended to attract news coverage and, thereby, encourage public support and financial contributions. If the people running the event depend solely on the media to form the audience and the majority of the reporters invited were suddenly reassigned to cover a more dramatic or spontaneous news occurrence—an explosion and fire at the mayor's office, for example—the groundbreaking would be left without an audience. If, however, an audience of medical center supporters and representatives of community and medical organizations were included, the event would still be a success, regardless of the number of media representatives attending. In addition, photos and a release could be sent to the media, enabling them to report on the event they could not attend. The audience of nonmedia people, thereby, would "ensure" the success of the event.

Press Conferences and Press Parties

A press conference (also referred to as a *news conference*) is called when the material to be presented to media is related to a timely news event of such significance that it is important that representatives of the company or organization involved are available for questioning by the press.

In contrast, a press party is an event where the press is entertained while being introduced to news about an organization's products, personnel, and/or plans. Press parties usually have a theme related to the information given. They often involve a meal or cocktails, and their atmosphere is more social and less businesslike than that at press conferences.

PRESS CONFERENCES

In many instances, it is more effective to hold a press conference than to circulate news to media in written form. It is, however, a great deal more expensive, and conferences should only be staged for stories that merit the expense.

At the conference, the press should be provided with a tightly written account of the proceedings which they can use to create their own stories. This means that the PR/publicist must know what has been "said" at the conference before it takes place. Questions should be anticipated; one or two should even be "planted." A detailed rehearsal should be held.

The ideal press conference, then, is much like a skillfully directed drama and should leave its audience entertained as well as instructed.

EVENTS, PRESS CONFERENCES, AND PRESS PARTIES

In planning a press conference, proper procedure requires notification of editorial desks at least a week in advance of a selected date. Notification is usually accompanied by a fact sheet that clearly sets forth the nature of the news to be handled, principals who will be present, and the date, time, and place. If people to photograph are going to be present, the fact sheet sent to media should include the information for the benefit of those responsible for photos. Also, an advance release should be delivered by messenger to each invited medium containing the essentials of what is to be covered at the conference.

If possible, the conference should be held in the offices of the organization calling the conference. Sometimes, if a large attendance is expected, meeting rooms in hotels are used. In either case, the conference room should be the right size and private. If a large turnout is expected, the room should be arranged in theater style with chairs facing a long table where key individuals who are to speak will sit. If a smaller group is expected, the attending press can sit around a long table, joining the speakers as if at a board meeting. Only executives or qualified staff, designated in advance, should speak.

Important press conferences usually call for the presence of representatives from the broadcast media. In such instances, sufficient electrical connections and facilities for lights and cameras should be provided. Some practitioners have found that the glare of lights and cameras are confusing and discordant notes, particularly for print reporters, and have opted to hold two press conferences—one for print media people and one for radio and television reporters.

The conference should be well rehearsed and contain no surprises for those staging it. The highest ranking speaker (i.e., if a company, the chairman of the board; if a less formal grouping, the individual in whose name the meeting has been called) should preside and refer questions to others on the staff when appropriate. The personnel present must be prepared to answer a barrage of questions, some which might even be embarrassing. If there is any doubt about the group's ability to handle such questions, the conference should not be held.

The best press conferences are amicable as well as businesslike occasions. It is often advantageous for the PR/publicist to introduce the client to key press correspondents before the formal presentation begins. In order to do this, the PR/publicist must know the names of the journalists attending and the media they represent. It is advisable, therefore, to ask all attendees to sign in at the door upon arrival to avoid any confusion concerning which journalists are in attendance. When signing in, attendees should be presented with press kit folders or envelopes containing copies of handouts covering the issues to be discussed and other relevant documents. Photographs should be displayed and numbered so that press representatives may easily select prints they desire.

The hallmark of the press conference should be a free disclosure of information between the principals and the press. If off-the-record information is to be presented, a designated spokesperson should establish its parameters at the very beginning of the conference.

PUBLIC RELATIONS/PUBLICITY

    While the conference should be professional and well organized, it should not be overstaged. Questions and answers should have a feeling of spontaneity. It is the PR/publicist's responsibility to rehearse the principals so that their answers to questions will project this feeling. He or she, however, should stay in the background. The media come to a conference to see and hear the story directly from the principals.

    In summary, then, a press conference is a special meeting called to make announcements of great importance. Such conferences should be called sparingly because the press will only respond to them if their subject is deemed to be of real significance. Press conferences provide a forum at which members of the press can get important information all at the same time.

    Before deciding to hold a conference, one should ask:

- Is the announcement of true significance?
- Is the information complicated or sensitive enough to deem it necessary for reporters to discuss it directly with the principals?
- Are the news stories expected to result from the conference worth the time and expense of staging the conference?

9-3. *Master photographer Alfred Eisenstaedt at his exhibition opening at the International Center of Photography (ICP) being interviewed by a television news reporter. Note Eisenstaedt's photographs displayed on the walls of the gallery and the crowds surrounding him at this important reception for the press and ICP members. (Photo courtesy of ICP.)*

- Are there qualified personnel available who can effectively handle a discussion/confrontation with the press?

PRESS PARTIES

Press parties are usually pleasant social affairs with no pretense of projecting an "earth-shaking" news story. Still, there must be a sound reason for holding them. Typically, they are used to present a new product or line, celebrate the opening of a new store or office, add a corporate division, or introduce new management. Although attending press usually enjoy the social aspects of a press party, they will become impatient if the point of the meeting is delayed too long. The trick is to make these occasions brief, lively, and meaningful from a PR/publicity view.

Like press conferences, press parties are held so that all the relevant press contacts can attend at the same time, and are timed to coincide with the public announcement of the news. Press parties are best scheduled for the breakfast, lunch, or cocktail hours and kept short so as not to interfere with the working day.

There are certain industries in which press parties and receptions are an important part of the on-going PR/publicity strategy. In the fashion industry, particularly, seasonal openings of new lines are launched with press receptions. This is because this industry introduces collections at least four and, in some cases, eight times a year, and a press reception is the most practical and expedient way to show the new styles. In addition, the fashion industry has a glamour image and the party-and-show format is an appropriate way for it to project its style news. Other industries use such showings as well, but the fashion industry depends on this PR/publicity technique the most.

10
Corporate PR/Publicity Functions

Large corporations use the services of PR/publicists in diverse ways. Many use them to publicize their products and policies on a regular basis. Those that are publicly owned and have stockholders rely on these practitioners to prepare annual reports and other materials for financial investment promotion. These organizations as well as those that are privately owned use PR/publicists to help with speech writing and to prepare executives for public appearances and media tours. In addition, PR/publicists are also called upon to write position papers, develop institutional advertising campaigns, and organize lobbying efforts.

In many companies, the PR/publicity function is represented in the senior management group. Today, big business's success, in large measure, depends on the image and goodwill it can generate among its various publics. PR/publicists have the skills and training to help top management do that job effectively.

Specifically, PR/publicity can be used to help a company name become better known, to enlarge the market share of products and services, to reinforce marketing, to express the company's position on controversial issues, to make philanthropic activities known, to report financial status, to help employee relations, and more. The actual function in an individual corporation is determined by the nature of the business and the style of management.

Looked at in another way, the PR/publicist functions to help guide and maintain a positive, corporate identity. By corporate identity is meant the total perception of the corporation by its competition and its many publics, including customers, employees, and the communities in which it maintains offices and/or factories. Corporate identity is affected by many aspects of the company's business life and activities. Some of the things that can affect corporate identity include the following:

- Advertising
- Annual reports
- Employee benefits
- Office environment and location
- Packaging and stationery
- Perceived management competency
- Newsletters to employees
- Press releases
- Product quality and customer service policies
- Size
- Social and community interests.

A fact of human psychology is that many times one impression engenders another—a situation that presents opportunities for the PR/publicity function. If a company has established a good identity in one or more areas of its business, it tends to be equally perceived in other areas. For example, if the company has made significant philanthropic contributions to a national charity and makes a product that is known to be healthful—a breakfast food containing nothing artificial, without any added sugar or salt—the company would probably be perceived to be kind to its employees, concerned about the community in which it has manufacturing facilities, and to have a caring management. These facts may or may not be true, but the positive spill-over from the points publicized would suggest that they were. Of course, the converse is also true. The company that is perceived poorly in one area, will have the burden of that poor reputation spilling over into other aspects of its business.

Company Culture, Logos, and Trademarks

Company cultures reflect the values, beliefs, reputations, and management styles that differentiate one company from another. They are the distinct identity and tone that are most often set by the chief executive officer's business style. Some companies are known for their family feeling, others for their high quality personnel standards, others for a sophisticated systems approach to management. Because a company's culture projects its total image, it is important that the PR/publicist understand the culture and establish that it reflects the best aspects of the company. To do this, PR/publicists survey various publics related to the company: employees, customers, competitors, and so on. In addition, they refer to printed materials that define company policies, such as annual reports and house organs as well as any articles printed in the media.

KLM Royal Dutch Airlines — *The crown motif for KLM Royal Dutch Airlines suggests the traveler will get "royal" service.*	**Mayflower means moving** — *Mayflower Mover's ship suggests that long-distance moving is a company tradition and that there will be "smooth sailing" for one's belongings.*
The Wool Bureau's stylized symbol is based on a skein of wool, and implies quality and durability that synthetics cannot offer.	**the cellar (macy's)** — *The arrow motif for Macy's Cellar suggests that the down-under area is chic and exciting—not a bargain basement, but a place for new ideas.*
MAXWELL HOUSE COFFEE — *Good to the last drop* — *Maxwell House's coffee cup says it all: "Good to the last drop."*	**PARKER** — *The narrow lines of Parker Pen's logo are graphically appealing, and the arrow suggests precision writing instruments.*

10-1. *A logo or trademark is a means of instant identity.*

If the current company culture is consistent with management goals, PR/publicists will seek to project it in their efforts. If it is not consistent, they will then work to define a more appropriate culture and use PR/publicity as a means of communicating it. Often management consulting firms play a role in this process as well, but it is eventually the PR/publicist's responsibility to relay the new culture to the public.

Consider the contrasting culture that two competitive companies in the same industry might have. In one, the culture might be a nurturing one with the reputation that it is a nice place to work and that the company takes care of its people. In the other, the culture might reflect a tough competitiveness epitomized by a "workaholic" president who often puts employees on the spot and calls meetings in the middle of long holiday weekends. The attitudes of employees, customers, and the general public will be vastly different because of the contrasting culture. These differences will affect a PR/publicist's function.

Other ways a company's culture or style is represented are through logos and trademarks. Logos are the distinctive signature or way of writing the company name. Trademarks are the symbols the company uses on its products and publications, and they are registered with the government to ensure exclusivity. In the past, these evolved casually from original trade symbols or company letterheads. Today, companies hire professional designers to develop logos and trademarks which are reflective of current philosophy and long-term management goals. For example, consider the contrast between the old-fashioned script Coca-Cola signature and the sleeker, contemporary Coke lettering. PR/publicists, although usually not responsible for the design of such symbols, incorporate them in most of their printed materials. In addition, they may have an input in establishing the design concept.

Institutional Advertising for PR/Publicity Purposes

One of the things that companies do in situations where they are fearful that a controversial stand in one area will affect other aspects of their reputation is to run institutional advertising to defend or project a positive identity and image. Institutional advertising is also used for PR/publicity purposes where an organization wishes to express a specific point of view. In the planning and execution of such campaigns, the practitioner sometimes gets involved.

Institutional advertising is usually aimed at a specific public. For example, in a labor/management dispute, management might buy media space to present the business or community public with the company's side of the story. Such ads are most effective if they have a single objective. They are difficult to write. The heading and format must be provocative and induce thorough reading of the text. Institutional PR/publicity ads often appear on editorial pages of newspapers. Their message can also be conveyed in the form of an "editorial reply" on radio or television.

PR/publicity institutional advertising represents the voice of management. Such ads stress one or more of the following: industry leadership, business competency and performance, social and community responsibility, warmth and style of organization, size and scope, company service, product quality and value, progressive management, and current technology.

Annual Reports

One of the most important areas in which PR/publicists work with publicly owned companies is in the conception, production, and distribution of annual reports.

THE PFIZER HEALTHCARE SERIES

Do you know anyone who can pump 2,000 gallons of blood through 70,000 miles of blood vessels every day?

We do. It's you.

Every day, of every year, of your whole life, your heart is pumping 2,000 gallons of blood a day through 70,000 miles of blood vessels. And your heart usually does it without fuss or complaint.

A time comes when the job gets tough, as after age 35 or when burdens (like overweight) are added or when vessels that feed the heart muscle lose their ability to bring enough blood to meet oxygen and nutrition needs and remove wastes. Your heart's signal is a condition called angina pectoris.

The symptoms of angina can be any one or more of these:
- A sense of tightness or heaviness in your chest
- A pain in your shoulder or neck
- A sense of fullness, a feeling of "indigestion"

These symptoms are different for different people and at different times in any one person. The important thing is to pay attention, your body is telling you something is wrong. Your heart is giving you a signal to act promptly. See your doctor because angina must and can be treated.

The diagnosis of angina pectoris can be made only by your doctor.

The treatment of angina depends upon a doctor's diagnosis and on the type of angina pectoris you may have. Is it the kind that's caused by spasm? Or thickening of coronary vessels that feed the heart? Or by both?

What's to be done?
Your doctor can help you reduce your cardiac workload by reducing weight, cholesterol, tension and stress. And he has a full range of medications that can relieve coronary spasm, improve the flow of blood to the heart and normalize heart rhythms. You can also help yourself with proper rest and relaxation, time for pleasure and recuperation and a program of moderate exercise.

If your condition is accompanied by elevated blood pressure, your doctor has other medicines that can bring it within normal range. In certain instances, surgery may be called for. Obviously you can't be your own doctor. You need a support system. We call it...

Partners in Healthcare

You are the most important partner.
Only you can spot the warning signs and report them to your physician. And it's you who must decide to accept the guidance and counseling of your physician, nurse and pharmacist. When medicines are prescribed, only you can take them as directed.

Your doctor interprets the warning signs, orders your tests, and makes the diagnosis.
Your physician also prescribes the best medication for you among those available—considering each drug's characteristics—and monitors your progress.

All those who discover, develop and distribute medicines complete the partnership.
Pfizer's ongoing research brings you essential medicines for a wide range of diseases. Through our development of these and many other medications, we are fulfilling our responsibility as one of your partners in healthcare.

Pfizer PHARMACEUTICALS • A PARTNER IN HEALTHCARE

10-2. *This is one of a series of health care columns appearing in newspapers, placed and paid for by Pfizer, a major pharmaceutical manufacturer. Such materials, acting as institutional ads, have enhanced the image of Pfizer as a concerned leader in the industry, offering information of public service to the community at large.*

Top management take their annual reports very seriously and are often obsessed with the idea they can be nothing short of "perfect." It is easy to understand why. The annual report is the final yearly representation of the current management of the company. It not only represents the company as a whole, but is a testimonial to the CEO (chief executive officer) and his or her management style as well. The stakes are high in the financial world. The impression of the annual report can win or lose members of the financial community, the loyalty of shareholders, and the approval of the SEC (Security and Exchange Commission). Consider the functions of the annual report: it is a stockholder information source, policy statement, defense against take-over, sales promotion tool, and an employee information source.

Because the report performs so many functions, its effective handling requires many talents. The person responsible for producing the report should have writing and editing skills and be knowledgeable in graphics, photography, printing, finance, and management as well as PR/publicity. The basic things to consider in writing the report are telling the truth even if it is unfavorable, keeping the report as short as possible yet complete, writing in easy-to-understand language and, in general, making the result interesting and informative. Those reports that are most successful reflect these considerations. Good annual reports are hard to produce, require excellent professional skills, and take more time to produce than is usually allotted them.

In many companies, the responsibility for developing and producing the annual report is the responsibility of the PR/publicity department. In other instances, it may be handled by an independent firm specializing in annual report publishing, an advertising agency, or an internal advertising department. No matter who has the final responsibility for seeing it through, the annual report is always a collaborative effort, drawing upon the skills and talents of a company: accounting for financial facts and figures; senior management for philosophy and future direction statements, PR/publicity and advertising for image and graphic concept.

In essence, the annual report is a key reflection of the public image of a company. That is why an understanding of its function is vital to the PR/publicist.

PLANNING AND PRODUCING ANNUAL REPORTS

The first step in preparing any annual report is to develop a concept and theme. Here, the PR/publicist usually consults with key company personnel, and from the discussion emerges a general idea of what is to be said and how. This phase in the planning process can take anywhere from one to four months. At the end of this phase, approval should be secured from management.

The second step usually involves outlining the report completely, then writing the text with the exception of the final financial accounting which is done right before press time so that the latest figures can be included. How the figures are to be shown—their graphic design—is determined during this phase, however. This is usually a one- to two-month job.

The next step involves design, layout, art, and photo assignments. These activities should be planned against the outline. They take the skills of experienced professionals. This step takes about three months. Printing time will vary depending on the size of the report and the final number required, but at least five weeks should be allocated for printing and binding.

Assembly and distribution will require as little as two weeks if streamlined mailing services or computerized machinery are used, and as much as one month if more manual labor is involved.

Obviously, there is some overlap in these phases, but it can easily be seen that each part of the process requires time.

ELEMENTS OF AN ANNUAL REPORT

Not all annual reports are the same, but most contain the following elements:

Cover. The cover should interest the prospective reader. A good cover is a determining factor in whether a report is read. Elements of cover design include color, graphics, an effective photo or illustration, and paper stock.

The concept for a cover motif which best reflects the image of the company is discussed with a graphic designer who then submits a series of ideas in the form of rough layouts. These are then reviewed by management and a final choice made. Finished photography and artwork are then prepared.

Highlights. This section presents a quick rundown of the past year's progress. It is used mainly in longer reports to give the reader, up front, the vital financial picture.

A "Highlights" section is presented somewhat like a fact sheet and will summarize, preferably on one page, the following information: sales, earnings, taxes, employment, shareholders, plants and facilities, new products or divisions.

The Chief Executive Officer's Letter. This is the most carefully read part of any annual report. It should be short; no more than two pages. It should be warm, friendly, conversational in tone. It should explain current conditions, describe the future and arouse interest in the company. In general, the CEO's letter should promote readership of the rest of the report.

In most instances, CEO's do much of the work in this letter, although they will often dictate concepts for a first draft to be worked on by PR/publicity writers and will seek help in final wording. How much others are involved in this letter depends on the personal style of the chief executive officer.

Management Profiles. This section calls for a rundown of the organization's management. Pictures of all key officers should accompany descriptions of their duties and areas of responsibility. It is important to stress top management's

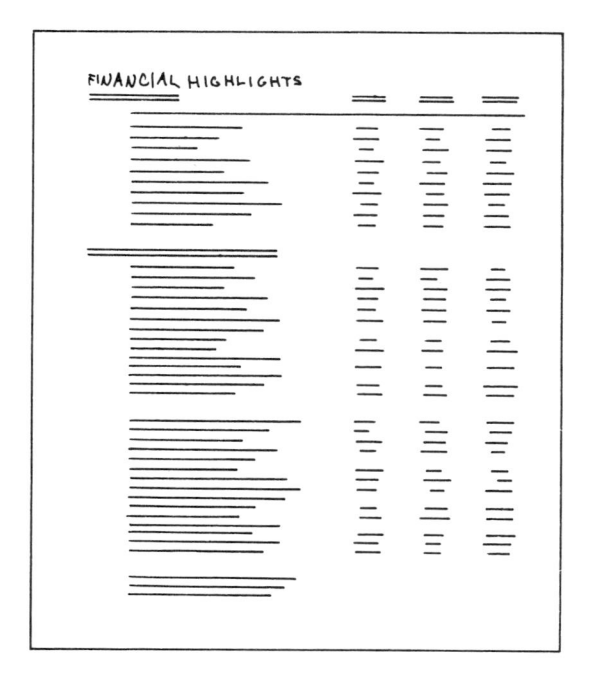

10-3. *The financial highlights page of an annual report presents a quick summary of the year's operations in outline form. Corresponding figures for one or more previous years are usually presented as well. Such a summary is especially useful when the annual report is relatively long and complicated.*

10-4. *The chief executive officer's letter is a personal presentation of the material in the annual report. It should be short, crisp, to the point, and friendly. It should reflect management philosophy.*

professionalism and qualifications and to highlight any newly appointed members of the management team. The photographs used should be varied in format, i.e., different poses. It is a mistake to have all such photos look alike and to have everyone in the "same blue suit." The variety of style and talent in a management team should be reflected in this section.

Main Text. The text of an annual report is the explanation of the company operations within the past fiscal year. Subjects covered in the text vary with the nature of the company's business. Some of the topics covered in the text of a report might include: sales, expansion potential, product development, customer relations, distribution facilities, unfilled orders, dealer relations, product changes, advertising and sales promotion campaigns. Writing this section requires particular skill because complicated processes must be made easy to understand, company mistakes defended, and problem areas honestly discussed—all, if possible, in an "upbeat tone" and all without losing the reader.

Revenue and Income Figures and Diagrams. Figures should be listed in a clear, easy-to-understand format and should be accompanied by charts or graphs for an at-a-glance view of the financial status of the company.

The Balance Sheet. The balance sheet is a standardized form of corporate assets and liabilities as determined by accounting practices. Also, it must conform to certain legal requirements. Because the average stockholder finds the balance sheet hard reading, explanatory notes referring to it are usually added to the financial statement section.

PRODUCTION GUIDELINES

In the production of an annual report, the PR/publicist should consider the following:

1. *Start early* and avoid compromising quality because of time pressure. It is best to start planning about a year in advance and to consider the events and policy changes projected for the year ahead in the initial planning.
2. *Develop a unique theme* or concept for each report. Seek the early participation and approval of senior management in concept development. This will ensure that the report reflects current management priorities and interests.
3. *Identify the key individuals* who will guide and approve the report. Establish a timetable for their review of each phase in its development. This will keep the report on schedule and help avoid the "held up in committee" disputes and delays.
4. *Set up sample pages for approval* of typeface, layout, and amount of text versus white space. Words alone cannot adequately describe a graphic concept, so do not depend on them. *Show* management what you are planning to do.

5. *Select photographs and illustrations* for their informational value and visual appeal. Annual reports are not company scrapbooks. Be discriminating and select only visuals that serve a purpose. Do not slip in a poor photo; each visual counts and affects the total impact of the report. It is essential to use experienced professionals to take photographs and do illustrations, and to have them work against a checklist of planned visuals you have discussed with them.
6. *Strive for a readable writing style.* According to research, the average shareholder devotes approximately ten minutes to reading an annual report with the chief executive officer's letter the most carefully read section. Writing should be clear, concise, and straightforward. For variety, some PR/publicists will engage professional writers who are not report specialists to write certain sections. For example, consider the verve a novelist might bring to a company history or the insight a veteran newspaper reporter could add to a management profile. If such special writers are used, it is essential that their work be carefully edited to fit into the total report theme and style.
7. *Design the mailing envelope.* Do not give it short shrift. It is the first thing a shareholder sees. Try to give it the same visual motif and/or color(s) as the report cover.
8. *Make the report impressively neat and well organized.* Even a low budget report should reflect professionalism and good taste. Beware of producing a report that is too lavish. Such reports can backfire and irritate stockholders who may question the budget allocation for a lavish printing job, especially in a year when there has been a share price decrease or low dividends.
9. *Make sure that all the key personnel preview the report* before it is distributed to the public. Management should be familiar with their report, so they can be prepared to answer any questions that it will prompt from the industry as well as the financial community.

EVALUATING ANNUAL REPORTS

It is hard to get an objective, honest evaluation of an annual report from those who have participated in its development and production. There is a tendency to get too close to such a project, and, if not directly involved, others in the organization often are diffident about criticizing a colleague's work. In recent years, corporations have subjected their reports to public opinion polls and postcard questionnaires soliciting reader reaction.

These techniques are useful, but recently some companies have developed rating systems that help objectify the evaluation of the report. These systems are based on a series of criteria for evaluation, including cover design, quality of photos and illustrations, text copy, figure presentation in charts and maps, printing quality, and so on. For each designated area a rating sheet based on a scale of one through five, or excellent to poor, is used with space provided for comments to explain the rating given. The rating system approach has been found to work best if relatively sophisticated investors—people who are used to reading annual reports—are surveyed.

Quarterly Reports

Most quarterly reports appear in a newsletter format. At one time, these reports were simply financial updates for government and financial industry use. Today, quarterly reports are used as an investors' update as well. Consequently, they also include text explaining progress in the quarter under review or projected moves and developments for the next quarter. Some even include questionnaires, the results of which can be helpful in giving management some insight into how the average investor perceives the company.

Some of the advantages of producing quarterly reports include the following:

1. They are timely; the information in them gets to shareholders and other audiences soon after events have taken place.
2. They are not restricted in format as is the annual report, allowing for more flexibility in presentation.
3. Unlike annual reports, whose issuance calls for a certain amount of fanfare, they are low key and provide a good way to report sensitive information to which a great deal of attention is not desirable.

Annual Meetings

A fact of corporate life is the annual meeting of the organization's stockholders, usually held at the corporate headquarters. These meetings provide an opportunity for management to report on the financial status of the corporation and indicate future plans. They also provide an opportunity for company executives to hear shareholders' opinions regarding company activities. This can sometimes present management with questions that are very difficult or embarrassing to answer without adequate preparation. Sometimes, PR/publicity practitioners participate in rehearsing company executives in queries that might come from the floor. Practitioners are also usually involved in making such arrangements as providing for the press, handing out appropriate informational material, arranging for refreshments, and, in general, making sure that things take place on schedule.

In many ways, an annual meeting is like a special event, requiring similar planning as discussed in Chapter 9.

Speech Writing

The degree to which individuals work on their own speeches varies. In many instances, PR/publicists will assume a major role in speech writing.

It is important to keep the speaker's personality and position in mind. The writer must ask, "Can this speaker deliver the speech that I have written?" The writer should strive to reflect the speaker's convictions, scope of knowledge, and language style. If the speaker's qualifications to speak on a designated topic are not obvious, it is a good idea to work an explanation into the opening of the speech. This can be an engaging introduction as well as a means of establishing credibility.

An interview with the speaker is the best way to start constructing the speech. Next, the rough draft is made and submitted for the speaker's comments and editing. It is important that the writer make a point of telling the speaker that the speech is to reflect the speaker's style and that criticism is welcomed and encouraged.

If humor is to be included in a speech, it is important to consider: Is it in good taste? Does it serve a purpose in the speech? As an opener, to modify a point? Humor for humor's sake is not effective; nor is name dropping and irrelevant quotes from famous people. Every part of the speech should contribute to the effectiveness of the whole message.

It is important to find out how the speaker plans to deliver the speech. There may be a difference in the way it will be written if it is known whether it will be read word for word from typed sheets or spoken with greater spontaneity from note cards.

Endings should be strong and provocative, if possible. Perhaps the ending should be a question the audience is left to consider, a prediction for the future, a phrase from a poem or song—something unexpected and unique. The idea is to leave the audience with something to think about.

In general, sentences should be short and the writing style reflective of the speaker's delivery style. Adjectives should be used carefully and selectively. In addition, examples should be as visual as possible in order to bring more scope to the ideas presented.

The most difficult speeches to write are those for executives who tend to speak too much as well as for those who tend to be laconic. In either case, the speech writer must strive for a result that is in keeping with the speaker's personality. It is probably easiest to limit the long speaker through honest discussion and rehearsal than to encourage the naturally brief speaker to "pour it on." The latter can best be served by creating a brief formal statement and then providing the opportunity for questions from the floor. This, too, will require rehearsal plus a certain amount of role playing on the part of all involved.

There is an old adage that when making a speech you should: "First, tell 'em

> **Checklist for the Speech Writer**
>
> 1. Write for the client. Reflect his or her point of view, not yours. Remember you are a technician.
> 2. Press for personal discussion with the person for whom you are writing the speech.
> 3. Submit outlines to save time and clarify ideas and sequences.
> 4. Speak up if research does not support the points your client wants to make.
> 5. Keep the speech within acceptable limits. Write for the delivery style of the speaker. One person can deliver a five-page speech in a much shorter time than another because of differences in rates of speech.
>
> **Guidelines to Give the Speaker**
>
> 1. Know what you want to say. The decision about the theme of the speech is yours, not the writer's.
> 2. Meet with the writer in person. This gives the writer the ability to really write for you.
> 3. Be prepared to edit and possibly rewrite some parts of the speech yourself. The writer will need your personal thoughts and direction to produce a good speech for you.
> 4. Encourage a free exchange of ideas with the writer. Solicit the writer's ideas about the speech. Do not allow your position to create a barrier and cause the writer to be diffident about telling you what he or she honestly thinks.
> 5. Allow a good deal of time between the assignment and the speech—time for revisions, time for rehearsing.
> 6. Report back to the writer after the speech. Let the writer know how it was received. It will help for future projects to report honestly about the results.

what you're going to tell 'em, tell 'em, then tell 'em what you've told 'em." Most effective speeches adhere to this advice.

The following is a general outline for a speech:

- Opening
- Introduction of the subject(s) to be discussed
- Main points with examples
- Exceptions to the points being made
- Summary or conclusion
- Thought-provoking closing (if appropriate).

11
Broadcast Techniques and Speaker Aids

It is essential for the PR/publicist to know how to present concepts and personalities in a way that is appealing to broadcast media. This is because of the multitude of radio and television talk shows that air PR/publicity stories and guest appearances and the many opportunities for placement available on cable television stations.

PR/publicists must be familiar with the routines of radio and television production and know how to develop scripts and visual materials appropriate for broadcast use. They should also know how to prepare an individual (their employer or client) for a broadcast interview. Equally important is a knowledge of the qualities of a successful film, tape, or slide presentation. In addition, PR/publicists should know how to develop effective audiovisual aids for a speaker, whether for broadcast or general presentation.

Broadcast Techniques

WRITING FOR BROADCAST

The basic rules for writing press releases (previously discussed in Chapters 4 and 5) also apply to broadcast, but only more so, particularly in terms of brevity. This is because television and radio stations (except for those radio stations with an all-news format) usually allot less time for news programming than newspapers allot space for stories.

Most stations that provide news announcements between broadcast features, such as interviews, music, talk sessions, and other locally created programs, will handle individual news items as "briefs," rarely devoting more than one minute (about 150 words) to each story. Even the most important stories of the day will rarely merit more than two or three minutes of broadcast time.

Another characteristic which separates broadcast news from print news is its sense of immediacy. TV and radio stations are equipped to handle news *instantly*. Consequently, releases aimed at electronic media should be handled separately from those slated for print media. While the latter can go through the mails, assuming that the deadline is not too close, material for radio and TV stations should be hand-delivered. In some instances, if the contact has already been established, the information should be phoned in.

As with print, notice of future events should be submitted well in advance to give the news editor and/or the program director sufficient time to figure his or her programming.

THE BROADCAST PRESS RELEASE

The PR/publicist accustomed to writing releases for print media (most PR/publicists are so oriented because newspapers and magazines offer greater placement possibilities) must make a considerable change in style if he or she wants to get material on the air. Writing for broadcast represents a particular challenge.

First, the writing has to be relaxed, informal, almost conversational in tone. Since the viewer/listener does not have the option of going back over what has been shown or said, the meaning of the words used must be understood immediately. Second, in keeping with the broadcast media's concept of immediacy, much greater use is made of the present tense. This, of course, is done only when appropriate. Another precept is to use short, declarative sentences (in reality, how most people talk) and words that can be easily pronounced.

The following example shows the comparison between a lead written for a release going to print media and one going to broadcast media.

Lead for Print Release: William Jones, president of Regal Industries, will be honored as the textile industry's "Man of the Year" at the Waldorf-Astoria Hotel on Thursday evening, May 1, according to an announcement by the company.

Lead for Release Going to TV or Radio Station: There's a new "Man of the Year" in the textile industry. It's Regal Industries' president William Jones, who will be so honored at a dinner tonight at the Waldorf-Astoria.

THE BROADCAST INTERVIEW SCRIPT

Broadcast interviews are frequently used by PR/publicists to dispense news and information about their clients. To prepare the client for the interview and as an aid to the show's personnel, PR/publicists frequently work out a rough script.

> **Guidelines for Writing for Broadcast**
>
> - Use simple, declarative sentences.
> - Avoid tongue-twisters.
> - Avoid words with lots of "S" sounds.
> - Be brief, yet do not forget the "Five W's."
> - A lead, whenever possible, should be written in the present tense.
> - If there is any question of the word being mispronounced, place the phonetic configuration next to the usual form, e.g., Mr. Smythe (Sm-eye-th).
> - Read the press release aloud and time it before sending it to the station. Make sure it is of proper length for the selected show.
> - Watch the use of "he," "she," "they," "it." If there is any question as to the identity of the referent, it is best to repeat the name or the word.
> - Remember, even more than a print release, putting together a release going to a radio or television station requires great care. Rewrite, rewrite, rewrite!

This script is edited by the show's production staff to fit their specific time and style requirements. Written in such a way as to indicate the interviewer's questions and the guest's answers, it is rarely followed verbatim, but acts as a guide for both parties concerned.

By writing a script for the show, the PR/publicist enhances the chances of the story being used because the story is being delivered to the show producers in a ready-to-use form. Also, because the PR/publicist has written the script, there is a better chance of the story being told from the point of view that will be most beneficial to the client. The emphasis on certain points and the flow of questions and answers might be considerably different if the show's staff were to devise it from releases and other material. It is definitely to the PR/publicist's advantage to prepare such scripts.

The heading for the script should read: "Suggested script for: <u>name of interviewee</u>." The length, indicated on the script, should be appropriate for the interview time allowed by the medium. The script should reveal all the information a client wishes to share with the interviewer and the audience. The contact name, address, and phone number should appear on the script.

In general, writers should consider the nature of the show(s) for which they are developing a script and try to make their script consistent with the show's style. Humor and human interest will help to make a script appealing. The sales "pitch" should be as subtle as possible.

Sometimes, such scripts are written and then prerecorded by the PR/publicist and/or company personnel and sent to the radio or television station to be aired. If sent to a television show, such recordings are usually accompanied by props and/or visual materials.

```
Pat Rodriguez
Hartman & Delaney
(213) 862-9034

Running time:  5 min.

Suggested Script for Alan Dee, costume jewelry designer
```

COMMENTATOR:	What fashions do we have to look forward to in jewelry?
ALAN DEE:	Fashion, as such, has changed and is continuing to change. Today, fashion is returning to classic lines, simple, elegant designs, and basic colors. The texture of a fabric can make a dress fashionable.
	It's the same thing with jewelry. Jewelry is an accessory to fashion and works as part of a whole, but it's not meant to stand alone. So, classic, simple jewelry is what is on the fashion horizon.
COMMENTATOR:	Does the present economy have anything to do with influencing fashion jewelry?
ALAN DEE:	Yes. Definitely. With money as tight as it is these days, no one really has money to throw around. People have to, and rightly so, look at jewelry with an eye on it as an investment. Even ladies who, in days gone by, took pride in the fact that they wore only real gold, and real gems, have taken to mixing that same real jewelry with some of the new and compatible costume jewelry.
	I must say that I'm reluctant to use the word "costume" because so many women think of costume jewelry in a sense that really no longer applies. They think of brash and brassy objects that turned necks green, ear lobes green, wrists and fingers green.

More

11-1. *Suggested script for a broadcast interview. This brief script will help the show to organize the interview and give the PR/publicist the opportunity to suggest the question sequence and to highlight important points the guest wishes to cover.*

Those days are just about gone. Finishes are far more durable today than years ago. For example, our "Eternum" finish is not just gold color, its made of 24-karat gold and has about 4 to 5 times the gold found in standard finishes. It looks like real gold because what you're looking at is real gold.

We tried an experiment. We made two pairs of earrings in the identical design, but we made one pair of 14K gold, and the other with "Eternum" finish. It's just about impossible to tell them apart without looking for the 14K stamp. Don't you agree? (Shows earrings for comparison.)

COMMENTATOR: (Commentator comments freely and then asks:) How can we achieve a fashion look, though, without running out and spending a lot of money on classic jewelry?

ALAN DEE: By adding one or two very basic items to an already existing collection. Let me show you. Here are a few of the things I've been talking about. None of the pieces I have here sells for more than $____ (price of highest). And here are a few things, the kind that might be around from fashions that have died. Let me show you how, using a little ingenuity, I can create a whole fashion jewelry wardrobe.

(Alan Dee will drape chains and other pieces, explaining what he's doing as he goes along, and illustrate what he's said on a model, the commentator, or someone from the audience.)

COMMENTATOR: So, all it really takes is a few of the basics, and a mirror to create a fashion look in jewelry on a modest budget.

VISUAL MATERIALS FOR TELEVISION

The PR/publicist who seeks exposure for a product on television must provide visual materials. These fall into two categories: (1) demonstration materials and samples; and (2) prerecorded films and tapes and "preshot" slides.

Demonstration materials and samples are used to show the actual nature of the product and how it works. These materials are given to the show's staff ahead of the actual airing so that they can become familiar with the product. If necessary, fresh materials are supplied for the actual show. In addition, samples of merchandise are often distributed to the program's production staff as a goodwill gesture.

Slides, films, and tapes for on-the-air use can be used by themselves or in conjunction with a guest appearance or interview. Usually, these slides, films, and tapes are not angled to a particular show, but are based on a generally interesting theme. Such materials are developed so that they can be used in soliciting coverage on a broad range of shows. For example, a film that shows all the steps in shoe manufacturing, developed for a large company that makes men's, women's, and children's shoes and boots, could be used in several ways. It could be shown on a show in which a woman's shoe designer was presenting new fashion trends, or it could be used equally as well by a children's shoe company executive discussing support for the growing child's foot.

Because materials of this nature are expensive to produce and to copy, PR/publicists usually write synopses of them to accompany a query call and/or letter. Order forms for films, slides, and tapes accompany the synopses. This arrangement saves time, helps prevent any last-minute foul-ups, and does away with the publicist having to provide copies of expensive materials that do not have any chance of being aired.

The exact nature of such visuals varies from project to project. In general, the better known the subject (product or person), the fewer background materials accompany the synopses. With a nonfamous guest or an obscure topic or product, these materials have to "sell" the idea.

PLACING PR/PUBLICITY ON A TV TALK SHOW

There are a series of steps the PR/publicist must follow when making a TV talk show placement. First, the practitioner must know the show well before contacting them. This means watching it regularly for at least two weeks to see the variety of formats used and the nature of materials aired and discussed in interviews. No source book can give the same insight as actually watching the show.

As the PR/publicist watches the show, he or she takes notes on the ways that the client could be adapted to the show's format. Ideas not directly related to the current project, as well as those that are, should be included; they may be useful for future reference.

It is necessary to find out who is the right person to contact. It varies from show to show. Sometimes it is the producer, sometimes the host or hostess, sometimes the talent coordinator. Source books may help, but all names should be checked by phone.

The contact is then called and asked if he or she would like to hear the idea on the phone or would prefer a written inquiry. The way the contact works should never be assumed—ask. The practitioner needs to prepare for any initial contact. He or she should be ready to sell the client, product, or concept on the spot, if necessary.

Whether the contact is made by phone, mail, or in person, the practitioner presents the concept in a way that will appeal to the show. He or she must stress *why* and *how* the person being suggested and the product or concept they are to discuss will help the show and enhance it. As much visual material about the personality or idea as possible should be included, but without trying to sell inappropriate demonstrations to straight talk shows.

The PR/publicist has to know the lead times that shows require. Most shows need three weeks even if they are pretaped. A very timely guest, such as the doctor who has discovered a cure for a dreaded disease or the fire chief who directed operations that saved the lives of hundreds of people, can be scheduled within a day, however. The PR/publicist should also know the differences among shows. He or she should not assume that the noon news show in one city is going to be the same as in another city.

The practitioner must learn to take rejection gracefully and, at the same time, try to pave the way for a future chance to get exposure on the show.

TRAINING FOR THE TV INTERVIEW

Even the most experienced speaker can be intimidated by the television interview. Training for broadcast interviews is usually part of a PR/publicist's responsibility. Because of the increasing trend toward company spokespeople making media appearances, some businesses have formed that are solely involved in training people for media interviews.

Whether training is done by the PR/publicist or such a company, the best technique is role playing. No matter how much a person is told about how to act in a media interview situation, more can be accomplished by simulating the actual interview process. Ideally, one should work with a video tape system, but if that is not available, a tape recorder with two microphones will do. The atmosphere in the room used for the training session should be as much like that in the actual studio as possible, and the participants should enact their roles seriously. The goal is to be able to play back the interview in order to critique the results.

The session should begin with an introduction or welcome by the person playing "interviewer," and then go on to a discussion of the interviewee's business or story. The interviewer should attempt to stump and provoke the interviewee,

THE ROWLAND COMPANY, INC.
Public Relations
415 Madison Avenue, New York, New York 10017

INTRODUCING FRAN SHERWOOD

If you were a Cordon Bleu-trained chef; a TV-food specialist (who'd had more than one celebrity host eat the props); a professional party cook catering to the likes of Dustin Hoffman and Ira Levin; the creator of a cook's "Survival Course for Men"; a long-time food writer (House & Garden, Glamour, Bride's); an experienced photographic food stylist and recipe-tester and had spent years living and studying in the food capitals of Europe--would you stand to gain from updating your basic cookbook library?

"Yes," says food authority Fran Sherwood, "if you want to stay up-to-date with our fast changing lifestyles. This is a very exciting time to be involved with food and cooking. In just a few short years, we've seen many of our long-standing eating and cooking habits change. We've become very much more sophisticated about nutrition, and our ideas about what constitutes a 'good meal' have been altered as Americans traveled more, ate out more, and generally experienced a more diverse menu."

Fran says that a quick look at a cook's vocabulary can give anyone a better idea of just how eating and food preparation have changed recently. "Words like high-fiber, microwave oven, and polyunsaturates just didn't matter a decade ago. But now, with the fitness movement and more women working out of the home--to say nothing of the money crunch and the fact that we're all more aware of conserving energy--it's clear why the cookbook you used in the 1960's just won't work in the 1980's."

More

11-2. *Materials used to present a personality for a guest interview. The biography highlights the personality's qualifications to be interviewed. The close-up photograph (usually an 8½ x 11-inch black-and-white glossy), on the facing page, shows good looks and an energetic smile. The series of questions suggests an outline for the interview.*

THE ROWLAND COMPANY, INC.
Public Relations
415 Madison Avenue, New York, New York 10017

QUESTIONS FOR FRAN SHERWOOD

Like so many American women, Fran Sherwood is a working mother living in a large urban area. But, unlike most homemakers, Fran Sherwood is also a Cordon Bleu-trained chef, the owner of a successful party catering business and cooking school in New York, a professional TV and photographic food specialist, and the author of many articles about good food and how to get it. She's with us today to share some of her knowledge and to give us some tips on how to enjoy food, 1980's style. Welcome, Fran Sherwood.

1. Have the cooking and eating habits of Americans changed much in the last few years?

2. What would you say today's consumer looks for when preparing a meal?

3. You taught a cook's "Survival Course for Men." How did that come about?

4. What are your students most uncertain about?

5. Are most cookbooks designed to meet our current cooking needs?

6. As a working mother, do you think your cooking needs are typical?

7. Have there been changes in the way we entertain?

8. How can a first-time cook feel more comfortable?

9. How can consumers learn to take better a

10. Why are so many people intimidated by "

> **Advice for a Radio or TV Interview**
>
> - Look and sound confident (even if you are not).
> - Speak with control.
> - Be polite.
> - Smile, but not too much.
> - Try to be relaxed and friendly, like a guest in a house.
> - Be understated, rather than overstated.
> - Do not read as if from a script; however, it is all right to glance at notes on file cards if the program allows it.
> - Answer questions you are asked, not those you wish you had been asked.
> - Make short statements. Do not go on too long.
> - Use humor with discretion.
> - When interviewed, do not look at the camera. Look at the person doing the interviewing.
> - Be forthright. If you cannot answer questions, say so. Never lie.
> - Dark suits are better than light suits.
> - Women should wear little or no jewelry. It may hit the neck microphone usually worn for interviews.
> - Men should be careful as they "hike" their trousers. The calf should not show. Wear knee-length socks.

trying to make the situation as realistic as possible. It should be based on the style and format of the type of show on which the spokesperson is scheduled to appear. During the playback, the tape should be stopped at key points in order to comment on both strengths and weaknesses. If possible, a second session should be scheduled shortly after the first, at which time the role playing is repeated, asking a somewhat different set of questions. The playback should again be evaluated.

In spokesperson training, the PR/publicist should be honest and critical. Candor is a must. The flattering of ineffective spokespersons just because they represent major clients or are company superiors, does them and the practitioner a disservice. If possible, additional training sessions should be held for each new project, as well as "refreshers" if there has been a considerable lapse since the spokesperson last tackled a broadcast interview.

Sponsored Films and Tapes

Sponsored films and tapes are useful to a PR/publicity program. Such material is produced with the intent of developing favorable attitudes and reactions, as well as arousing public awareness on an issue of social importance to the sponsoring organization, stimulating and instructing employees, and/or educating a selected public about products or services.

To get the best PR/publicity value from such films, the practitioner must get the maximum exposure possible. There are producers who, in addition to creating, can provide distribution services for films and tapes. Thus, a distribution can be "ordered" which will reach a specific number of people with certain common characteristics; i.e., a public. Television stations, both commercial and cable, use these films, but require that they be of appropriate length to fill their time slots. The best film lengths are between twenty-three and twenty-eight minutes to fill a half-hour slot, and fourteen minutes for a short segment. Today, the nontheatrical film and tape business is more than a billion dollar industry, and the growth of cable will lead to a sizable increase in the next decade.

As a form of communication, the advantages of film and video tape are distinct. They combine sight, sound, and drama to maximize the message and, if done well, they command sustained attention to the message. In addition, there are certain actions that can be depicted on film or tape that words and still visuals cannot represent. Films and tapes can provide a sequence of events that is easily understood. They can present objects in a selected setting that is flattering and tells the client's story most effectively.

Sponsored films and tapes can have additional PR/publicity uses. Particularly interesting sections of annual reports can be filmed for stockholder presentations, manufacturing processes of complicated products and machinery can be recorded on film to make it easier for the press to follow, plants and office facilities can be toured from afar by showing views and close-ups of people at work.

Before allocating time and funds for a film or tape production, consider why it is being produced; the public it is possible to reach with it; how long it will be useful; how soon before it will become dated; and a realistic budget for production and distribution.

Evaluate the professionalism of the staff making the film. Ask to see films they have made for other clients, and check references on their ability to meet deadlines and stay within budget. A nonprofessional film can do more harm than good.

Tapes and Films for Other Uses

New video technology has made the taping and editing of events and presentations readily available for PR/publicity purposes. Many large agencies and in-house PR/publicity departments have video cameras and video tape recorders at their disposal. Obviously, the type of company using this technology is one with substantial funds and a large volume of news to project. The fashion and retail industries, particularly, make use of this type of video equipment. Examples of this include video demonstrations and presentations in large retail stores, such as cooking demonstrations and fashion collections presented on tape.

Closed circuit and cable television offer substantial PR/publicity opportunities. Sequences and full programs that will inform or instruct the selected publics can be produced and then aired on a cable television station. Such programs can also be offered to institutions and community groups to use for educational and/or entertainment purposes. For example, a practitioner might produce for a client, a travel magazine, a program about how one of its editors lived for six months with a primitive tribe. This could be shown over a series of local cable TV stations and then sent on a type of "shuttle system" to a series of Chamber of Commerce lunch meetings. Or the PR/publicity department of a medical equipment company could produce instructional films on using its new resuscitation kit. These could be shown at schools via closed-circuit TV or at community Red Cross meetings.

Looking ahead, as the number of cable television stations continues to grow, the demand for interesting programming will be greater and the PR/publicity potential considerable. However, as with other projects, it will remain important to analyze the cost effectiveness of such productions in terms of the specific publics cable television can reach.

New technology has also made it possible to produce sophisticated multiscreen, multimedia presentations that combine film, tape, and slide sequences with unique sound and lighting effects. Some even use smoke screens and fragrance blasts. These presentations are most commonly used to depict new products and company profiles and to feature educational, historic and civic information to large groups of people. As production costs are high and technical expertise is required, PR/publicists usually work with outside production companies on such projects.

Speaker Aids

Audiovisual techniques are useful to PR/publicists making a presentation personally and to speakers representing clients or organizations. Some of these basic techniques, such as the use of chalk boards and flip charts, are not as glamorous as others. However, they are effective in helping the speaker to project a clear message. Because their use is so common, it is possible to underestimate the need for rehearsal to ensure familiarity with such equipment and the proper timing and sequence of the presentation.

There is nothing worse than a speaker who fumbles when using presentation aids. Consider the flip chart page that repeatedly rips as it is flipped, the blackboard that will not be completely erased, slides that appear upside down, or the audio tape that is "out of sync" with the visual shown. No matter how polished the speaker is, his or her use or misuse of such aids can determine the effect of the presentation. Because of the fear of inviting such disasters, many speakers shy away completely from using presentation aids.

But using audiovisual materials need not be a disaster. They do add dimension to a presentation. Also, they assist the speaker in keeping the audience's attention. However, the speaker must be practiced in coordinating the A/V aids to the speech, and the PR/publicist doing the counseling must call attention to the details in order to avoid pitfalls. Consider some of the most common problems in using speaker aids.

Slides. The worst problem is when slides are in a projector upside down or backwards. This can be avoided by personally viewing the entire sequence before the presentation, marking the slides with dots or numbers on the section of the mount or frame that pokes up above the plastic tray. In this way, the slides can be easily replaced, in sequence, should the slides accidently fall out of the tray.

Films and Video Tapes. Fumbling to adjust sound and image is distracting, and most of the audience will pay more attention to such actions than to the beginning of the presentation. Films and tapes should be wound to the starting point before the audience arrives. The focus should also be preset to ensure that the video is clean. The correct volume adjustment depends on the size of the room and the number of people present. If it is not possible to pretest and set the volume ahead, a good way to start is with the volume turned halfway up, and to move from there. If tape is used, the picture will probably be played through a television screen, so it is essential that the screen be clearly visible from every seat in the area. If the room is big, the tape can be projected onto a large screen for easier viewing. If films are shown on a standard projector, it should be shielded or placed in such a way that the mechanical noise is minimized.

Flip Charts. Flip charts are an excellent aid to a speaker making a presentation to an audience of ten or less, but the easel holding the charts must not be wobbly. It should be secured to the floor, if need be, with heavy "gaffer" tape, in a position comfortable for the speaker and permitting a clear view for the audience. If marking pens are used, the speaker should practice using them until he or she can do so comfortably. The pages should be handled carefully to avoid ripping. If the speaker is to use a chart pad for writing, the pad should be checked to see that it actually is blank. It can be embarrassing to flip the page of a chart pad during the course of a presentation and come upon an already marked page. As a final note, extra pens, in a variety of colors, should be available.

Chalk Boards. Chalk boards are good for groups of up to twenty or more. Plenty of chalk and clean erasers should be on hand. If the speaker is going to provide a good deal of information, he or she should work from two boards, giving the audience time to take notes from one board as the other is erased, ready to hold additional material.

Lecterns. Lecterns help provide speakers with a place to stand as well as a place for notes. A lectern must be the right height for the speaker. If it holds a light and/or microphone, they must be in good working condition. The mike cord

> **Consider the Importance of the Script**
>
> No matter what the form, all scripts function to provide basic structure and sequence to a presentation whether it be prerecorded or "live." A good script is one in which the visual images and words enhance each other; one in which the sequence is logical and interesting. Scripts take many forms, from elaborate screen scenarios to ad-hoc guides for narrating slides.
>
> In film and video tape production, the script is the foundation for success. It provides order, visual sequence, and story line. It is the starting point for a production. It gives form to the ideas portrayed by the camera.
>
> Scripts used for television and radio production are written to suggest an interview sequence or an announcer discussion. They give the PR/publicist the opportunity to present the spokesperson and his or her story in the most favorable light possible.
>
> For slide shows, the script is the backbone of the presentation, and even if the narration seems spontaneous and casual, the basic thinking behind the sequencing of the slides and the descriptions demands the same skills as writing a line-by-line script.
>
> It is best to hire the services of a script writer for films and tapes since their success is so dependent on a professional, somewhat slick result. In the case of suggested scripts for broadcast and for slide presentations, the PR/publicist often develops these without outside help.

should be long enough to allow the speaker to take the microphone off the lectern and move about. If the presentation is to be longer than ten minutes, a pitcher of water, a glass, and a napkin should be on the lectern.

EXTENDING THE IMPACT OF AUDIOVISUALS

The reach and impact of films, slides, tapes, and live presentations can be extended by developing and distributing coordinated posters, booklets, and novelty items. The experience of seeing a film or listening to a discussion will be enhanced by giving the audience something to take away with them. Providing such materials literally forces the audience to take the message home, prolonging its impact.

Depending on the situation, it may be more effective to mail the coordinated materials out soon after the presentation. Pamphlets and booklets summarizing the points made may remain in a home or office as a reference and reminder of the sponsoring organization long after the original presentation. For this purpose, some companies even produce novelty items such as tote bags, pens, and datebooks with design motifs coordinated to the subject of the A/V presentation.

12
PR/Publicity Planning

Every PR/publicity effort requires a plan that includes goals and objectives, an action strategy, budget, and timetable. Sometimes, a plan for one project can be modeled after a previously successful one, but just as a mass-produced suit will not fit as well as a custom-tailored one, so the wise PR/publicist seeks to create a special plan that truly fits the needs of his or her client.

No two plans are exactly alike. The size of the client or organization, scope of the project, management style of the company—these are all variables that affect the specifics of a PR/publicity effort. There are, however, some general considerations involving flexibility, timing, and implementation that go into developing a plan of action for any program.

Flexibility is essential. Things usually do not work "exactly" as anticipated, and the very nature of the PR/publicity business requires that the practitioner have an accommodating and flexible attitude.

Proper timing must be considered. Stories that appear too late—after the public's interest has peaked, or those that appear ahead of their time—do not accomplish objectives as well as those that are properly timed.

Finally, the PR/publicist who developed the plan must oversee its actual implementation. Even if experienced staff members are entrusted to activate the plan, the professional who developed it should check progress regularly to ensure its proper implementation and to provide direction when necessary.

Establishing a Plan

Establishing a plan does several things. It helps clarify pertinent PR/publicity goals and objectives. It provides the basis for a working schedule and direction. It lessens the chances of misunderstanding by management. It keeps the practitioner and the staff's efforts centered on those PR/publicity opportunities that are consistent with the overall reach of the program.

The determination of goals and objectives for a plan springs from a penetrating study of what has gone on before and a calculated guess of what is going to happen in the future. It is here that the instinctive judgment, experience, and creativity of the practitioner are tested.

ELEMENTS IN A PR/PUBLICITY PLAN

Most PR/publicity plans include the areas listed in the outline below. The order and relative importance of each section are determined by the nature of the project. Plans submitted by out-of-house PR/publicists will also include a section on credentials.

1. Situation analysis
   - The industry
   - Company background or personality profile
   - Competition
   - Prospects for the future
2. Goals and objectives
3. Relevant publics
4. Media available
5. Events or other special activities
6. Budget and/or fee
7. Personnel and equipment required
8. Timetable
9. Criteria for evaluation
10. Procedure for reporting to management

SITUATION ANALYSIS

Effective PR/publicists are not magicians who cast spells on reporters and the public to make news and generate goodwill for clients. Rather, they are strategists who depend on research to plan and enact programs logically.

Research concerning the organization, its environment, its policies, people, problems, and reputation is the foundation of a sound PR/publicity program. Experienced practitioners know that it is impossible to structure and implement a program without having intimate knowledge of the organization and the environment in which it functions. Research is time-consuming and, at times, dull, but it provides the facts needed to develop meaningful goals and objectives and is the foundation upon which successful campaigns are built.

The information gathered from research is used to construct a situation analysis and to study PR/publicity potentials. Some of the points considered are:

- Current standing of the organization—rank in industry, gross sales figures, number of employees, and so on.
- Reputation in the eyes of trade and consumer publics.
- Management style—democratic, authoritarian, laissez-faire, from-the-top, by group, and so on.
- Past PR/publicity campaigns—what image have they created?
- Strengths and opportunities—identification of policies and programs that can project a favorable image.
- Weaknesses and problems—identification of the activities and policies that need modification or could be obstacles to favorable PR/publicity results.

In order to answer these questions, the PR/publicist acts like an investigative reporter, interviewing key people and studying relevant material in order to get vital background information. Within the organization, senior management is usually the initial source for information, but valuable insights frequently come from interviews with middle management and on-line employees as well.

Like the reporter, the PR/publicist should examine all points of view with an open mind, and facts should be drawn from every corner of the organization. A financial analysis can lead to good insights as can a review of the company's legal status. Production and research and development (R&D) also can give the practitioner a sense for the style of the company and a long-term view.

In addition, the company's advertising agency, its suppliers, its retailers, and its customers are excellent sources of information. Editors of trade and business publications, industry association heads, and other experts can also provide information. It is also useful to survey secondary sources of information—what has been written about the company and its industry in periodicals and books—and to review other printed material, such as annual reports, brochures, and marketing proposals.

GOALS AND OBJECTIVES

The terms "goal" and "objective" are often confused. In this text, goals are defined as the desired end result of the PR/publicity campaign; objectives are the things that must be done to reach the established goals.

The determination of goals and objectives establishes the order of priority in a plan. It is important to relate them to the overall purposes of the client or organization as well as to current PR/publicity opportunities. For example, there would be no point in creating a program aimed at enhancing the reputation of a suburban branch of a central city store if the overall plan was to eliminate that branch in a short period of time. Often, PR/publicists set forth programs that promise too much. This can be self-defeating. Because of the unpredictable nature of PR/publicity itself, it is better to be realistic, promising less and providing more.

Unfortunately, many potentially successful programs have been suspended because the PR/publicist and the client or organization were not working with the same goals in mind. For example, suppose a company in the paper packing products business hires a PR/publicist. The chief executive officer says that she wants to make news about the company's growth potential and impressive recent sales records, but really means that she desires personal acknowledgment for the company expansion under her leadership. The two goals are quiet different. In one instance, emphasis in PR/publicity releases would be placed on the company as a whole, in the other on the individual as a leader. They would result in a totally different approach by the PR/publicist and generate different kinds of news stories.

In a second example, the situation might be the exact opposite. Suppose that an attractive and articulate senior partner of a small, but rapidly growing law firm is viewed by the PR/publicist as a perfect spokesperson for building the firm's reputation. Consider the ramifications if, in reality, he turned out to be camera and interview "shy" and continually canceled interviews with press representatives because he was "unavailable." In such a case, the total effort might be jeopardized because the PR/publicist and the senior executive did not really view the method of achieving company recognition the same way.

One can see, then, the necessity of discussing goals and objectives thoroughly with the client or organization before any work takes place. This is especially important if the individual time of company personnel is required. Surprises and hidden agenda can upset management and destroy a potentially effective program. Many practitioners report that they submit written objectives and plans of action before they start any project to make sure that there is no misunderstanding as to the methods of procedure and hoped-for outcome.

DEVELOPING EFFECTIVE GOALS AND OBJECTIVES

There is an art to developing effective goals and objectives. They should be established after basic research has been completed and the PR/publicity problem or project has been identified. PR/publicity objectives that have little relationship to the long-term goals of the client or organization are counter-productive.

For example, a community hospital has goals of attracting more patients to its children's clinic and raising money for a new playroom in the clinic. These goals would be well served by PR/publicity objectives seeking to establish a free educational lecture series for parents in the community, and as a result, generating news stories about innovative architectural plans for a unique new playroom facility. Because the objectives are specifically tied to the two goals, the accomplishment of the goals would be greatly aided by meeting the objectives.

The best objectives are specific and indicate the plan of action to be taken to meet them. If objectives are too broad and general, they will seem vague, leading to equally vague plans of action. Consider these broad objectives in comparison to the more specific examples that follow:

Broad and Vague PR/Publicity Objectives
- To enhance the image of the company.
- To attract new customers.
- To establish identity in the community for the candidate.

Specific and Precise PR/Publicity Objectives
- Change the image of the company from conservative to more progressive.
- Attract new customers in the eighteen to thirty age group who live in the community but work elsewhere.
- Establish recognition of the candidate as a major philanthropist in the community.

Note how the second set of objectives suggest action and would probably lead to a more specific plan and program of implementation. Such objectives do more than merely provide a general direction; they serve as a source of ideas and enable the PR/publicist to plan specific projects to meet them.

In addition, goals and objectives should be set forth in order of importance and with respect to the time period in which they are expected to be achieved. If possible, some consideration as to how to evaluate the results should also be part of the process of their formulation. Management responds best to measureable results of PR/publicity effort.

Although it has been acknowledged that a large part of any PR/publicity program can be considered successful if it promotes general "goodwill," the more measureable the results of the goals and objectives, the better. Results can be measured in terms of numbers of people in the publics reached, number of news stories that appear in media, sales increase, or more sophisticatedly, in the degree of attitude changed. Suffice it to say, the true professional considers methods of evaluating results when developing the initial set of goals and objectives for a project. (See Chapter 13, "Evaluating and Merchandising Results.")

SELECTING PUBLICS AND APPROPRIATE MEDIA

The careful selection of a public or group of publics is another essential element of any PR/publicity program. In a sense, it is like choosing a target market for an advertising campaign. One must define the public by a common interest, attitude, lifestyle, or location. In addition, a consideration of the public's motivations and their existing attitudes about the organization or client seeking exposure is important.

FIRST YEAR PLAN: "LO-CAL ITAL"

PROJECT DEFINITION:

    To publicize the opening of a new chain of gourmet fast food restaurants offering calorie-controlled portions of pasta, vegetables, salad, and cheese dishes along with fruit, desserts, and beverages. The decor in each of the six restaurants is clean, white, modern formica and contrasting red and green trim (the colors of the Italian flag). There are long service counters and booths for those eating at the restaurants. Colorful straw fruits and vegetables hang from the ceiling to give a festive feeling. Cleanliness is stressed and apparent. The food is served on plastic-coated white paperware with a red and green striped border and the LO-CAL ITAL logo in green. Take-out food is packaged in matching Chinese food-type containers. Prices are moderate. Each of the six branches opening are in and around Baltimore, Maryland.

PR/PUBLICITY GOALS:

1. To create initial consumer interest in the restaurants and take-out service.
2. To attract attention of people who might wish to open franchises in new locations.

PR/PUBLICITY OBJECTIVES:

1. To generate publicity in local media about the opening of each LO-CAL ITAL.
2. To generate PR/publicity about the concept in the food industry and business media.
3. To create a series of special events to maintain news about LO-CAL ITAL.
4. To demonstrate proof of the low calorie and high nutritional value of the food.

ACTIVITIES:

1. Pre-opening publicity about the LO-CAL ITAL concept, who developed it, and why.
2. Arrange an attention-getting opening event--perhaps with an Italian tie-in.
3. TV appearances and stories about the chef who created the concept.
4. News about celebrities and local personalities who have ordered take-out food from LO-CAL ITAL and/or eaten at the restaurants.
5. A benefit tie-in with a local charity.
6. The hospital food programs that are using the take-out service.
7. Recipes in gourmet magazines.
8. Feature in a Baltimore area publication about a local new business.
9. Christmas gift concept, e.g., gift certificates.
10. New Year's Eve take-out service.

12-1. *Example of PR/publicity plan. Note the precise project definition, which is the result of situation analysis, and the goals and objectives specified. Such well-defined statements clarify the project and provide a guide for evaluating progress and results. The activities listed are designed to meet the goals and objectives. The subsequent pages of this plan contain more proposed activities, relevant publics, a budget, and the other elements necessary to the "Lo-Cal Ital" project.*

In the same way that an advertising campaign will be most effective if the ad message is geared to the motivations of specific customer types, so a PR/publicity program is most effective if the news is directed to the interest of specific publics. Equally important is using the appropriate media to reach selected publics. In order to do this, the PR/publicist must know the characteristics of the media relevant to the project and know their reach and influence on their audience.

In the process of determining the audience for a PR/publicity program, the practitioner seeks to define as many publics as possible and then refine the list to meet the objectives. It is best to start with the broadest possible range of people who might be reached so as not to miss any opportunity. There are some general points to consider in defining all the relevant publics:

- *Who are the people to be reached?* Age? Sex? Education? Income level?
- *Where are they located?* In cities? Small towns? On farms? In the military?
- *Which groups are the most important?* The salespersons? The workers?
- *When is the best time to reach them?* Market season? Leisure time?
- *What influences their opinions?* Political parties? Social gossip?
- *How are they best reached?* Through local media, national media, or a combination?
- *Can they be influenced by reaching other groups?* Husbands through wives? Parents through children?

The more PR/publicists know about each identified public, the more effective the news angles that can be formulated to reach these publics. As much as possible, the message should be personalized to be specifically relevant. The trick is to focus in on each public and engage and involve them. People with different roles in one broad public should be approached individually and as a group. For example, if one wants to reach executives in the toy manufacturing industry, it would be most effective to consider the designers, salespersons, and factory workers as different publics as well as parts of a whole and look to develop stories for media that reach them in both ways. In the same sense, for example, it is wise to think of reaching those who might attend the theater in a certain city by distinguishing the tourist from the full-time city resident and the city resident from the person who works in the city and lives in a suburb.

EVENTS OR OTHER SPECIAL ACTIVITIES

Events have been discussed in detail in Chapter 9. It is relevant to mention here that one considers many types of events and activities and selects only those that meet the defined goals and objectives of the program. It is useful to consider a broad range of possibilities and then refine the choices. A listing is a useful starting point for event development in a plan.

The following is a checklist of events and activities that can be used in any PR/publicity program:

- Consumer clinics
- Contests
- Conventions
- Demonstrations
- Displays and exhibits
- Employee discount programs
- Fashion or product shows
- Handbooks and manuals
- Letters and bulletins
- Parades
- Personal appearances
- Plant tours and open houses
- Posters
- Scholarships
- Speaker's bureau
- Specially made films and tapes
- Specially written books
- Sponsoring of civic events
- Sports competition
- Studies, surveys, and reports

BUDGET, PERSONNEL, AND EQUIPMENT

Every PR/publicity plan should contain budget, personnel, and equipment requirements. This point seems obvious, but all too often these elements are not carefully worked out in the early stages of plan development.

If a client or organization approves a project and finds out later that it will cost considerably more in time and manpower than originally anticipated, the practitioner could well be in trouble. Management does not look kindly on cost overruns. Consequently, the whole PR/publicity program could be in jeopardy.

Informed clients know that it is hard to project PR/publicity costs exactly, but the wise practitioner provides management with broad estimates at the start of each project and makes sure to come in with reasonable accuracy. This is essential for the agency or the free-lance PR/publicist engaged in a "one-shot campaign" for a prospective client and vital for the in-house practitioner working against a yearly budget.

Specifically, management needs an estimate of funds required for the production of press material; costs for printing, photographic reproduction, mailing, and so on. Expenses for hiring additional personnel, such as photographers, artists, specialty writers, and spokespeople, must also be included. Equipment, from simple office machinery and supplies to sophisticated audiovisual systems, must be accounted for. Expenses for press contact work, such as telephone, travel, and entertainment, should also be supplied.

Properly planned budgets help the PR/publicist and management control a program. They bring the priorities in the program into focus and help in the cost/return evaluation. It is best to define the budget by specific techniques and activities to be used rather than by general functions. For example, it is easier to understand and adjust expenses projected for a series of public information pamphlets if the expenses are broken down into categories such as printing, photography, typesetting, etc. Obviously, the details of breakdowns presented in written plans will vary, but it is best for the PR/publicist to check details carefully so that gross figures quoted are realistic.

PR/publicity budgets should be large enough to warrant top management involvement, but not so large as to be a burden.

Budgets should be re-evaluated if:

- Results are not equivalent to expenses
- Specific objectives are not being met and long-range results seem unpredictable
- Results are good and new opportunities are on the horizon, but the allocated funds have been used
- Those in senior management controlling the "purse strings" are not informed as to results and new potentials and are keeping at a static level what should be a responsive budget.

TIMETABLES

Timetables for PR/publicity can be organized in any convenient way: as a month-to-month checklist, on a daily calendar basis, or according to the client's or organization's fiscal year. Timetables give order to a program and provide a guide for implementation. They enable a practitioner to anticipate heavy working periods and to plan effectively to meet projected deadlines.

In general, it is a good idea to leave some "free" time in a program. This gives the opportunity to respond to spontaneous press requests and to deal with fast-breaking news stories. In addition, the creative tasks of writing and event planning are time-consuming; extra time in a plan allows for necessary flexibility, just in case the proper phrases and event ideas do not come as quickly as anticipated. The implementation of some projects can be very involved. For example, a seminar, survey, or contest can take hours and hours of work to plan, and the time necessary for making arrangements can be overwhelming. Experienced PR/publicity professionals give themselves ample time to allow for contingencies.

EVALUATION AND REPORTING TO MANAGEMENT

Gathering results and evaluating and merchandising them is of great importance. (This will be discussed in greater detail in Chapter 13.) Consequently, any PR/publicity plan should have a section that indicates the criteria for determining success or failure and a schedule of points along the way in the program at which evaluations can be made.

Ideally, a plan should specify that PR/publicists report to management often and seek direction on a regular basis. The nature of the reports may vary—some are informal, brief memos and phone conversations; others, formal written summaries of work in progress and results. Whatever the style agreed on, it is vital that there be an effort to maintain an open line of communications. This is important so that there is recognition of the PR/publicist's day-to-day efforts on a project. It often takes many months of behind-the-scenes work to produce results, and regular reporting helps the PR/publicist to justify his or her activities to management.

Most successful programs produce steady and continuing results and have a cumulative effect. Those are easy to chart and evaluate. But, sometimes even with the best of plans, the most experienced PR/publicists, and highly supportive and well-informed management, things just do not work as expected. In such a situation, evaluation periods built into the plan help those involved analyze what has "gone wrong" and determine what modifications might save the effort before it is too late.

WHY SOME PROGRAMS DO NOT MAKE IT

Hundreds of PR/publicity programs are undertaken by practitioners throughout the year. A disproportionate number of them fail. Why? According to experienced professionals, they fail for one or more of the following reasons: lack of time allocated to research and development; lack of clearly defined and agreed upon objectives and goals; lack of honest communication and full disclosure between management and the practitioner. There are others, of course, such as too much management red tape, resulting in an inability to get clearances on time. However, the preceding reasons are the most important ones.

Proposals Precede Plans

PR/publicists write proposals in order to sell their services and secure a new client, or to sell a new campaign to the management of a company for which they are already working. In proposal writing, there is a need to persuade the reader of

> **Points to Consider in Formulating a Plan**
>
> - What is the company history or individual's background?
> - Why is PR/publicity desired?
> - What are the products, services, or ideas involved?
> - What are the news angles?
> - Who are the people in the organization with whom the PR/publicist will work?
> - What publics should be reached?
> - What messages should be sent?
> - Is there current or proposed advertising or promotion that could affect this program?
> - Are there any projected changes or developments that might affect this program?
> - What media could be approached?
> - Are events and other special activities appropriate?
> - What is the budget?
> - What time period is realistic?
> - What kind of results are expected?
> - What criteria can be established to judge success or failure?
> - Has there been any previous PR/publicity activity that could affect this program?
> - Does management understand the unpredictable nature of PR/publicity?

the writer's understanding of the nature of the problems and to present a program that will satisfy defined PR/publicity goals. The style in which the proposal is written as well as the manner in which the proposal is presented are also important because they serve as samples of the quality of material a PR/publicist can produce. In short, the proposal functions as an important sales tool for the PR/publicist.

Proposals are most often written by agencies and free-lancers seeking a PR/publicity account. Occasionally, an in-house staff PR/publicist will write one to convince management of a desired change in strategy on a new campaign concept. The basic reasoning used in writing proposals is comparable to that used in developing a PR/publicity plan. The emphasis usually is on long-term and overall goals and benefits rather than on short-term objectives, but the nature of the program is the determining factor.

The best proposals are based on careful research and discuss specific concepts and ideas, not vague generalities. They should also be logical, insightfully written, and impressively neat. The writing of such proposals is time-consuming and takes considerable skill. Consequently, many PR/publicists charge prospective clients a fee for writing proposals on speculation.

> **Five Basic Suggestions for Writing Proposals**
>
> 1. Outline the proposal, as in a report, with major and minor headings.
> 2. Add points to the proposal, heading by heading, with an eye to building a logical argument for your plan.
> 3. Strive for clear, concise words and avoid needlessly complicated phrasing or terminology.
> 4. Reread and edit many times over. Try to think as though you were management reading and considering the proposal. Be critical and rewrite for maximum effect.
> 5. Proofread carefully. Make sure that the final version is effectively organized and perfectly typed.

There are many variables that effect the length and style of a proposal, including: the nature of the project for which it is being written (the longer the duration and the more involved the activities, the more appropriate a longer proposal); the writing style of the prospective agency or consultant; and the preferences or specifications of the organization or individual for which the proposal is being written.

Although forms for proposals will vary from project to project, most contain the same basic elements. They are:

1. A brief statement about the company indicating its current public image and any historical facts that have contributed to that image.
2. A concise definition of the problem or opportunity for a PR/publicity effort.
3. The long-term goals for the program.
4. Specific PR/publicity objectives listed in descending order of importance.
5. An outline of a plan of action and a detailed discussion of how it will solve the problem and/or maximize the opportunities to generate news and goodwill.
6. Projected time and cost factors.
7. Exhibits or samples of PR/publicity materials, if appropriate.

13
Evaluating and Merchandising Results

More and more PR/publicists, whether they are agency-connected, independent, or part of a corporate structure, are being asked to show hard evidence that their programs are working. Much of this approach grows from the state of the art in areas closely related to PR/publicity—marketing and advertising, where greater emphasis is being placed on statistical proof of results. Justifying PR/publicity undertakings through gut-level reaction or superficial documentation is getting short shrift from larger, more sophisticated clients. It is only a matter of time when the demand for pinpointed accountability will filter down to the smaller organizations utilizing the services of PR/publicity professionals.

A number of reasons have been advanced for PR/publicists giving result measurement a very wide berth. First, many of their programs have objectives and goals so lacking in specificity that it is not possible to measure to what degree they have been achieved. Another reason is methodological—many of the programs are too small or too short in duration to allow the measurement of results. Still another is economic; the cost involved in checking results, in many cases, would be almost as much and, in some instances, more than the program itself. And a final reason is the very human factor that many practitioners are afraid to admit that their efforts may have little value.

Measuring PR/Publicity Programs

One of the built-in problems in evaluating PR/publicity programs is that some are relatively difficult to measure. Quantitative activity is, by and large, more conducive to concrete analysis than qualitative activity. For example, a campaign to increase the attendance at a county fair by 10 percent can readily be ascertained by checking the attendance records of one year against another. At the community level, a program to get at least a 50 percent turnout for a school board election or, at an industrial level, a project to increase the number of employee suggestions for raising production can also be measured by comparative figures.

A more difficult task is encountered when one seeks to evaluate a qualitative change, a shift in position on a matter of more extensive public concern. For example, consider a program whose goal is a change in attitude toward a public institution, or a nationally known producer of home appliances which seeks a new image. It is here that problems are compounded. In the words of researcher Burns Roper: "Measuring public relations effectiveness is only slightly easier than measuring a gaseous body with a rubber band."

STORY USE

Each PR/publicity project should have its own goals and objectives. The evaluation of the results depends on how well they are met. There are, however, certain general observations that can be made.

Some stories, because of their dramatic aspects or the prominence of the people featured, will result in a much higher rate of media pickup than others. Similarly, a large company with substantial business influence is apt to generate better pickup than a smaller, less prominent one.

A general rule of thumb for print is that a usage of a story by at least one-fifth of the media to which it has been offered would indicate a very successful PR/publicity effort. In broadcast, the same benchmark prevails, although the figure is more approximate because of the nature of the medium.

Sometimes, PR/publicity is secured which exceeds all expectations and produces results whose impact is so great that they must be judged independently. For example, an appearance on a major network talk show will have immediate impact upon millions of viewers simultaneously. The same is true of the cover story of an important magazine.

Evaluating Qualitative Programs

Programs whose objectives (short term) and goals (long term) are expected to lead to changes in opinions and attitudes can be evaluated in several ways.

One method of evaluation is through the use of *public opinion surveys* in which the goals and objectives are delineated, a public defined, a random probability sample decided upon, a questionnaire formulated, and the results tabulated, interpreted, reported, and applied to decisions.

One problem with an approach of this nature, if administered at the end of a campaign (which is usually the case), is the absence of a benchmark to measure the opinions and attitudes *prior* to the programming.

Although the concept of pre-testing (which does provide a benchmark) and post-testing has many advantages and its worth is quite obvious, it is not too popular with PR/publicity organizations because: (1) it is very complicated; to do a statistically projectable study, it is necessary to contact the same group of respondents twice—once for the pre-test, and once for the post-test—and the chances of getting answers from the same people in a real-life situation are very remote; (2) it is very expensive; and (3) if the results should show that the program was not successful, after such an expenditure of time and money, the sponsoring organization would be very loath to present those facts.

Another method of evaluating qualitative programs is the *survey panel* in which the same group of people are interviewed over a period of time. This has the advantage of being more manageable, compared with a public opinion survey, because of the smaller number of people (usually less than thirty) involved. Disadvantages are apparent, however. Should one or two members of the panel withdraw, the results would be affected tremendously. Also, a smaller group of people is less representative of the larger public.

Some practitioners are of the opinion that evaluations of qualitatively based programs should not be restricted to any one period of time. Rather, they should be on-going in order to track attitudinal changes. As a result, one could get a better understanding of what is working and what is not. Consequently, these practitioners recommend *short telephone surveys*—not more than ten minutes—based on a questionnaire and directed toward the targeted public. They argue that using a random digit-dialing technique, which could reach listed as well as unlisted numbers, would result in reaching a statistically representative sample of people. A variant of this technique, but one not used as frequently because of the problems involved in getting a projectable rate of return, is the *periodic mailing of questionnaires* to a random sampling of the specific public.

Another approach to dealing with qualitative evaluation, but not necessarily restricted to it, is referred to as the *audit*—a sort of looking from within and without.

In the *internal audit,* a practitioner's program is periodically scrutinized by peers within the PR/publicity organization with the purpose of focusing on what has been done, what results have been achieved, and what the future plans entail. While this procedure, somewhat related to practices in an advertising agency, has worked in various situations, it has the disadvantage, particularly in a smaller organization, of taking people away from their duties a disproportionate amount of time. Moreover, it can set up psychological conflicts—with staffers being defensive about their programs.

A variation of this procedure, the *external audit,* usually involves a third party, an outside consultant or group of consultants. Depending on the situation, the approach can call for a good deal of preliminary research ultimately leading to

PUBLICITY REPORT

From: BILL CHANG COMMUNICATIONS

Publication	Theme or Merchandise
	Lilac Jewelers' Progress Report: 3/12
GLAMOUR	Fashion Editor will visit store this week. Shopping Editor awaiting new merchandise.
MADEMOISELLE	Fashion Editor will cover story after July 4th. Shopping Editor will call for next editorial spot.
NEW YORK TIMES	Men's Fashion Editor will cover new store and is especially interested in men's jewelry.
PLAYBOY	Men's Fashion Editor waiting for jewelry to use in fall editorial.
CHANNEL 5 NEWS	Possible TV story.
PENTHOUSE	Men's Fashion Editor waiting to see jewelry.
WEIGHT WATCHERS	Fashion Editor will visit store this week.
SEVENTEEN	Fashion Editor will visit store.
REDBOOK	Would like to see jewelry for Christmas gift editorial.
WOMAN'S DAY	Has jewelry. Is considering it for Christmas editorial.
HOUSE BEAUTIFUL	Waiting to see things.
TOWN & COUNTRY	Waiting to see things.
BRIDES	Interested in seeing items for gift section.
WOMEN'S WEAR DAILY	Will cover shop.
COSMOPOLITAN	Will cover shop after July 4th.
NEW YORKER	Will cover shop with next appropriate story.
MODERN BRIDE	Going this week.
SPORT	Men's Editor will visit store.
NEW YORK	Will take an item on men's jewelry.
MCCALLS	Will consider item for gift section.

13-1. *This progress report for a jewelry chain with a national mail-order business reflects the many on-going activities involved in generating PR/publicity. Such reports are usually prepared on a regular basis. They suggest the scope of the practitioner's efforts as well as any confirmed story placements.*

an examination of the program's short-term objectives and long-term goals, its activities and targeted publics. The advantage of such an approach is, of course, its objectivity.

Content analysis is another form of measurement which, while qualitative, also has many quantitative aspects. It consists of a periodic review of usage, or pickups, in terms of location of the medium in which there has been a placement, the kind of medium, its circulation, its date of publication, the length of the mention involved, and whether or not the client was favorably or unfavorably treated and to what degree. While it is possible for individual practitioners to do content analyses on their own, because of the large number of variables involved, it often becomes a matter requiring the services of a computer. There are firms that specialize in handling this for practitioners.

QUANTITATIVE RESULTS ARE NOT NECESSARILY EVALUATION

After finishing a program, many practitioners and their clients have been happy to move onto other projects, ignoring a thorough quantitative *and* qualitative evaluation of the program most recently completed. While this condition is changing and more complete evaluative processes are being employed with greater frequency, quantitative measurement has enjoyed some popularity by practitioners. In fact, reporting results in terms of "how many" and "how often" often takes up a sizeable portion of their time. Too often, however, there is little emphasis on the meaning of the results.

The problem, as thinking professionals point out, is that communication is one thing, but the results of that communication in terms of observable action is another. The fact that thirty newspapers in New England picked up material from a press kit and ran stories is not in itself a complete validation of the program that gave birth to that press kit. Rather, it is a report of the activity of that program. However, until such time as all clients will insist on true evaluations of their programs and, moreover, will permit budgets for such evaluations, practitioners are justified in providing statistical condensations of PR/publicity activity.

Looking to the future, one can predict that computers will allow PR/publicists and management more opportunity for concrete measurement and analysis of results. With advanced systems, it will be possible to detect subtle changes in buying habits and attitudes, indicating the impact of a PR/publicity program on selected publics.

ADDITIONAL CRITERIA FOR EVALUATION

Much of management's judgment of the value of a PR/publicity program, or even of the PR/publicity organization itself, is based on contact—both personal and written. Through this contact, often informal in nature, the knowledgeable professional lets management know the "blow-by-blow" of the current activity; what the problems are and how they can be solved; and suggestions for further PR/publicity activity.

Formal reports concerning PR/publicity activity are usually written and sent to the client or organization management either weekly, monthly, semi-monthly, or in the case of a full-fledged review, presented every year or every six months, depending on the situation. This complete review is sometimes elaborate and, depending on the nature of the client, may be complete with audiovisual effects and charts. Often included are clippings of newspaper and magazine placement together with the tapes of television and radio placements, where appropriate.

Merchandising the Results

In many instances, the reprinting and documentation of stories that have appeared in media (particularly if they are significantly treated) and distributing them to specific and strategic publics, i.e., boards of directors, stockholders, sales staff, and customers, can have a more beneficial result than the original placement. Not incidentally, the practitioner plans for these merchandising uses and allocates part of the budget for disseminating both print and broadcast results.

DOCUMENTATION OF PRINTED RESULTS

The practitioner seeking print documentation can secure copies of the publication when the story appears. This is easy to do when working with a national magazine, trade publication, or local newspaper that can readily be purchased. However, it is more difficult when one is working with many PR/publicity outlets across the country. In these instances, the PR/publicist can either employ a press clipping service or request clips directly.

Press Clipping Services. Press clipping services can supply documentation of any printed material in which a specific name or event is mentioned. The PR/publicist supplies the service with a copy of the press releases and other news material and a list of the media to which they have been sent. Members of the service staff read the publications, clipping and remitting pertinent material. Press clipping services are usually used by companies who initiate, on a continuing basis, sizable PR/publicity campaigns. The price of these services is based on a yearly flat fee for reading plus an extra charge for each clipping secured. Well-known clipping services include Burrelle's Press Clipping Bureau and Luce Press Clippings. In addition, mailing houses (see Chapter 8), such as PR Aids and Derus Media Service, include a clipping service.

Requesting Clips Directly. It is also possible for PR/publicists to obtain results of a mailing to many out-of-town papers without having to use a clipping service. This can be done by using any of the following techniques:

1. Writing a brief request to the editor for clips of any material used.
2. In a press mailing, enclosing a card on which the editor can indicate if he or she plans to use the materials, and when.
3. Including a postage-paid reply envelope to make it convenient for the editor to return clips of used materials.
4. Phoning the editor, asking if he or she expects to use the material; then asking that the editor notify the PR/publicist in advance so that copies can be purchased.

MERCHANDISING PRINT PLACEMENTS

Many practitioners make copies of press clippings, mount them on regular size paper, reproduce them, and send them out to where they are capable of doing the most good, together with a brief note explaining the background and circumstances. More specifically:

- Articles can be reprinted in house organs or circulated directly to employees to increase incentive and company pride.
- Articles that are especially significant can be used to increase credibility among editors. For example, an inclusion of a prestigious article about a company in a major business publication can give more credibility to a general newspaper mailing.
- PR/publicity results can be included in annual reports to enhance the company's image.
- Stories can be reprinted and mailed out to impress customers with the image of the company.
- Results can be tallied and copies of the printed material given to salespersons as an additional sales tool.

Some practitioners, in order to impress the recipients with their newspaper or magazine placement, compare such results with the cost of the equivalent space in the specific publication, pointing out that such pickup has additional credibility because it came to readers in the guise of editorial material rather than as an advertisement. Others advance their case by multiplying the cost of the equivalent space by a certain factor, said to represent the impact of editorial endorsement, and then come up with a figure.

While such mathematical machinations are practiced somewhat extensively, there are publicists who feel that comparisons linking advertising and PR/public relations are counter-productive and muddle an already somewhat beclouded situation regarding the difference between the two areas.

DAILY NEWS

Supervisor Genevieve Kelly and Kelly Brown wait on corner before crossing 65th St. and Columbus Ave.

A symbol of independence

The Jewish Guild for the Blind marks White Cane Day with national salute

By DAVID HARDY

THE JEWISH GUILD for the Blind marked "White Cane Safety Day," a national salute to the rights of the visually impaired, by staging a public demonstration on ways the public can help blind persons avoid curbside accidents while traveling.

"The white cane is a symbol of the independence of visually-impaired men and women, it's their instrument of pathfinding and signals the presence of obstacles and changing contours," explained Genevieve Kelly, a training supervisor for the Jewish Guild.

The guild has provided safety training for about 300 visually-handicapped persons.

According to Kelly, if a member of the public comes upon a blind person about to cross an intersection, "You should approach a blind person from the left. Never take a blind person's arm without first asking if they want assistance. If help is desired the blind person will place his or her left hand on your right arm and then you can guide them across the street. As you approach the opposite curb advise the blind person of it."

Guide's arm and cane at curb help to cross busy intersection in heavy traffic

Instructor Rich Patek shows Adam Shapiro how to avoid fixed objects as Peter Rodriguez listens nearby.

Genevieve Kelly demonstrates proper way to escort blind.

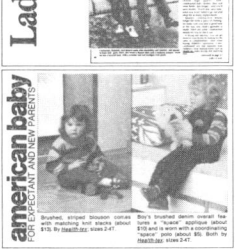

13-2. *Reprints of PR/publicity results. The example on the facing page is a simple reprint of a newspaper article about the Jewish Guild for the Blind, which could be given to employees, supporters, or the press. The four pages, above, are from a sales promotion mailing piece for Health-tex, a children's wear manufacturer, which highlights their PR/publicity efforts.*

BROADCAST DOCUMENTATION

Because placement of PR/publicity materials via the broadcast media is so filled with a "now-you-see-it, now-you-don't" aspect, proof of usage is usually more difficult for practitioners to pass on to their management.

Conscious of this situation, broadcasters recently have been taking more pains to provide practitioners with greater facilities for documentation of any PR/publicity materials used. Contrary to reaction from most print media, broadcasters will usually comply with a request of usage, self-addressed letter or card. However, since broadcast stations—whether television or radio—are very busy places, first-time requests may be overlooked. In those cases, a follow-up communication is in order.

Specifically, documentation of broadcast usage can be obtained in the following ways if one has advance knowledge that their story will be used:

1. Some stations will tape a TV segment for a fee. Radio stations will do the same, and in some instances, it can be provided free.
2. Broadcast monitoring services are available to make tape recordings of television and radio PR/publicity. Additionally, they can provide scripts and descriptive material of the visuals shown. In many instances, arrangements must be made in advance, although in some major markets, on-the-air material is recorded on a routine basis. Radio-TV Reports, Inc., New York, is one of the organizations which, for a fee, will provide documentation of radio and television PR/publicity pickup.
3. In the case of a prerecorded film, tape, or slide package, the PR/publicist can request an affadavit indicating dates the material was used.
4. Reproduction of a desired TV segment is also available in the form of photographic stills arranged like a storyboard with appropriate dialogue under the photos.
5. An easy way to get a record of radio PR/publicity material is to find out when the program is being aired, and then have it recorded using a cassette or reel-to-reel recorder. Often, permission is needed from the station or program if it is to be replayed for any commercial use.

MERCHANDISING BROADCAST PLACEMENTS

As in print, broadcast placements can be promoted. One way is to estimate what a comparable amount of time would cost in advertising and equate the time utilized by the PR/publicity material.

Another method is to estimate the thousands of people listening or viewing the placed materials and divide that into the cost of producing the materials. The result would be a cost-per-thousand figure, a calculation much used in media and advertising and well known in corporate circles. Such a procedure is available from suppliers who specialize in the production and distribution of broadcast publicity materials.

In addition, television tapes and films can be shown on internal video systems. This is particularly good for sales meetings, showrooms, conventions, and at point-of-purchase displays.

Editorial Surveys

From time to time, PR/publicists will ask the media contact with whom they work for feedback on the quality of their releases and visual material and suggestions of story themes for future use. If they have established a personal relationship with the editorial contact, this can be done in an informal, spontaneous way. However, if they are working over long distances with editors whom they do not know personally, or if they would prefer the opportunity to get a written response from media contacts in their own city, PR/publicists can send out an editorial survey. Such surveys are usually well received by the press. In addition to providing the PR/publicist with information about the editors' preferences and interests, they also serve to point up the professionalism and sincerity of the PR/publicist's efforts. Results can be compared from city to city. Tallies can be taken of those responding; who, for example, can use color photographs, or who prefer line drawings to black-and-white photos for fashion stories, and so on.

The editorial survey form shown in Figure 13-3 was sent to family/style editors of 500 major daily newspapers in the United States by a PR/publicity firm. The response was impressively high; almost 300 editors filled out the forms and sent them back. The results were then summarized in a report and tabulated so that the agency could use them in many of the ways listed previously.

It is also advisable to survey editors by phone or in person. In order to do this, PR/publicists should have a good working relationship with their contacts. Sometimes, an individual contact's spontaneous comments tell a great deal about general attitudes and can give a PR/publicist new insights as to how to serve media more effectively.

PR/publicists can also request specific suggestions and critiques as to the effectiveness of their efforts. Obviously, it takes confidence to solicit such opinions, but the advice can greatly improve the PR/publicist's ability to do a good job. Although editors welcome occasional requests for direction and evaluation, they can become annoyed by constant calls for advice that may seem as if the PR/publicist were asking the editor to do his or her job.

Editors receive a great deal of PR/publicity material. In the final analysis, they are the ones who must determine its usefulness to their medium. They are intimately involved with the business of PR/publicity. Requesting their thoughts can provide a PR/publicist with valuable feedback and direction.

LOIS BEEKMAN ASSOCIATES INC.
PUBLICITY SERVICES
605 PARK AVENUE   NEW YORK, N.Y. 10021

Dear Editor:

To best serve your needs, we need information from you. Please, would you take a moment to fill out this simple check list.

EDITORIAL INTEREST	STRONG	MODERATE	LITTLE
Men's Fashion	✓		
Women's Fashion	✓		
Boys' Fashion			✓
Girls' Fashion			✓
Teen Fashion			✓
Teen Fads			✓
New Consumer Services	✓		
New Products	✓		
Unique Uses for Familiar Products		✓	
Family Health News	✓		
Decorating Ideas		✓	
Food Ideas and Recipes		✓	
Features on Universal Family Concerns	✓		
Features on How Products Are Made		✓	
Health, Hygiene, and Physical Fitness News	✓		
Features on Money-Saving Ideas	✓		
Human Interest Stories with a Relevant Message		✓	
Products and Trends from Foreign Lands			✓
New Self-Education Materials	?? Don't understand		

Other subjects of particular interest to you and your audience: *Behind-the-scenes stories about books, movies, and theatrical productions. Women's rights issues, pro and con. Divorce and single parenting help. Feel free to call if you have good "special" material on these topics.*

13-3. *This editorial survey was prepared for several reasons: to acquire specific information about individual editor's interests and preferences, to get an overall feeling about the needs of family/style editors around the country, to establish recognition of the PR/publicist's name with the press, and to impress clients and management with the PR/publicist's professionalism and the number of contacts that have been made.*

VISUAL MATERIAL PREFERENCES	YES	NO
Can you use photographs?	✓	
Can you use line drawings?	✓	
Can you use charts and diagrams?	✓	
(For TV) Can you use slides?	—	
(For TV) Can you use movies?	—	
Can you credit sources who supply such materials?	✓	
Can you credit retailers who carry products featured?	✓	
Can you use color materials?		✓

Do you travel to trade shows, market weeks? _yes_
How many times a year? _2_
List markets covered in person. _New York, Dallas_
Can you use in-depth market information features? _no_
List products of special interest to you. _____

If materials are of high quality, do you run them without rewriting or editing? _It's rare that I don't change something_
Are you especially interested in materials that don't necessitate a great deal of your time in rewriting? _yes_
Do you prefer to gather information from many sources and create your own store? _Depends on subject and time_
(For TV and Radio) Can you use scripts? —
Preferred Length:

Janet Zipulki   _Style Editor_   _Ellenville Examiner_
Your Name   Title   _Ellenville, Tenn._
                                                  Publication

Please send us a tear sheet when you use any of the enclosed materials. Thank you for your cooperation.

14
The PR/Publicity Picture Today

The need for PR/publicity was never more pronounced than today. Society is undergoing vast changes in population density and mobility, family structure, ethnic configurations. Not a day goes by that some statute is not enacted, some decision made by either a governmental agency, private enterprise, or concerned group of citizens that requires communication and clarification. An expanding society requiring more and more interaction among its components—government, business, schools and colleges, labor organizations, special interest groups, and so on—mirrors a continuing need for those communication skills embodied in PR/publicity.

That the growing importance of PR/publicity is recognized is apparent in the steady growth of the number of programs in use in industries, institutions, social agencies, government bureaus; the number of books and articles written about the subject; the increase in the number of college curricula where PR/publicity is either a major course of study or an elective to be taken with liberal arts sequences; and the number of applicants for positions in the field.

The Revolution in Communications

Consistent with the growing importance of PR/publicity and adding to its dimension is the coming revolution in communications—a movement of such magnitude that it has been equated with the development of printing, the telephone, and the telegraph. Involved are such electronic developments as electronic mail, word processing, videotex, interactive cable television, computer-generated graphics, and other new technologies—all tools on which practitioners, alert to the challenge and potential, can capitalize in order to dispense knowledge and information.

Electronic Mail. Mail will be one of the first areas affected by the electronic revolution. It is estimated that by 1985, 11 billion messages will be sent electronically from one video display terminal to another as compared with about 3 billion in 1983. While its use as a means of distributing press releases and other PR/publicity mailings is restricted because of the expense involved, its future looks good. Currently, the primary application of electronic mail is for communication between governmental and commercial institutions, but home mail-delivery service is in the wings, awaiting the introduction of low-cost receiving terminals.

The Word Processor. Central to many of the electronic technologies available to the practitioner is the word processor, an instrument of infinite potential. In addition to automatically producing form and standard letters from a memory bank, it can edit by shifting paragraphs and making corrections of all types. The word processor also has many transmitting and receiving capabilities. When connected with the proper equipment by telephone line, it can "talk" to another word processor, gather information from a computer stored in some far off data bank, and send press information directly to newspapers.

Developments in Television. The expanded use of cable television and the movement to increase the average home TV set's capacity from twelve channels on upward will, no doubt, increase the opportunity for practitioners to provide information more carefully targeted to specific audiences. This new means of communication, called "narrow casting," as opposed to "broadcasting," will permit cable network channels to be geared to isolated and specific publics, such as people over fifty, religious groups, ethnic groups, hobbyists, and so on.

Another development in broadcasting is a television service delivered directly to homes via satellites circling Earth. Competitive with network broadcasting, this new system, referred to as DBS (Direct Broadcasting Service), will enable viewers to receive programs from small roof-top dish antennae and watch them over ordinary television sets.

Teletext. Teletext is a system in which graphic and printed material, imbedded inside the standard TV signal, is decoded and received on a home television screen. Teletext has the potential of developing into a regularly published electronic newspaper, a condition that can have great implications for the PR/publicist. The failure of some outstanding newspapers could well be an indication, according to some observers, that the conventionally printed word cannot be entirely relied on to disseminate entertainment and information in the future.

Videotex. Videotex is, in many ways, similar to teletext, except that it is a two-way form of communication in which information is sent via telephone or cable hook-up from the originating source to a home television screen. Utilized at the present time as a means of offering consumers the chance to purchase products immediately by signalling on a knee pad (a hand-held control), videotex has the potential of developing into a valuable means of story placement via personality interviews, product promotion, and direct response.

On balance, what do these new developments in electronic technology mean for the PR/publicist? On one level, it brings closer to reality the concept of a home video center where members of the family, in the privacy of their own home, will be able to receive all sorts of information, tailored to specific tastes, and to react instantly in terms of issues ("What do you think of the President's policy on Social Security benefits?"), and products and services ("I would like to buy that new swimsuit shown in the current issue of *Glamour* and on sale at Macy's").

On another level, it evokes images of a PR/publicity writer working at home on a story featuring the sources of a new fabric design to be brought to market by her client. Momentarily stumped, she activates her word processor; checks in with the data bank at some well-known university library; gets the necessary information; writes the piece, changing paragraphs, punctuation, and words as often as necessary; ends up with a perfectly typed version; presses a control and gets multiple copies of the article to send to a list of weekly newspapers; presses another button and interfaces with the computers in a series of major newspapers throughout the country; and sends off the article. The revolution in communications has arrived.

Getting a Job in PR/Publicity

The field of PR/publicity is attracting more and more people because of the diversity of tasks it offers and the growing demand for the services it provides. Fresh from college, they write letters and knock on doors seeking PR/publicity positions in commercial and industrial organizations, labor unions, schools and colleges, government units, and volunteer agencies—either "in house" or with an independent PR/publicity agency. The competition for such jobs is keen at all levels, but particularly at the entry-level notch.

The activities of PR/publicity personnel, whether they are part of the corporate structure (in-house) or part of an independent agency, vary in accordance with the client or organization they serve and the programs they must generate. A producer of textiles may need to run a fashion show to focus the attention of retailers, designers, and dress manufacturers on a new fabric brought to market. A hospital anxious to raise money for a new maternity wing might need to sponsor a week-long festival climaxed by a gala dinner-dance. A governmental agency, promulgating a new regulation, might require a press conference to explain the law's intricacies to the press.

THE JOB LADDER

Because the work of PR/publicity organizations varies so much, job titles can be misleading. Most entry-level positions carry a designation such as "assistant."

At a PR/publicity agency, an assistant could be an assistant account executive. In such a position, depending on the size of the agency, that individual will assist in the preparation of news releases, writing of magazine articles, preparation of materials for radio and television, helping to set up press conferences and press parties. In short, the assistant would assist in everything.

Assistants in PR/publicity agencies may work their way up to an account executive, who may handle one or two accounts; then to a vice president, who would supervise a number of account executives and their accounts; then up the bureaucratic ladder to senior vice president, executive vice president, and so on. In an in-house situation, the ladder is usually from assistant to regular staff member to senior staff member, then public relations director, an elevation that is often rewarded with the title of vice president.

In each of the steps upward the emphasis is more and more on the planning of programs, the consideration of objectives and goals, budgeting, and the analysis and evaluation of program results. In large organizations, there is usually a greater emphasis on specialists, with each specialist engaged in a particular type of activity: audiovisual production, art layout, in-house television production, speech writing, fund raising, market research, and so on. In smaller organizations, as much of this as possible is done by the staff. The remainder is handled by freelancers or consultants.

EDUCATIONAL REQUIREMENTS

While there are exceptions to the rule, most entry-level positions in PR/publicity call for a college degree from either a two-year or a four-year institution; the latter is preferable. Because of the diversity of tasks a PR/publicist is called on to do, entrants into the field should have a broad educational background and a multiplicity of skills or the potential for mastering them. The educational background should include courses in the social sciences—sociology, history, psychology, political science, history. Also of importance are speech, journalism, public relations and publicity, and business administration. The latter should include finance, accounting, and marketing.

If students have some idea of what field of PR/publicity they would like to enter, they might take courses relating to that specialty. If a student is aiming for a career in financial PR/publicity, for example, he or she would do well to study economics and money management. If one's goal is health agency work, the study of hospital management would be recommended.

EXPERIENCE

One of the difficulties encountered in getting a job in PR/publicity is that most employers ask for an indication of experience. While some students will have had the opportunity to work on a part-time basis in some communications organization during their undergraduate days, most will not. As a substitute, most employers will accept a summer internship working for a radio or television station, a PR/publicity agency, or a newspaper as a substitute. Also they will accept extra-curricular participation, such as working on the college newspaper or radio station, as a sort of on-the-job training. Other activities that find favor with prospective employers is working in a store as a salesperson, working in some capacity as a fund-raiser, or participating in student government affairs.

Attitudes and Skills

An extensive study of personnel in the PR/publicity field, including account assistants, account executives, corporate vice presidents, and vice chairmen of PR/publicity agencies was recently undertaken to determine what, in their estimation, were the skills and attitudes necessary for getting an entry-level job in the field. It was found that the successful candidate for an entry-level job should possess the following attitudes and skills:

- *A curious mind.* The need to answer the question "Why?" is perhaps more important in the PR/publicity field than in any other.
- *An acceptance of nonrecognition.* The PR/publicist works hard, often under great pressure, without worrying about personal public recognition (the by-line of the story).
- *The ability to get along with one's client.* This is important, but it does not necessarily mean making a "buddy" of the client.
- *The recognition of two bosses.* The PR/publicist must recognize that in dealing with media he or she has two bosses—the editor of the magazine or newspaper or the station manager where the practitioner is trying to place a story and the organization or client who pays the salary. To satisfy them both, the PR/publicist has to be a diplomat.
- *Self-confidence.* The successful PR/publicist exudes self-confidence and enthusiasm and tries to instill it in others.
- *An ability for detail.* The success of many a program and project depends on the completion of many details. The practitioner must develop an attitude that nourishes follow-through and attention to detail.
- *An ability to write.* The practitioner must be able to write so that the reader will understand the message as intended.
- *A knowledge of business.* A knowledge and understanding of how business operates so that the practitioner can participate in a financial decision that the client must take.
- *Creative thinking.* A thinker who can examine many sides of a situation, a

creative problem-solver who sees the different alternatives involved and brings previous knowledge to bear to solve the problem.
- *The ability to speak.* The ability to speak face-to-face or over the telephone, in public or in private, and get the message across as intended.
- *The ability to listen.* The skill to listen intently, no matter how long and involved the message, and be able to understand and synthesize it.

Observations by an Assistant Account Executive

As valuable as it is to have someone describe a field and the entry-level career opportunities in a broad and general sense, it is equally helpful to have some first-hand information from a person who has just entered the PR/publicity field. Following are some thoughts on establishing oneself in the field from a young woman with an entry-level job that involves traveling for business in the home furnishings industry:

Pay. The pay is not terrific, but generally better than at an editorial magazine job. Also, consider benefits, such as travel, paid meals, and so on.

Dress. You will hardly be able to dress the way you are supposed to, on your salary. A couple of suits, nothing too sexy, "comfy" shoes, and make sure they all *travel well.*

Personality. Welcome to the world of being the friendliest person on earth—no matter what. Always smile, introduce yourself to everyone, be ready with ample chit-chat. (Try keeping up with a weekly news magazine; it will give you something to talk about.)

Industry "Savvy." A lot of talk will be going on about the industry you have just entered—you may be a whiz about PR, but know nothing about the furniture industry, automotives, and so on. Always look attentive, do not yawn, and after a couple of markets, you will catch on.

Entertaining. Taking people out to breakfast/lunch/dinner. Make a reservation and be punctual, if not early. Have plenty of money or credit cards. You may want to frequent one certain restaurant where they will get to know you, know that you bring your important clients there, and so on. On the sensitive matter of taking out persons of the opposite sex, lunches and breakfasts are safer. Always call to make a reservation, and explain to the maître 'd that you, Ms. X, are taking an important client, Mr. Y, out to dinner, lunch, or whatever. Remember that he is just as likely to feel the slightest bit awkward about this, too. When you see the waiter coming over with the check, flag him down in a lady-like manner. If the waiter neglects to hand you the check, pick it up before your client does. Remember, you're *not* on a date. Concerning certain chivalrous activities, e.g., opening doors, helping with one's coat, and so on—you cannot ignore biological differences, but hopefully, all rules of courtesy will apply, and such chivalry should not be one-sided.

Social Life. You are supposed to be the friendliest person on earth. However, your good nature is not to be taken advantage of. Mention any "abuses" to your boss, when you are sure that is what they are. Do not give anyone the "wrong idea." Keep business and pleasure separate—no matter how pleasurable your business is. Especially, do not give away company secrets to clients, editors, or journalists with whom you are friendly. This could mean trouble.

"Dirty" Work. Menial tasks have to be done by the "low man/woman on the totem pole." Grin and bare it—in time, you will have an assistant of your very own to bully around.

Competition. Your co-workers may begin to resent you—especially if you do especially well. You may be the new kid, younger, and so on. Hang in there, be "chummy" but do not give them any ammunition, and just remember, someone has got to take over the company in ten years.

Another Professional View

By means of comparison, Kathy M. Hyett of the Public Relations Society of America has this advice to offer students thinking of entering the field:

On Job Satisfaction. It's not an easy job, but then this is not an easy profession. If you want to go into public relations because you like to work with people, sell Tupperware. If you want glamour and intrigue, try espionage. If you believe that the power of communication can solve the difficult social, political, and economic problems facing the world, then, by all means, choose public relations.

How Much Will You Make? Not as much, say, as a brain surgeon, or president of IBM, maybe, but enough to live a comfortable life.

Find a Mentor. Mentors are extremely important to your professional growth. They see you through the peaks and valleys. They help fill in the gaps your education may not have provided. They help you evaluate your strengths and advise how to overcome your weaknesses. A few years ago, I was asked by the U.S. Department of Energy to arrange a press conference for our annual meeting. I had never done a press conference before (of course, I didn't let anyone know this). I called my mentor and within an hour, I had a complete set of guidelines for running a press conference. It went beautifully.

Join a Professional Organization. Never underestimate the advantages of networking. Besides contacts, they provide a national reservoir of people, talents, and skills that can prove instrumental in helping you advance in your career.

Take Chances. No educational program prepares you for this. It's one thing to make a classroom decision that might affect your grade. It's another to make one that will affect hundreds of people and even your job. Risk-taking is essential in any business. Learn how to do it prudently—through analysis of the situation. And in the end, trust your gut reaction.

Maintain High Visibility. Volunteer for the tough jobs—the ones that no one else wants. Volunteer to serve on committees. Contribute ideas and help do the work. I don't know of anyone who has made it in this profession by working 9-to-5 days alone.

Do All That Is Required to Get the Job Done. I have stuffed registration kits until midnight, fixed Xerox machines, run postage meters, typed manuals, and collated information packets. I'm not saying I enjoyed doing it, but every professional I know will agree that there are times when you pitch in and get the job done any way possible.

Know Where Your Career Stands in Your Life's Goals and Priorities. If it's number one, fine. If it falls somewhere in between a family and a social life, that's fine, too, but be aware of the tradeoffs for any situation.

Conform to the Workplace's Culture. Learn the politics—and fast. It's not the most pleasant part of any work situation, but it is critical to survival. Know who the *real* players are and become a part of their team.

Ethics and the PR/Publicity Process

Much has been made of ethics as they pertain to PR/publicity. Concern springs from the fact that the PR/publicity process is difficult to understand, particularly for students. One reason is that it goes under different names: publicity, public relations, public information, corporate communications, public affairs, consumer service, customer relations, issues management. Another reason is that in addition to the diversity of names, the process provides so wide a diversity of services that, in totality, it represents the communications spectrum.

A relatively young craft, it has been dogged by suspicion and disbelief. Many misconceptions have sprung up about it. Its practitioners have, at various times, been called hustlers, cocktail party con artists, hacks, flacks, image merchants, syrup dispensers.

While some of these names may have been deserved because of the antics of a few of its members—every field has its charlatans, the ambulance-chasing lawyers, the bogus doctors, the dishonest politicians—the fact remains that the PR/publicist, acting as a communicator and an interpreter of communications performs a very vital function.

The ultimate goal of PR/publicity is the dissemination of information to influence public opinion, a practice of persuasion which is part and parcel of the democratic process. The question of ethics, however, arises in the nature of the information that one is called on to disseminate.

To make an honest and fair attempt to persuade people to a point of view or to a decision by reason or emotion and then to abide by the resultant consensus is very much in keeping with the American tradition. But what constitutes honesty and fair dealing? How wrong is it to put one's best foot forward? Take the well-known example of pouring water into a glass until it is midway between the top and the bottom. Is the glass half empty? Is it ethical to call it half-filled?

Ethical issues are involved in every area of corporate and professional activity. They are not necessarily restricted to the practice of PR/publicity. The doctor, the lawyer, all face ethical problems—instances where their personal concepts of what is right and what is wrong run into conflict with the very practical aspects of making a living. How they solve those problems depends on their own moral concepts and the code of ethics and licensing body of the profession to which they belong.

It may be a little harder for the PR/publicist, who has no official code for guidance and no prescribed licensing machinery to judge the moral pros and cons of a situation. Granted, it is wrong to distort the truth, to send out a release saying that a new product is meeting with a great deal of success at the retail level when in reality it has not had rapid acceptance. But how about saying that it is "moderately successful?" That does not make news. At what point does one draw the line between deceit and salesmanship?

This is particularly the situation when dealing with a profit-motivated organization, where hard-headed businesspeople look for results in terms of dollars and cents. This is not to say that such management deliberately sets out to muddy the waters, or agrees to offer scholarships, fund an art program, establish a library purely to improve their corporate image. Quite possibly, many large corporations in this day and age have a strong sense of social responsibility. But too many have not; too many are inclined to travel the path of expediency when confronted with a problem of ethics. And it is here that the practitioner can do the most good. He or she can ask, if we do such and such, how will it look? What will be the public's reaction?

Most PR/publicists serve their clients or organizations as an advocate—just as a lawyer is an advocate of his or her client to represent a certain position, to achieve a certain goal. But the lawyer's conscience must square with the case he or she has to prepare. So it is with PR/publicity practitioners, whose ethics must coincide with that of the client or organization represented. If the practitioners find that the activities in which they must engage are contrary to their personal code, then they have no alternative but to resign the account or, if in a corporate situation, to quit the job.

Admittedly, these are hard decisions to make. But if the practice of PR/publicity is ever to achieve the true professional status it seeks, its practitioners must adhere to a code of conduct. Social responsibility, in the largest sense, is a basic cornerstone on which much of the field's concepts rest.

One of the most important forces for the establishment of ethical conduct and increased professional recognition is the Public Relations Society of America (PRSA), the largest of the several groups of practitioners in the country. The Society has promulgated a code of professional standards and tries to enforce its precepts on its membership. It also has an accreditation program for members, which involves written and oral exams, the satisfactory completion of which gives them a "degree status" (ARPS) as an indication that they have met professional standards.

THE LICENSING OF PR/PUBLICISTS

For a number of years, the licensing of PR/publicity personnel has been a matter of much discussion among practitioners. Its advocates claim that such licensing is necessary before PR/publicity can gain the offical status of a profession, recognized by either state and/or federal government.

Others feel that because of the problems involved in defining PR/publicity it would be difficult to create a viable set of statutes required for licensing. Further, they argue that it would probably be in violation of the First Amendment to the Constitution. An alternate proposal for an independent body consisting of practitioners and representatives of the public has been proposed. So far, no concrete action in either direction has been taken.

In PR/publicity, as in any other field, it is primarily its members who set the standards of work and morality. As the field continues to grow, it will be the professionalism of the practitioners themselves that will build the ethical standards and maintain them at the highest possible level.

Glossary

A

Account Executive: In a PR/publicity agency, a person in charge of the PR/publicity activities for one or more clients. In an advertising agency, a person who is a liaison between one or more clients and the agency.

Activity Reporting: Enumerating PR/publicity results without evaluating their effectiveness, i.e., listing the number of articles secured without regard to number of people reached, etc.

Ad: See *Advertisement*.

Advertisement: A paid, nonpersonal message by an identified sponsor used to influence and/or promote sales, services, and the acceptance of ideas.

Advertising Agency: A company that provides advertising, promotion, and marketing services to its clients. Some agencies provide PR/publicity services as well.

AM Radio: A form of broadcast in which the electromagnetic waves vary in amplitude. AM signals travel much further at night than during the day. Compare with *FM Radio*.

Angle: The distinctive interest element that makes a news or feature story worthy of public notice. Also called *peg* or *slant*.

Annual Report: A yearly financial statement required by the Securities and Exchange Commission. Such reports often appear as glossy, magazine-size pamphlets and include management profiles, and product pictures along with financial data, and are used to promote the company to stockholders and media.

AP: Associated Press—a news-gathering organization.

Audio: Sound or pertaining to sound as compared with video or sight.

Audiovisuals: Materials that present information in visual and audible forms, i.e., narrated slide presentations, videotapes, films.

B

Beauty Photograph: A close-up shot of a model usually in connection with featuring a cosmetic product.

Bio: In PR/publicity, a written statement about an individual's career, education, and accomplishments.

Blowup: An enlargement of a photograph or illustration.

Booking: An appointment made with a model for either a photographic or art session. Also called a *sitting*.

Books: Trade or professional slang for magazines.

Border: The thin, white, unprinted strip around a photograph.

Brainstorming: A conference technique in which one of the members of the group presents the other participants with a problem which is then explored through unrestrained discussion.

Broadcast: Transmission of a radio or television signal. Also, pertaining to radio or television media.

Broadside: A promotional message printed or drawn on one side of a large piece of paper.

Brochure: A small pamphlet or booklet, usually printed.

Budget: A sum of money allocated for a PR/publicity program.

B & W: Black and white (as compared with color) photograph or illustration in which the total gradations range from black to gray to white.

By-line: Names of writers or reporters appearing directly above their printed stories.

C

Cable Television: A method of sending out televised messages to homes by specially installed cables.

Campaign: A collection of ads or commercials with a common theme.

Caps: In typography, capital letters or upper case letters as opposed to smaller or lower case letters.

Caption: A written description accompanying a photograph or illustration. Frequently referred to as *cutline*.

Center Spread: Two facing pages where the printed matter can extend over the center fold or binding. Also called *double truck*.

CEO: Chief Executive Officer—the senior executive of a company with final responsibility for its operations, profits, and losses.

Circulation: The number of copies of a specific publication distributed within a given area.

Clean Copy: Copy needing little or no revision.

Client: The individual or company engaging the services of a PR/publicity or advertising agency.

Clipping Service: A company that supplies PR/publicists and their clients with clippings of articles or photographs placed in media outlets.

Column: A department of a publication that is regularly published. Also, a vertical row of type.

Computer-Generated Graphics: Various shapes and forms, in color or black and white, created by an artist using a computer.

Consultant: See *Free-lance*.

Consumer: Someone who is the ultimate buyer or user of a product or service.

Contact List: Names of persons at media with whom one can establish a working PR/publicity relationship.

Contact Sheet: A group of small size, black-and-white pictures obtained by direct printing of strips of film negatives on a piece of photographic paper.

Contact Techniques: The various written and spoken means by which a PR/publicity practitioner communicates news or feature information to a medium.

Contrast: In photography, the degree of difference between the highlights and shadows in a film negative or photographic print.

Cooperative Events: A planned occurrence in which more than one organization is featured and shares expenses as well as credit. See *Event*.

Copy: Any written, typed, or printed material used as text.

Corporate Image: The impression of a company held in common by one or more of its publics.

Cover: The front page or binding of written material. Also, to attend an activity with the intent of reporting it.

Creativity: The ability to recognize relationships and make connections between seemingly unrelated concepts, resulting in original thought.

Credit Line: A line of type accompanying a picture or story, giving its source.

Cropping: Changing the size or proportions of a photograph or illustration.

Cutline: See *Caption*.

Cuts: News and features materials in audio form provided to radio stations by the wire services.

D

Day Book: A listing of newsworthy events compiled by the wire services and transmitted by teletype to the various media.

Day Side: Newspaper personnel, i.e., reporters, photographers, etc., who work during the day.

Deadline: The time when all materials (ads, copy, visuals) must be at a medium if they are to appear in the next edition or issue. Also, the time when a newspaper or magazine goes to press.

Derus Media Service: Media service that supplies newspapers with feature stories and "fillers" in ready-to-print form or mats.

Direct Broadcasting Service: A television service delivered directly to homes via satellites circling the Earth. Viewers receive programs via dish antennae.

Double Spread: In a newspaper or magazine, two facing pages.

Double Truck: See *Center Spread*.

E

Editing: The process of making written or visual material suitable for publication or presentation.

Edition: Newspapers or magazines printed during a single press run.

Editorial Credit: Where merchandise featured in a release and mentioned in a published story can be found at the retail level. Sometimes known as a *store credit*. The name of the manufacturer is also included.

Editorial Survey: A gathering of media editors' opinions as to the newsworthiness of materials sent out by a specific PR/publicity practitioner.

Editor-in-Chief: The creative head of a publication who has managerial responsibility for its contents.

Electronic Mail: The transmission of nonvoice communication from one location to another via video display terminals.

Employee Public: The group of individuals working for a particular organization.

Equal Time Rule: Federal regulation requiring broadcasters to provide air time to all serious candidates in a political campaign.

Evaluation: The process by which PR/publicity events and programs are examined and judged as to their worth.

Evaluation Criteria: The benchmarks used to judge the worth of a PR/publicity event or program.

Event: A planned occurrence, specialized activity, or "happening" usually characterized by publicity. Also called *special event*.

Exclusive: A notation at the top of a publicity release sent to a newspaper indicating that the recipient is the only newspaper in the area or city that has received such information.

External Audit: An examination of a PR/publicity program by someone outside the originating sources, e.g., a consultant.

External Media: Those forms of communication that circulate outside of their originating source, e.g., a newspaper leaves its plant and is circulated throughout the city.

F

Fact Sheet: PR/publicity material used to present essential facts about a subject, most often in a non-narrative, outline form.

Fairness Doctrine: Federal regulation requiring broadcasters to provide air time for opposing viewpoints on public issues.

Fashion: A prevailing custom or style, most often associated with dress.

Feature Release: A story submitted to a media outlet highlighting a person, place, or thing in a manner that emphasizes human interest. Usually lacks the urgency of a news release.

Feature Syndicate: Organization that specializes in servicing newspapers with stories that emphasize the "human" side of the news.

Film Strip: See *Slide Film*.

FM Radio: FM or frequency modulated radio, more static free and better tonal quality than AM radio. However, the signal does not travel as far. Compare with *AM Radio*.

Format: Size, shape, and general makeup of a medium.

Free Association: Unrestrained thought.

Free-lance: An independent professional who takes individual assignments from different sources, e.g., media, companies, PR/publicists, but is not in their employ. Sometimes called a *consultant*.

G

Gaffer Tape: Heavy duty, pressure-sensitive, silver, cloth adhesive tape used in photographic and art studios.

Galley Proof: Typed material that has been set and reproduced in sheet form for reading and correcting before pages are made up.

Glossy: Photograph with a shiny surface or finish necessary for newspaper reproduction.

Goal: The desired end result of a PR/publicity campaign which is attained by accomplishing a series of objectives.

Grainy: A property of a photograph characterized by a granular appearance.

H

Halftone: Photoengraving plate photographed through a glass screen in the camera which breaks up the reproduction of the plate into dots or screen. This makes possible the printing of shaded values as in a photograph or wash illustration.

Happening: See *Event*.

Headline: Copy line above a news or feature release which summarizes or introduces the story.

Head Shot: Photograph of a person from the shoulders up. Often sent out with a bio.

House Organ: Publication, usually in magazine format, in use in large companies to foster communication between management and employees.

I

Idea Event: A planned occurrence developed to influence the way people think about a subject, e.g., open houses at plants, hospitals, schools.

Illustration: Visual material, usually artwork, often distributed with a publicity release to media.

Image: The overall image that a person, place, or thing projects. Also see *Corporate Image*.

Independents: Stations that are not affiliated with a television or radio network.

Instant Replay Video: Home equipment used to record television programs for later viewing.

Institutional Advertising: Advertising aimed at image-building.

Institutional Event: Planned occurrences designed to enhance an image over the long term; usually does not feature merchandise or services in a direct way.

Internal Media: Forms of communication whose circulation is restricted to their originating source, e.g., a college newspaper circulated on campus.

Internal Public: See *Employee Public*.

Interpersonal Communication: Communication between two or more people in which they exchange words and gestures.

Interviewer—Interviewee: The two roles in the interview process. The interviewer asks questions; the interviewee responds.

Intrapersonal Communication: Problem-solving in which people rely on their own reasoning and do not communicate with others.

Intuitive Reasoning: A quick insight which results without any formal reasoning process.

J

Journalistic Style: Manner of writing used by newspaper reporters, characterized by a lead, short paragraphs, and relative objectivity.

Junket: A trip for the press sponsored by a special interest group in the hope of getting favorable publicity.

K

Kill: To delete part or all of written copy.

Kinescope: A recording on film made of a live or videotape television performance, electronically reproduced from the kinescope tube. Often used to document PR/publicity results. Sometimes referred to as *kinney*.

Kinney: See *Kinescope*.

L

Lead: The beginning paragraph of a PR/publicity release.

Leaflet: A printed handbill, usually folded, and containing four sides.

Licensing: Practice of giving permission to an individual or organization to reproduce or utilize a name or trademark, usually for a monetary consideration.

Line Cut: A letterpress printing plate made from a line drawing by a photoengraving process.

Line Drawing: An illustration made with pen, pencil, brush, or crayon. Impression of shading is obtained through varying the width of single lines or crosshatching them.

Listening: As applied to the PR/publicity practitioner, the ability to concentrate and understand what is being said.

Lobby: A group of private persons engaged in influencing legislation.

Location: A site appropriate for PR/publicity pictures.

Logo: See *Logotype*.

Logotype: Name, symbol, or trademark of a company or product combined in a single lettering or design. Usually referred to as *logo*.

M

Mailing Service: An organization used by PR/publicists to distribute their materials to media outlets. Some services will also reproduce and assemble materials in addition to distributing them.

Management: Those persons who have responsibility for determining organizational policy and planning and/or directing operations.

Marketing: The sum total of all activities connected with bringing a product or service to the ultimate consumer. This includes research, development, production, distribution, and promotional activities.

Mass Media: Although the broad definition includes books, motion pictures, and advertising, PR/publicists are most concerned with four mass media: newspapers, magazines, radio, and television, which lend themselves most readily to PR/publicity placement.

Masthead: In magazines and newspapers, the listing of the publication's name, executive staff, and their responsibilities. Usually runs each issue in a boxed format.

Mat: Papier-mâché mold of a typeset story which, when cast into metal, can be reproduced by letterpress printing.

Mat Finish: A dull surface on a photograph. Some magazines prefer mat finish photographs for reproduction.

Mat Service: An organization that takes PR/publicity material, sets it in type, and offers it to interested newspapers in a ready-to-print, cardboard mat form, free of charge. Cost is borne by participating PR/publicist.

Media: Means through which PR/publicity messages are transmitted, i.e., newspapers, magazines, radio, television, posters, speeches, house organs, etc. See *Mass Media*.

Medium: One of the media. Singular form of the word *media*.

Merchandise Event: Specialized activity created specifically to promote and sell more of a product. See *Event*.

Merchandising: Presenting a product, service, or idea so as to make it attractive, more accessible, and/or more desirable. The term is often used in the sense of "selling."

Model: A person serving as a subject for a photographer or artist. May be also employed in fashion shows and other activities.

Model Release: An authorization by a person who has posed for a photograph or drawing, allowing commercial or editorial use of that likeness.

N

Network: A chain of radio or television stations interconnected for simultaneous broadcast of the same programs.

News: A person, event, or situation considered a choice subject for journalistic treatment. Anything that "disturbs" the status quo.

News Angle: The aspect of a story that is emphasized in its writing and which makes it pertinent to a specific public. Also referred to as *peg* or *slant*.

News Bureaus: Offices of news services such as AP and UPI, situated in important population centers.

News-Feature Release: A written story usually based on an item of current news and distributed to media. The treatment of news in a news-feature release is more detailed and elaborate than in a regular news release.

Newsletter: A written report that usually provides forecasts, analyses, or other information to special publics.

News Release: A story submitted to a media outlet, based on an easily identifiable and urgent news angle. It may also be used to identify all types of press releases. See *Press Release*.

Nonprofit: An area of PR/publicity activity concerned with such social institutions as charities, hospitals, schools.

O

Objective: Things that must be done to reach established goals in a PR/publicity program.

Off the Record: Information given to the press in an interview, but not to be made available to the public.

Order of Diminishing Importance: The manner in which a news release is written with a summary of the most important facts in the lead and the subsequent paragraphs dealing with information of lessening importance.

Outlet: A media source, i.e., newspapers, magazines, radio, television, etc.

P

Package Producer: A producer, not on the staff of a radio or television network or station, who puts together a program in the hope of selling it to the broadcast media.

Peg: See *News Angle*.

Personality Event: A "happening" that builds recognition and enhances the reputation of an individual or group.

Plan: See *Program*.

Post-Testing: A means of examining the results of PR/publicity activity after the program has been completed.

PR: Abbreviation for *public relations*.

PR Aids: A service employed by PR/publicity practitioners to assemble, collate, and mail PR/publicity materials.

Press: Reporters and editors of print and broadcast media.

Press Conference: A meeting called to simultaneously inform the various members of the press about an event or news subject. Format permits questioning by the press of the company or individual calling the meeting.

Press Kit: Usually a file-sized folder with pockets inside the cover to hold press releases, fact sheets, and photographs. Given or mailed to media.

Press Party: An informal meeting called to present an item of news to the press.

Press Release: A written story, usually following a standardized format, prepared for issuance to the print and broadcast media.

Press Room: An area given over for use by members of the press. Contains tables, chairs, typewriters, telephones, and other facilities.

Press Table: A table at a luncheon, dinner, or banquet, usually near the speaker's table, reserved for members of the press.

Pretesting: A means of determining the attitudes and opinions of a specific public to provide a benchmark or measurement for further testing.

Print Documentation: Proof, usually in the form of a clipping, that a PR/publicity story has appeared in a newspaper or magazine.

PUBLIC RELATIONS/PUBLICITY

Program: A procedure or *plan* for solving a PR/publicity problem.

Promotion: A planned occurrence or event to bring public attention to a specific product or idea.

Proposal: A plan written by PR/publicists to sell their services and secure a new client, or to sell a new campaign to the management of a company for which they are already working.

PR/Publicity: The technique employed to make news for an individual or organization.

PRSA: Public Relations Society of America, an organization of PR/publicity practitioners who have established a code of professional standards for its members and conducts an accreditation program.

Public: Any group of people that a PR/publicity program is intended to influence, i.e., stockholders, teachers, retailers, teenagers, etc. Also referred to as *target audience* or *target market*.

Publicity: An organized effort to make known some person, product, place, or idea, either by word-of-mouth or by being featured in media.

Public Relations: The total image projected by an organization or individual. Advertising, packaging, customer relations, and all corporate policies are parts of public relations.

Public Relations Society of America: See *PRSA*.

Publisher: A person or organization engaged in the publishing of printed material. Also, the head of a publication who is responsible for its overall profit and loss.

Puff: An approving or flattering mention in a media outlet without regard to its relative news value.

"Put to Bed": The "closing" of an issue of a magazine or an edition of a newspaper after which no additional material may be inserted.

Q

Quarterly Report: Statement of a company's sales and earnings for three months, issued for the first, second, and third quarters of the year.

Query Letter: A letter containing a story idea and submitted to an editor in the hope of stirring interest.

R

Reach: The number of people who read, watch, or listen to a newspaper, magazine, television, or radio program.

Regional Edition: An issue of a newspaper or magazine in which the news is either partially or wholly concerned with a specified geographical area.

Release: To issue material and provide information to the press. Also, a PR/publicity story sent to media.

Release Date: The date on which information issued to the press is to be exposed to the public.

Reprint: A copy of a printed article often used to document PR/publicity results or as a sales promotion tool.

Retouch: To improve by artwork the quality of an illustration or photograph.

Rough: A preliminary sketch or layout.

S

Sales Promotion: A planned occurrence or event to bring attention to a specific product or idea so as to increase its sales. See *Promotion*.

Script: A text for a broadcast interview written by the PR/publicity practitioner as a guide to the interviewer. Also, a typeface that resembles handwriting.

Shots: Photographs.

Sitting: See *Booking*.

Situation Analysis: An examination of the background and current status of an organization conducted prior to presenting a PR/publicity program or proposal.

Slant: See *News Angle*.

Slide: Image on individual transparent film frame for projection onto a screen. Slides are often used as aids to an oral presentation. Usually in 35 mm. size. Also see *Transparency*.

Slide Film: A length of transparent film divided into separate image frames for projection onto a screen and often accompanied by voice explanation. Also called *film strip*.

Special: A notation at the top of a press release indicating that the information contained therein has been written specifically for the recipient.

Special Event: See *Event*.

Specialized Media: Media that are edited primarily for a specific public, such as a business, profession, trade, or occupation.

Sponsored Films and Tapes: Materials that a PR/publicist will provide to a TV or radio station for demonstration purposes or for use on interview and guest appearance shows.

Spot News: News that is unexpected and requires immediate dissemination.

Store Credit: See *Editorial Credit*.

Studio: The workroom or establishment of a photographer or artist.

Stylist: A consultant, usually free-lance, who advises and assists a photographer or artist in areas of dress, decorating, or beauty.

Syndicate: An organization which, either in conjunction with a newspaper or as an independent, buys and sells news stories, features, photos, and other materials for the use of media.

T

Take(s): A series of photographic shots taken under a particular set of circumstances, e.g., a specific kind of lighting, camera angle, etc. For PR/publicity purposes, the photographer usually shoots a number of takes.

Target Audience: See *Public*.

Target Market: See *Public*.

Tear Sheet: Page containing an article or advertisement torn from a newspaper, magazine, or other periodical after publication.

Teletext: A system in which graphic and written information is imbedded inside the standard TV signal, decoded, and received on a television screen. A separate decoder is required on the receiving end. Teletext, in comparison to Videotex, is a one way form of communication. Also see *Videotex*.

30: A mark used to designate the end of a story. The symbol ### is also used.

Timetable: A plan of PR/publicity activity laid out according to the times certain events are expected to take place.

Trade Publication: A type of business periodical concerned with marketing and merchandising functions in a specific industry.

Transparency: A framed film containing an image that can be projected onto a screen. Comes in a variety of sizes. Color transparencies are the best form in which to distribute color PR/publicity photographs to print or broadcast media. Also called a *slide* when in 35 mm. size.

Typeface: In type, the design and style of letters having a "family" relationship, such as Bodoni, Caslon, etc. Often named for the original designer.

Typo: A typographical error occurring through the use of a typewriter or typesetting mechanism.

U

UPI: United Press International—a news-gathering organization.

V

VCR: Video cassette recorder. An electronic recording device that records video, audio, and control signals on either ¾-inch or on ½-inch video cassette.

VDT: Video display terminal. A means of receiving or displaying information via a cathode ray tube (CRT). The VDT usually consists of a keyboard and a screen which can be linked to a computer network through a telephone line.

Verbal: Expressed or communicated in spoken words (as opposed to written).

Video Disc: Record-like circular plate used in instant replay video.

Videotex: A two-way form of communication in which graphic and written material is sent via telephone or cable TV hookup from an originating source to a television screen. This permits the user to receive and transmit information. Compare to *Teletext*.

VIP: "Very important person." In PR/publicity usage, someone associated with management or intimately associated with the client.

VTR: Videotape recorder. A reel-to-reel electronic recording device that records video, audio, and control signals on videotape.

W

Wash Illustration: Brushwork producing a softer picture, made with diluted India ink or color with a brush. Offers varying gray tones.

Word Analogies: List of words bearing a relationship to the main thought.

Selected Bibliography

Books

Bernays, Edward L. *The Engineering of Consent.* Norman: University of Oklahoma Press, 1956.

Blake, R. and E. Haroldson. *A Taxonomy of Concepts in Communication.* New York: Hastings House, 1975.

Bush, Chilton R. *Newswriting and Reporting Public Affairs.* Radnor, Pa.: Chilton Book Co., 1970.

Carlson, Robert O. *Communications and Public Opinion.* New York: Praeger Publishers, 1975.

Center, Allen. *Public Relations Practices: Case Studies.* Englewood Cliffs, N.J.: Prentice-Hall, 1975.

Crane, Edgar. *Marketing Communications: Decision Making as a Process of Interaction Between Buyer and Seller.* New York: John Wiley & Sons, 1972.

Darrow, Ralph J. *House Journal Editing.* Danville, Ill.: Interstate Printers, 1975.

Dichter, Ernest. *The Strategy of Desire.* New York: Doubleday, 1960.

DuBrin, Andrew. *The Practice of Managerial Psychology.* Elmsford, N.Y.: Pergamon Press, 1972.

Dyer, Frederick C. *Executive's Guide to Effective Speaking and Writing.* Englewood Cliffs, N.J.: Prentice-Hall, 1962.

Gibson, D. Parke. *$70 Billion in the Black: America's Black Consumers.* New York: Macmillan Publishing, 1978.

Gordon, George N. *Persuasion: The Theory and Practice of Manipulative Communication,* New York: Hastings House, 1971.

Hall, Mark W. *Broadcast Journalism: An Introduction to News Writing.* New York: Hastings House, 1978.

Hill and Knowlton, Inc. *Critical Issues in Public Relations.* Englewood Cliffs, N.J.: Prentice-Hall, 1975.

Hough, George A. *News Writing.* Boston: Houghton Mifflin, 1975.

Jones, Gerre. *How to Prepare Professional Design Brochures.* New York: McGraw-Hill, 1976.

Kahn, Gilbert R. *The Effects of Audiovisual Career Exploration to Develop Career Maturity in Publicity and Public Relations Students.* Philadelphia: Temple University, 1980. Unpublished doctoral dissertation.

Kanter, Rosabeth Moss. *Men and Women of the Corporation.* New York: Basic Books, 1977.

Kotler, P. *Marketing for Nonprofit Organizations.* Englewood Cliffs, N.J.: Prentice-Hall, 1975.

Lerbinger, Otto. *Designs for Persuasive Communications.* Englewood Cliffs, N.J.: Prentice-Hall, 1972.

Lesly, Philip. *Lesly's Public Relations Handbook.* Englewood Cliffs, N.J.: Prentice-Hall, 1978.

Little, Jeffrey B. and Lucien Rhodes. *Understanding Wall Street,* Cockeysville, Md.: Liberty Publishing Company, 1978.

Martin, Dick. *Executive's Guide to Handling a Press Interview.* New York: Pilot Books, 1977.

Robinson, Edward J. *Public Relations and Survey Research.* New York: Irvington Publishers, 1969.

Ross, Raymond S. *Persuasion: Communication and Interpersonal Relations.* Englewood Cliffs, N.J.: Prentice-Hall, 1974.

Sager, Arthur W. *Speak Your Way to Success.* New York: McGraw-Hill, 1968.

Spiro, Herbert T. *Finance for the Non-Financial Manager.* New York: John Wiley & Sons, 1977.

Stone, Christopher D. *Where the Law Ends: The Social Control of Corporate Behavior.* New York: Harper & Row, 1977.

Sullivan, Frank. *Crisis of Confidence: Utilities, Public Relations and Credibility.* Canaan, N.H.: Phoenix Publishing, 1977.

Vance, Charles. *Boss Psychology.* New York: McGraw-Hill, 1975.

Wales, Larue. *Newsletter Design and Layout.* Ames: Iowa State University Press, 1977.

Weiner, Richard. *Professional's Guide to Publicity.* New York: Richard Weiner, 1978.

Welsh, James J. *The Speech Writing Guide.* New York: John Wiley & Sons, 1968.

Wright, Charles R. *Mass Communication: A Sociological Perspective.* New York: Random House, 1975.

Periodicals/Journals

Public Relations Journal. Public Relations Society of America, 845 Third Avenue, New York, NY 10022. Monthly.

Public Relations Quarterly. 44 West Market St., Rhinebeck, NY 12572.

Public Relations Review. Communication Research Associates, Inc., Suite 101A, 7338 Baltimore Blvd., College Park, MD 20740. Quarterly.

Public Relations Directories

O'Dwyer's Directory of Corporate Communications. 271 Madison Ave., New York, NY 10016. Annual.

O'Dwyer's Directory of Public Relations Executives. 271 Madison Ave., New York, NY 10016. Annual.

O'Dwyer's Directory of Public Relations Firms. 271 Madison Ave., New York, NY 10016. Annual.

Professional's Guide to Public Relations Services. R. Weiner, Inc., 888 Seventh Ave., New York, NY 10019.

Public Relations Register. Public Relations Society of America, 845 Third Ave., New York, NY 10022. Annual PRSA membership directory.

Index

A

Account executives, 2, 4
Advertising
  compared to PR/publicity, 8-11
  institutional, 152
  PR/publicity departments, 4
Advertising Age, 37
Affiliates, television, 42
AFL-CIO News, 32
Agencies, PR/publicity, 2-4
Albers, Jeanne, 94
American Broadcasting Company (ABC), 42, 44-45
AM radio, 44
Annual meetings, 159
Annual reports, 152-59
  elements of, 155-57
  evaluation of, 158-59
  planning and producing, 154-55
  production guidelines, 157-58
AP Newsfeatures, 41
Appliance Manufacturing, 37
"Art" press kits, 107
Associated Press, 40, 42, 128
Associated Press News Photos, 41
Attribution, press release, 64
Audiovisuals, extending impact of, 176
Audit, 191-93

B

Beauty photographs, 85-88
Beekman, Lois, 6
Better Homes and Gardens, 34
Bios. *See* Profiles and bios
Black Radio Network, 45
Black Star, 41, 128
Books, for business organizations, 72-73

Brainstorming, 22
Briefs, 164
Broadcast documentation, 198
Broadcast media, 41-45
  radio, 43-45
  television, 42-43
Broadcast merchandising placements, 198-99
Broadcast techniques, 163-74
  interviews, 164-65
  press release, 164
  sponsored films and tapes, 172-73
  talk show placement, 168-69
  tapes and films, 173-74
  training for TV interview, 169-72
  visual materials, 168
  writing, 163-64
Budget planning, 184-85
Business publications, 37-39
Business Wire, 128

C

Cable television, 43, 174
Captions or cutlines, 99-102
  do's and don'ts, 102
Chalk boards, 175
Closed circuit television, 174
Columbia Broadcasting System (CBS), 42, 44-45
Columns, 39-40
Communication
  levels of, 21
  photograph, 77-78
  revolution in, 203-5
  spoken word, 104-5
  written word (with eye appeal), 105
Company culture, 150-52
Contact list, establishing, 120-21
Contact sheets, 81
Content analysis, 193

Corporate functions, 149-61
   annual meetings, 159
   annual reports, 152-59
   company culture, logos, and trademarks, 150-52
   institutional advertising, 152
   quarterly reports, 159
   speech writing, 160-61
Creativity, defined, 20
Creativity development, 20-29
   ABC Company (case study), 26-29
   brainstorming, 22
   levels of communication, 21
   research and listening importance, 25-26
   techniques for, 24
   what makes news, 21
Cropping, 92
Cuts, 41

D

Dates on releases, 51
Davis, Hal, 5
Day books, 41

E

Editorial replies, 74
Editorial surveys, 199
Ehrlich, Susan, 25-26
Electronic mail, 204
Employment, 4-5, 128-30, 205-8
   attitudes and skills, 207-8
   educational requirements, 206
   experience, 206-7
   job titles, 205-6
   observations and professional viewpoints, 208-10
Equipment, planning, 184-85
Ethics, 210-12
Evaluating PR/publicity results, 189-94
   measuring programs, 189-90
   personal and written contact, 193-94
   qualitative programs, 190-93
   story use, 190
Evaluation, annual report, 158-59
Events. *See* Special events
Executive and personality photos, 84
External audit, 191-93
External media, 31

F

Factory photos, 89
Fact sheets, 65-67
Fashion and beauty photographs, 85-88
Fashion PR/publicity, 10

Feature release, function of, 56-57
Feature syndicates, 41, 126-28
Films and video tapes, 175
Financial PR/publicity, 10
Flip charts, 175
FM radio, 44
Free-lance consultants, 2, 4

G

Globe Photos, 41, 128
Glossy photographs, 79
Good Housekeeping, 34
Guest editorials, 75

H

Hand delivery contact technique, 120
Harper's Bazaar, 34
Hotel & Travel Index, 37
House and Garden, 34
House organs, 39

I

Idea events, 134-35
Illustrations, using sketches and, 98-99
Image/issue PR/publicity, 10
Independents, 42
In-house, PR/publicity, 2
Institutional advertising, 152
Institutional events, 134
Internal audit, 191
Internal media, 31
Interpersonal communication, 21
Interview contact technique, 120
Interviews
   broadcast, 164-65
   training for (TV), 169-72
Intrapersonal communication, 21

J

Journal of the American Dental Association, 37
Journal of the American Medical Association, 37

K

King Features Syndicate, 41
Kunis, Sol, 6

L

Lecterns, 175-76
Letters to the editor, 74
Letter writing, 73-74
Licensing, 212
Listening, importance of, 25-26
Locale and scenic photographs, 92
Localizing a release, 57-62
Local PR/publicists contact technique, 120
Logos, 150-52
Los Angeles Times, The, 32

M

McCall's, 34, 35
Magat, Dick, 26
Magazines, 34-37
  for business organizations, 72-73
  getting a story into (case study), 110-13
  organization, 35-37
  photographs, 78-79
  See also names of magazines
Mail contact technique, 119-20
Mailing houses, mailing in-house as compared to, 125-26
Mailing services, 125-26
Manuals, for business organizations, 72-73
Marketing
  meaning of, 6
  PR/publicity importance, 6-8
Mass communication, 21
Mass media, 31
Mat services, 126-28
Matte photographs, 79
Mechanical Engineering, 37
Media, 31-45
  broadcast, 41-45
  employment, 128-30
  establishing a list, 120-21
  feature syndicates and mat services, 126-28
  "freebies" and gifts, 130-31
  importance of right contact, 125
  knowledge of, 31
  mailing services, 125-26
  photo syndicates and PR wires, 128
  print, 32-41
  professional source books, 121-25
  questions to ask, 121
  techniques, 119-20
Media and consumer relations experts, 5
Media contact, 119-31
Meeting contact technique, 120
Men's Wear, 37
Merchandise events, 134

Merchandising PR/publicity results, 194-201
  broadcast documentation, 198
  broadcast placements, 198-99
  documentation, 194-95
  editorial surveys, 199
  print placements, 195
Modern Health Care, 37

N

National Broadcasting Company (NBC), 42, 44-45
National Public Radio, 45
New product development, fact sheets, 67
News, PR/publicity, 2
  making, 21
  See also Creativity development
News angles, 17-20
  creating, 18
  developing, 17-18
  evaluating, 20
New services, fact sheets, 67
News-event photography, 88-89
News-feature release, function of, 57
Newsletters, 39
Newspaper employment, 128-29
Newspaper Enterprise Association, 41
Newspapers, 32-34
  getting a story into (case study), 113-14
  organization, 33-34
News release, function of, 53
Newsweek, 34
New York Magazine, 35
New York Times, The, 32
Nonprofit PR/publicity, 10

O

Office photos, 89

P

Pamphlets, for business organizations, 72-73
Personality events, 134
Personality photos, 84
Personality PR/publicity, 10
Personnel, planning, 184-85
Person-to-person contact, 119
Photographs, 77-94
  captions or cutlines, 99-102
  compared to sketches, 96-98
  cropping and retouching, 92
  do's and don'ts, 93-94
  outlets for, 78-79
  releases, 93
  requirements, 79-80

standards, 80
types of, 81-92
value of, 77-78
what the press expects, 80-81
working with photographers, 81
Photo syndicates, 41, 128
"Pitch," 7
Placement techniques, 110-17
    getting a story into a magazine, 110-13
    guest on a TV interview show, 114-17
    newspaper story, 113-14
Planning, 177-88
    budget, personnel, and equipment, 184-85
    criteria for evaluation, 186
    elements in, 178
    establishing a plan, 177-78
    events or special activities, 183-84
    goals and objectives, 179-81
    points to consider, 187
    proposals, 186-88
    selecting publics and media, 181-83
    situation analysis, 178-79
    timetables, 185
Plugs, 40
Presentation strategy, 103-10
    press kit, 105-10
    spoken word, 104-5
    written word (with eye appeal), 105
Press
    PR/publicity photos and, 80-81
    relationship between the PR/publicist and, 5-6
    special attention at events, 139-40
Press clipping services, 194-95
Press conferences, 144-47
Press kit, 105-10
    contents, 110
    preparing, 107
Press parties, 147
Press releases, 47-64
    basic form, 47-50
    broadcast, 164
    dates on, 51
    do's and don'ts, 62-64
    feature release, 56-57
    localizing, 57-62
    meaning of, 47
    news-feature release, 57
    news release, 53
    questions to ask (before sending), 64
    tips, 62
    variations of, 51
    writing styles, 51-57
Press room, 139-40
Print media, 32-41
    business publications, 37-39
    magazines, 34-37
    newsletters, house organs, and columns, 39-40
    newspapers, 32-34
    supplementary news services, 40-41
Print placements, merchandising, 195
Product photos, 84-85
Product PR/publicity, 8
Professional source books, for media contacts, 121-25
Profiles and bios (biographies), 67-70
Proposals, 186-88
PR/publicity
    at an advertising agency, 4
    agencies, 2-4
    broadcast techniques, 163-74
    compared to advertising, 8, 11
    in contemporary society, 203-12
    corporate functions, 149-61
    employment, 4-5, 128-30, 205-8
    evaluating and merchandising results, 189-201
    in-house, 2
    kinds of, 8-10
    marketing importance, 6-8
    meaning of, 1
    media and, 31-45
    media contact, 119-31
    miscellaneous written materials, 65-75
    news, 2, 21
    news sense and creative ideas, 17-29
    organizational chart, 3
    photos, sketches, and diagrams, 77-102
    planning, 177-88
    presentation strategy and placement techniques, 103-17
    press conferences and press parties, 144-47
    press releases, 47-64
    "publics" or specific audiences, 10-12
    relationship with the press, 5-6
    scope of activities, 13-15
    speaker aids, 174-76
    special events, 133-44
PR wires, 128
Publicists, 5
Publicity releases. *See* Press releases
Publicity wire services, 41
Public opinion surveys, 190
Public Relations Newswire, 128
Public Relations Society of America (PRSA), 212
"Publics" or specific audiences, 10-12

Q

Qualitative programs, evaluating, 190-93
Quarterly reports, 159
Query letters, 71-72
Questionnaires, periodic mailing of, 191
Quotes, use of, 63

INDEX

R

Radio, 43-45
   employment, 129-30
   station organization, 44-45
Reader's Digest, 34
Redbook, 34
Releases, photo, 93
Research, importance of, 25-26
Results, PR/publicity
   evaluating, 189-94
   merchandising, 194-201
Retailers, special events and, 135-36
Retouching, photo, 92
RKO Radio Network, 45

S

Scenic photographs, 92
Seventeen, 35
Short telephone surveys, 191
Sirinek, Carol, 6, 26
Situation analysis, 178-79
Sketches, diagrams, and charts, 94-99
   compared to photos, 96-98
   and illustrations, 98-99
Slides, 175
Speaker aids, 174-76
Special events, 133-44
   classification of, 134-35
   fact sheets, 67
   insurance policy, 143-44
   management of, 138-39
   meaning of, 133
   opening ABC Shops (case study), 142-43
   organization for, 140
   planning, 183-84
   press facilities, 139-40
   retail importance, 135-36
   theme development, 140-42
Specialized media, 31
Specialized news syndicates, 41
Speech writing, 160-61
Sponsored films and tapes, 172-73
Store photos, 89
Supplementary news services, 40-41
Survey panel, 191

T

Talk show placement, 168-69
Tapes and films, 173-74
Telephone contact, 119
Teletext, 204
Television, 42-43
   cable systems, 43, 174
   employment, 129-30
   getting a guest on an interview show
     (case study), 114-17
   organization, 42-43
   photos, 79
   See also Broadcast techniques
Theme development, special event, 140-42
Time, 34
Timetables, 185
Trademarks, company, 150-52
Transportation photos, 89
TV Guide, 34
T. V. Publicity Outlets, 43

U

United Features Syndicate, 41
United Press International, 40, 42, 128
UPI Newspictures, 41

V

Video discs, 40
Video tape recorders, 173-74
Videotex, 204
Visual materials for television, 168
Vogue, 34

W

Wall Street Journal, The, 32
Wide World Photos, 41, 128
Wire copy, 40
Wire services, 40
Women's Wear Daily, 32
Word processor, 204
Writing for broadcast, 163-64
   guidelines for, 165

HM 263.E33

JUN -8 1990
OCT 08 1992